LETTER TO THE WORLD

ALSO BY SUSAN WARE

Beyond Suffrage: Women in the New Deal

Holding Their Own: American Women in the 1930s

America's History (coauthor)

Partner and I: Molly Dewson, Feminism and New Deal Politics

Modern American Women: A Documentary History

Still Missing: Amelia Earhart and the Search for Modern Feminism

LETTER TO THE WORLD

SEVEN WOMEN WHO

SHAPED THE

AMERICAN CENTURY

SUSAN WARE

W. W. NORTON & COMPANY

NEW YORK / LONDON

We gratefully acknowledge the following for permission to quote from the cited sources:
William Johnson and Nancy P. Williamson's *"Whatta-Gal": The Babe Didrikson Story* (New
York: Little, Brown, 1975). By permission of William Johnson. Margaret Mead papers
housed in the Library of Congress. Courtesy of the Institute for Intercultural Studies, Inc.,
New York. Dorothy Thompson papers held at Special Collections, Syracuse University,
© 1998 by Lesley Lewis, John Paul Lewis, and Gregory Lewis. By permission of McIntosh
and Otis, Inc. *My Lord, What a Morning* by Marian Anderson. Copyright © 1956, renewed
1984 by Marian Anderson. Used by permission of Viking Penguin, a division of Penguin
Books USA Inc.

For information about permission to reproduce selections from this book,
write to Permissions, W. W. Norton & Company, Inc.,
500 Fifth Avenue, New York, NY 10110

The text of this book is composed in Garamond No. 3
with the display set in Fenice
Desktop composition by Platinum Manuscript Services
Manufacturing by The Haddon Craftsmen, Inc.
Book design by JAM Design

Library of Congress Cataloging-in-Publication Data
Ware, Susan, 1950–
Letter to the world : seven women who shaped the American century
/ Susan Ware.
p.   cm.
Includes bibliographic references (p.) and index.
ISBN 0-393-04652-4
1. Women—United States—Biography. 2. Biography—20th century.
I. Title.
CT3235.W36   1998
920.72'0973—dc21   997-45923
CIP

W. W. Norton & Company, Inc., 500 Fifth Avenue, New York, N.Y. 10110
http://www.wwnorton.com

W. W. Norton & Company Ltd., 10 Coptic Street, London WC1A 1PU

1 2 3 4 5 6 7 8 9 0

To my parents
Charles Kline Wolfe, Jr.
and
Charlotte McConnell Wolfe

"I long to speak out the inspiration
that comes to me from the lives of strong women.
They make of their lives a Great Adventure."

—RUTH BENEDICT

CONTENTS

ACKNOWLEDGMENTS

RITING IS A solitary business, and I adore it. This book was written in a beautiful setting—an eighteenth-century farmhouse in New Hampshire that my husband and I bought in 1993. Friends who see my study for the first time, with its views of Kearsarge, Cardigan, and Moosilauke, inevitably say, "How do you get any work done here?" but I find the setting wonderfully conducive to the writer's craft. I hope to write many more books here. Keeping me company will be my Bernese Mountain dogs Kate and Jesse, who are always ready (as was the much missed Molly) to remind me that walks in the woods or watching frogs in the pond are just as important as writing.

If writing is solitary, doing research is the opposite, and I would like to acknowledge the help of archivists at the Manuscript Division of the Library of Congress, the Department of Special Collections at Syracuse University, the Department of Special Collections at the University of Pennsylvania, and the Bryn Mawr College Archives. My strongest debt is to Radcliffe College and the Arthur and Elizabeth Schlesinger Library on the

History of Women in America, my institutional base since I left New York University in 1995. Special thanks to Schlesinger Library director Mary Maples Dunn for her ongoing support.

Friends and colleagues offered generous support as I grappled with the question of how to make a collective biography more than the sum of its parts. Enormously helpful readings of the manuscript by Joyce Antler and Joan Jacobs Brumberg pushed me to raise the story another notch, and I am grateful for their advice and ongoing friendship. Professor Jeffrey Sammons of NYU and Professor Susan Cayleff of the University of California at San Diego offered leads on Babe Didrikson Zaharias. My editor at Norton, Amy Cherry, was the first person to read the draft, and her enthusiastic initial response gave me the needed confidence to see it through to the end. In New Hampshire, I would like to acknowledge the indirect contribution of the carpenters and stoneworkers of Derek Owen Associates, who took almost as long to restore our barn as it took me to write this book, perhaps because they were always willing to take a break when I felt like talking. And thanks to our "director of landscape," Bunny H. Van Valey, for her enthusiasm for the project.

I owe a special debt to my husband, Don Ware, for two quite different contributions to this book. The most important was his support of my decision to leave NYU to become an independent scholar and his unflagging interest in my research and writing, including a careful reading of the final manuscript. But I must also acknowledge, only partly in jest, how fortuitous it was that during my most intensive months of writing he was so immersed in a major legal case that he tolerated with humor and good grace my long absences from Cambridge. This book got finished sooner, and turned out better, because of him.

This book is dedicated to my parents, with thanks for raising a daughter who never doubted she could pursue any path she chose and in gratitude for their ongoing love and support.

HOPKINTON, NEW HAMPSHIRE

I N T R O D U C T I O N

CASTING CALL FOR THE
AMERICAN CENTURY

WANTED: Strong, independent characters for book about celebrated women who shaped twentieth-century American life and culture. Must be ambitious, opinionated, hard-working, and instantly recognizable around the world. Especially looking for applicants from the following fields: politics, the professions, film, sports, and the performing arts. Longevity of career, distinctive personal style, and loyal following a plus.

❦

ELEANOR ROOSEVELT WAS the first to answer the casting call, befitting her stature as the twentieth-century's most influential woman, although she had trouble finding time to schedule the audition and kept having her secretary, Malvina Thompson, put it off. Roosevelt's plate was always full to overflowing: there were causes to promote, columns to write, children and friends to see, the world to improve. She showed up wearing whatever she had worn at her previous engagement—as long as clothes were serviceable and comfortable, she cared little for fashion. Actually she was a bit reluctant to put herself forward for such a leading role—

she had learned from her years in public life to avoid being seen as personally ambitious, instead hiding much of her influence under the cloak of being her husband's stand-in. And yet, since Eleanor Roosevelt set the standard for public-spirited womanhood for the rest of the century, her widely admired life provided the logical place to start.

Dorothy Thompson auditioned for the part by writing a witty "On the Record" column about the trials and tribulations of modern women's lives. As one of the nation's most influential syndicated columnists in the 1930s and 1940s, she reached millions of readers with her trenchant prose and commentary. Foreign affairs was her specialty (at times she seemed to be leading a one-woman crusade against Hitler), but she also shared her lighter side in the Ladies' Home Journal, where she wrote about topics like her farm in Vermont and her lifelong battle with her weight (the "Size 20 situation," she called it). She had a special reason for wanting to be included: the other characters whose names were being bandied about were practically household names, but Thompson had fallen into eclipse at the end of her career and was far less well known. This could be her comeback ticket.

Like her friend Eleanor Roosevelt, Margaret Mead was so busy that she couldn't even schedule an appointment to talk about participating in the book. She was always heading off to the South Seas to do research, or speaking and lecturing in hamlets across America; she networked at conferences, in television studios, on planes, indeed wherever two or more people gathered. If she were to stay put anywhere for more than a day at a time, the grandmotherly anthropologist with a walking stick would be likely found tucked away in her corner turret office at the American Museum of Natural History in New York City, surrounded by assistants whose numbers were never quite adequate to manage both her thriving career and equally active personal life, which were intricately intertwined. As the best-known anthropologist of all time, and one of the country's most respected oracles for no-

nonsense advice on every topic imaginable, Mead would have been miffed to be excluded.

Katharine Hepburn showed up for the audition dressed in her trademark outfit of slacks, turtleneck, and jacket, her feet tucked in comfortable sandals and an old cap stuck on her head. Probably more than any other twentieth-century figure, Hepburn has come to stand for the independent, headstrong woman who gets her way. No matter what role she played on screen or stage, her personality and style blazed through; she retained her popularity and stature as a national icon for the entire span of her career. Off screen her life strayed from her liberated public persona, but like most celebrities she never could get her fans to believe there was a difference between the two. A book about important women in twentieth-century American life that did not include Hollywood would be woefully incomplete. As she had been doing all her life, Hepburn won the part.

Babe Didrikson Zaharias tried out next. Arguably the twentieth century's most gifted all-around athlete, male or female, she showed up dressed for a round of golf: skirt and sweater set, bobby socks and shoes, her hair styled in a soft permanent wave. This mature incarnation of Babe Didrikson Zaharias was a far cry from the brash, working-class Texas "Muscle Moll" with boy's body and cropped hair who won three medals at the 1932 Olympics but then had nowhere to go as a professional female athlete. Golf provided her ticket into a more respectable (and conventionally feminine) middle-class lifestyle, complete with a husband who doubled as her business manager. The Babe regularly and gleefully blew away her competition in whatever sport she chose, and easily grabbed a slot in this book.

Martha Graham was no stranger to performance. As her audition piece, she would likely have selected one of her dances choreographed from the point of view of a woman—perhaps "Letter to the World," based on the life and poetry of Emily Dickinson. An expert seamstress with a superb sense of style, Graham could have performed the audition in whatever street clothes she was wearing. To complete the effect, she would simply pull her hair back tightly from her face, touch up her exaggerated eye shadow and mascara, and top it off with a slash of bright red lipstick. She dressed to be noticed, and she danced to be noticed. A true creative genius, she could be aloof and intimidating, but there was never any question that she would get the part.

The contralto Marian Anderson had been singing in public since she was a child and she would have approached her audition with the same poise and dignity that characterized her entire performing career (as long as it was cleared first with Sol Hurok, her exclusive manager). Actually she would have much preferred to let her singing do her talking; she hated to draw attention to herself, dressing elegantly but conservatively on stage and off, and was so self-effacing that she could barely bring herself to use the first person in interviews or articles. Although a somewhat reluctant crusader, as an African American she was forced into that role by the emergence of race as one of the twentieth-century's most pressing moral and political dilemmas. Never one to pick a fight, she nonetheless realized the importance of symbolic breakthroughs, and she fought hard for her career. A book on women who shaped the twentieth century that only included white folks would have been, in her opinion, a poor sample. Her agreement to participate was yet another instance of leading by example.

After the auditions were over, last-minute doubts set in. What about Georgia O'Keeffe rather than Martha Graham? Should I include Margaret Bourke-White instead of Dorothy Thompson? Perhaps I should reprise Amelia Earhart, even though she was the subject of my last book? In the end I exercised my author/director's prerogative, and found my original seven choices sound. Now that the dramatis personae were set, it was time to plot the narrative.

🦌

THIS IMAGINARY AUDITION is not far off the mark in depicting how I chose the characters for this book. I set out to write about significant twentieth-century American women who influenced their times, whose accomplishments and lifestyles were widely reported in the press, and whose lives, both public and private, still speak to us today. How popular culture created and dispersed new images of female achievement and celebrity, and the impact that these models had on twentieth-century life and women's experience would provide the thematic core. I chose the format of collective biography to tell that story because individual lives are often the most compelling lenses to illuminate broader patterns and themes in history and contemporary life. And I deliberately cast my net widely to include subjects who represented a diversity of fields and professions in order to explore women's broad-based contributions to American society and culture over the course of the twentieth century.

Two aspects about my choices stood out immediately. Probably the most obvious was the fact that Marian Anderson was the only non-white woman in the book. This result primarily reflected the prevailing racism of American life at the time, a deep-seated prejudice that restricted African Americans and other minorities (including religious minorities such as Jews) to the margins of the emerging mass culture and national celebrity. Since my interest was focused on the way that individual women achieved their stature as popular culture icons, my sample was by necessity limited to those who had been successful in vaulting themselves into such national consciousness. Marian Anderson was the rare case of a black performer who found fame, wealth, and celebrity comparable to that of a white woman, but always with the difference of race lurking just below the surface.

The other singular characteristic about my group was that the subjects were all products of the same historical period—that is, they were born roughly within a twenty-five year span (1884 to 1911) and they had their greatest influence in the period from the 1930s to the early 1960s. Domestic-bound women born before the 1880s would have had few chances to excel in fields like politics, journalism, or the professions on a national level. On the other hand, women who came of age in the early years of the twentieth century, as these seven women did, found many more opportunities to lead and win public recognition for the kind of important, public lives that until then had been reserved primarily for men. In the 1920s and 1930s a rapidly expanding mass media was eager to broadcast the accomplishments of these women, especially if they were "firsts" or were pioneering in areas where women had never excelled before. As more women followed in their paths, which they invariably did as the century progressed, the news value of successive waves of women's individual accomplishments declined. As a result the postwar period proved a far less fertile climate for the creation of individual popular heroines and female icons than had the preceding decades.

These seven women popped into public consciousness at an auspicious time, but celebrity does not just happen. They all self-consciously created images that allowed them to win public acclaim, pursue rewarding and often highly remunerative careers, and emerge as leading opinion makers, cultural leaders, and path breakers in mid-twentieth-century popular culture. The key to their success, and to their impact on American culture and society, was their ability to package themselves in ways that the media found attractive and marketable. Each then worked long and hard to sustain public interest in her unusual individual achievements. For example, each wrote an autobiography at a time when celebrity memoirs were far less common, especially for women. Although luck was part of the story, things rarely just happened to these unabashedly ambitious women: they made things happen, and with their brains, not their looks. They also made sure they were well paid for their efforts, often earning as much as $100,000 a year in the 1930s and 1940s.

It is hard not to be struck by the remarkable longevity of these women's celebrated careers: with the possible exception of Dorothy Thompson, each remains an American icon even today. Unlike the brief shelf life of many contemporary American celebrities, these women sustained the public's interest decade after decade, and without living the kind of ostentatious lives associated with celebrities today. Their collective stories provide role models not just of how to succeed as a woman in a man's world, but how to maintain a following in a culture notoriously fickle in its loyalty to leaders and heroes. That these women managed to parlay their personal and professional life choices into public personalities that their followers and fans continued to embrace contradicts the widely held belief that popular culture simply casts women aside when they turn forty. More fundamentally, it suggests a wider acceptance of independent roles for women in popular culture in the middle years of the twentieth century than is generally recognized.

The carefully controlled images found in newspapers, magazines, films, newsreels, and autobiographies that kept these women squarely in the public eye were only the tip of the iceberg of these women's lives, but they were the only part that mid-century audiences heard about in a less media-intrusive age. One of the most striking differences between our times and the historical period in which these women were prominent was the latitude they were given to lead their personal lives outside the scrutiny of the media or a prying public. These private lives often diverged from or contradicted their carefully crafted public personas in revealing ways. Every woman profiled in this book led a private life far more unconventional than her public imagined.

The stories of these seven women, exceptional as they were, also reflect many of the daily dilemmas and ordinary challenges of modern women's lives. Though each was rich and famous, none could escape being female. As women they shared common concerns, such as getting an education and finding meaningful work, the need to be financially independent, the question of whether to marry and have children, maintaining female friendships, deciding how much allegiance to give to the forces of modern feminism, growing old. How these seven women struggled with the difficulty of reconciling their very demanding public careers with their desires for full and satisfying personal lives will sound remarkably familiar to many readers.

Perhaps the issue with the most contemporary relevance is the historical perspective these women's choices shed on the catch phrase "You can't have it all." Despite the overarching importance of their work and careers, these women were also drawn (at least in the abstract) to home and family. But when they tried to imagine combining family life with career, their imaginations faltered. With the exception of Margaret Mead, who balanced the personal and professional unusually well, domestic life and career remained an either/or proposition for many women achievers of their generation. Out of necessity and personal predilection, these seven women made their careers and public lives their top priority, and with few regrets. At the same time, they refused to distance themselves completely from conventional gender norms: domesticity is the right choice for most women, they seemed to say, just not for us.

Despite those public nods to conventionality, these seven women experimented with a wide range of personal relationships as they searched for love and affection. Perhaps most striking is the fact that four of them—Roosevelt, Thompson, Mead, and Zaharias—had important loving relationships with women as well as men. Katharine Hepburn and Martha Graham had long-term relationships with men who could not or would not marry them because they refused to divorce their wives. Marian Anderson married a man who had for a time passed as white. These women's strategies in forging unconventional relationships that filled their personal needs, and their ability to successfully hide or camouflage these liaisons from public scrutiny, remind us of how much more freedom celebrities used to be given to keep their private lives truly private.

In the end all seven characters did marry, often more than once. The most successful marriages were the ones that a mature Dorothy Thompson and never-before-married Marian Anderson entered into when their careers and reputations were secure. Katharine Hepburn was temperamentally unsuited for marriage, and Martha Graham wasn't much better. The problems in Eleanor Roosevelt's marriage helped propel her need to find useful and productive work, while

Babe Didrikson quickly outgrew her husband and manager George Zaharias (figuratively, not literally—the ex-boxer's weight ballooned to four hundred pounds during their marriage). The high number of divorces (Margaret Mead led the pack with three) attests to the difficulty that many ambitious and successful women had— and still have—in maintaining mutually satisfying relationships with men. And yet these women found fulfillment in their work, their friendships, and their celebrity.

But not necessarily in motherhood, a pattern shared by many female professionals and women achievers at that time. Eleanor Roosevelt's six children, of whom five survived infancy, were the exception: as the oldest of the group and the one who did not set her independent course until she was in her thirties, she came closest to a conventional family life. Only two of the other women, Dorothy Thompson and Margaret Mead, had children at all. Each of them had only one child and waited until what was then considered the advanced age of her mid-to-late thirties to tackle motherhood. Katharine Hepburn, Babe Didrikson Zaharias, Martha Graham, and Marian Anderson all chose to remain childless, in part because of the demands of their careers, but also, it seems, because they took advantage of a cultural shift in modern life that affirmed that not all women had to bear children to find fulfillment. In certain ways such personal choices could be profoundly political statements.

Other shared characteristics unified their lives as women. A striking number (Roosevelt, Thompson, Mead, Graham, and Anderson) were the first-born children in their families, and in many ways Katharine Hepburn became the eldest child after her older brother committed suicide as a teenager. Equally striking was the fact that six out of the seven kept their names when they married, though, of course, there was no opportunity for Eleanor Roosevelt to make that decision since she married a distant cousin with the same name. Babe Didrikson was the exception here, and her taking the name of her husband, George Zaharias, was a deliberate choice to bring her image more in line with conventional heterosexual norms. For all the others, keeping their names was a declaration of independence and personal autonomy.

Then there is the issue of aging. All but Eleanor Roosevelt and Margaret Mead publicly shaved years, sometimes decades off their birth dates starting at a relatively early age, which suggested a certain lack of comfort with the prospect of growing old so publicly. Aging has always been problematic for women in popular culture, and it was an especially compelling dilemma for the three women who were performers—Marian Anderson, Martha Graham, and Katharine Hepburn. They managed to remain active well into their sixties, seventies, and beyond by finding ways to use their celebrity to keep them before their loyal public at a time when many older women had difficulty getting creative roles. Babe Didrikson Zaharias did not have that challenge: she died of cancer at the age of forty-five, just as she was beginning to face the decline in her own athletic prowess, which was of course the key to her professional success and her financial security.

How to go on if one is no longer at the top of one's game was a problem shared by all these celebrities, not just the performers and athletes. The idea of retirement was so foreign to Eleanor Roosevelt and Margaret Mead that they clung to their brutal schedules practically until they checked into the hospital to die. All of these women were used to being on the front page, the lead story in a magazine, the featured speaker at a conference. That kind of influence, indeed power, proved difficult to cede voluntarily. But inevitably there came a time when each woman was forced to slow down, or sometimes to step aside completely. This struggle against age is a profoundly moving, and often sad, story. Like so many other stories in this book, it is also a woman's story.

There is a further resonance to these women's collective stories: their attempts to strike a balance between public and private were very much linked to the fortunes of feminism. On the whole, these accomplished and celebrated women did not publicly identify with feminism or women's causes, although most who lived long enough to see the revival of feminism grudgingly made their peace with the movement. (Eleanor Roosevelt, a lifelong and public feminist, was the exception here.) Instead they presented their accomplishments and successes as the result of individual achievement, regardless of gender. Moreover, their public pronouncements often supported very traditional roles for women (other women, that is), a sort of "do as I say, not as I do" message. And yet even as these very prominent women ignored or rejected the public side of feminism, in their personal lives they warmly embraced modern feminism's agenda of autonomy, productive work, and freedom from traditional gender roles. In effect they lived lives of "applied feminism" without swearing public allegiance to the cause.

This seemingly contradictory stance was very much in keeping with a specific moment in the history of modern feminism—the decades between the passage of the suffrage amendment in 1920 and the revival of the women's movement in the 1960s and 1970s, the very years when these women built their careers and enjoyed the peak of their influence and fame. In the absence of a broad-based feminist movement, women of achievement had little choice but to think in individualistic terms and to fight their battles, both personal and professional, on their own. Yet in order to make it as women in a man's world, they had to embrace many of the tenets of liberal feminism, especially a belief in women's equality and a commitment to breaking down artificial barriers set by sex. They were the forerunners of contemporary women who say, "I'm not a feminist, but . . . ."

Lack of identification with the feminist movement does not mean these women's lives hold no relevance for the history of modern feminism, however. The accomplishments of women such as Margaret Mead, Babe Didrikson Zaharias, and Martha Graham were widely and sympathetically reported in the media, allowing these exceptional women to serve as role models for ordinary women (and a not insignificant number of men) who followed their careers through newsreels, movies, radio, and print journalism. These women functioned as symbols of women's advancement even if they did not specifically identify with the cause of feminism; the media's celebration of individual achievement spread their message of the new possibilities for modern women's lives throughout popular culture.

This vicarious encouragement of women's aspirations was especially important in the decades of the 1930s, 1940s, and 1950s, which lacked active feminist movements. If popular culture so enthusiastically validated the achievements of remarkable individual women, especially in the critical middle years of the twentieth century, then perhaps the period was not so barren of feminist consciousness after all. The narratives of these women's lives are just as compelling today in another period of contention about the relevance of feminism to contemporary American life.

There is something almost voyeuristic about reading (and writing) biography, because it allows us to peer into the lives of exceptional characters and discover moments of truth and self-awareness not so far removed from our own lives. The public personalities and unconventional private lives of Eleanor Roosevelt, Dorothy Thompson, Margaret Mead, Katharine Hepburn, Babe Didrikson Zaharias, Martha Graham, and Marian Anderson give us a lens onto women's lives in twentieth-century America. These stories of remarkable renown are offered as testaments to what history and biography can teach us about the challenges and rewards of contemporary women's lives.

LETTER TO THE WORLD

"OF COURSE I KNOW — IT'S MRS. ROOSEVELT"

(A 1954 copyright Herblock Cartoon)

O N E

FIRST LADY OF THE WORLD: ELEANOR ROOSEVELT

*W*HEN ASKED BY reporters at age seventy-five to reflect on her life, Eleanor Roosevelt replied, "I think I must have a good deal of my uncle Theodore Roosevelt in me, because I could not, at any age, be content to take my place in a corner by the fireside and simply look on." She concluded emphatically, "Life was meant to be lived."[1]

That approach to life made Eleanor Roosevelt one of the most important, and most respected, women of the twentieth century. Columnist Raymond Clapper called her a "cabinet minister without portfolio—the most influential woman of our times" and in 1938 *Life* magazine anointed her the greatest American woman alive. The next year a Gallup poll gave her an approval rating of 67 percent, which was nine points higher than the president's. Of course she had her detractors, legions of them: "We Don't Want Eleanor Either" was a popular Republican campaign button in 1940. But even if the American public did not always agree with Eleanor Roosevelt's views, it respected her right to have them. In sharp contrast to the plummeting stature of most political figures, past and present, Eleanor Roosevelt's reputation has continued to rise in the three decades since her death in 1962.[2]

Eleanor Roosevelt always downplayed her own contributions to public life: "As for accomplishments, I just did what I had to do as things came along." Posing as a dutiful wife who was merely helping her husband deflected attention away from her own political skills and ambitions, which were prodigious. "I'm the agitator; he's the politician" is how she summed up the remarkably productive political partnership she built with Franklin over the years, one of the greatest two-for-one deals in American political history. When she went too far, Franklin would simply throw up his hands and say, "Well, that's my wife, and I can't be expected to do anything about her." According to Brain Truster Rexford Tugwell, no one who saw Eleanor Roosevelt lock eyes with her husband and say, "Franklin, I think you should" or "Franklin, surely you will not," ever forgot the experience. (She put it more benignly, "You don't just sit at meals and look at each other.") He did not always welcome or take her advice, but he always listened. In terms of politics they were a team.[3]

Eleanor Roosevelt was an inspiration for the nation's women. She constructed a public persona that combined traditional female virtues like concern with the home and family with nontraditional behavior like visiting coal mines, writing a newspaper column, and serving in the United Nations. "Mrs. Roosevelt Spends Night at White House," ran a newspaper headline, not entirely in jest. As Michigan journalist Esther Van Wagoner Tufty realized, "Eleanor Roosevelt caused more to be written by, for and about women than any other woman." She presented a model of womanhood that women of all classes, young and old, could admire. Hard-hitting *New York Daily News* reporter Doris Fleeson "was cynical about most people," remembered her daughter, "but she was never cynical about Mrs. Roosevelt. I think Mrs. Roosevelt represented to her the ideal of what women could be. She realized what Eleanor Roosevelt was or tried to be and she internalized it—made it part of her own work and life."

An eighteen-year-old factory worker from the Tennessee hills put it more succinctly: "Say, she's swell. Why, I'm not ashamed of being a girl any more."[4]

A 1942 Gallup poll noted that Eleanor Roosevelt was probably the "target of more adverse criticism and the object of more praise than any other woman in American history." As early as 1924 the Federal Bureau of Investigation had opened a file on her; by the end of her life it had grown to 4,000 pages. One of her most vocal critics was conversative columnist Westbrook Pegler, who could always get a laugh by ending a right-wing diatribe with "and I haven't mentioned Eleanor Roosevelt once."[5] Everything from the timbre of her upper-class voice ("Now, Franklin . . . ") to her prominent front teeth was fair game, but she rarely let it get her down. When journalist and close friend Lorena Hickok tried to give her pointers for facing photographers, Eleanor laughed them off: "My dear, if you haven't any chin and your front teeth stick out, it's going to show on a camera plate." Plus at five feet eleven inches she usually towered over everyone else in the shot. Surviving pictures confirm her self-deprecating diagnosis, but that didn't keep her from being one of the most photographed—and admired—American women of all time.[6]

The person behind the personage was more complex. Eleanor Roosevelt always claimed the two were quite separate, commenting about one political gig in 1933, "I drove up in the capacity of Eleanor Roosevelt, and only on arriving became FDR's wife." Eleanor's personal life was characterized by occasional depression and loneliness but also by a deep-seated capacity for friendship and love. She could not bear to be alone, and when her husband failed to provide the emotional sustenance she craved, she turned to a highly unlikely assortment of people on whom to bestow her affection, ranging from a woman journalist to a state trooper to a young student activist to a refugee doctor. In biographer Blanche Wiesen Cook's memorable evaluation, "In conventional terms, ER lived an outrageous life."[7] In a less intrusive media age, she got away with it.

Even though Eleanor Roosevelt remembered herself as gawky and shy, she cut a slim and quite charming figure as a young woman. No wonder Franklin was smitten. (Franklin D. Roosevelt Library)

EDITH WHARTON'S BOOKS about old New York, especially *The House of Mirth*, capture the world in which Eleanor Roosevelt grew up and from which she so dramatically and irrevocably broke free. Born on October 11, 1884, into a world of old money and privilege, her childhood was punctuated by illness and death, alcoholism and insecurity. Her parents, Elliott and Anna Hall Roosevelt, were bright young things in New York society, with her mother especially renowned for her beauty and charm. "My mother was one of the most beautiful women I have ever seen," began the first sentence of Eleanor's 1937 autobiography.[8] In contrast, the young Eleanor felt gawky and ugly, deeply wounded by being called "Granny" by her mother, despite the fact that photographs show she blossomed into a striking (if insecure) young woman.

Eleanor's alcoholic father was the center of her emotional life as a child but also the cause of a great deal of pain when he let her down, which was often. For long periods of time he lived apart from his wife and children (their first son Elliott, born when Eleanor was five, died as a child; a second son Hall was born in 1891); his infrequent visits were followed by the inevitable leave-takings, which were devastating for the young Eleanor. So attached was she to her father that when her mother died suddenly when Eleanor was eight, her first thought was that "my father was back and I would see him soon."[9] But he too was dead within two years, and Eleanor and Hall were sent to live with their Grandmother Hall at Tivoli, an estate north of New York City on the Hudson River. Seven years older than Hall, Eleanor began to treat him more like a son than a brother, a role she played until he too succumbed to alcoholism in 1941.

Eleanor spent six years with Grandmother Hall, who was then in her early fifties and the mother of five grown children. Eleanor grew especially close to her aunts Maude and Pussie, but her relationship with her high spirited (read: alcoholic) uncles

Eddie and Vallie was more problematic: at a certain point Eleanor's room suddenly sprouted three locks to shield her from their potentially predatory behavior. (When studying Eleanor Roosevelt's early life, one thinks often of Virginia Woolf, then Virginia Stephen, living as a daughter in a household where she likely was abused by her stepbrother.) In contrast to her tolerance of the high jinx of her children, Grandmother Hall imposed a strict regimen on Eleanor, dressing her in hopelessly outdated and unflattering clothes that just heightened her sense of social isolation. "I was the typical old-fashioned girl of my period," Eleanor remembered, brought up with "strict ideas as to the sphere of women."[10]

Against the odds, she did get the groundings of a good education. On the recommendation of a favorite Roosevelt aunt, at the age of fifteen she was sent to Allenswood, a school outside London run by a charismatic and forward-looking Frenchwoman named Mlle. Marie Souvestre. The outspoken headmistress saw something in the young Eleanor, and the adolescent blossomed under her attention; Eleanor's three years at Allenswood (1899–1902) were among the happiest of her life. Looking back, it is possible to see many attributes of her adult life—her social conscience and sense of duty, her ability to inspire others, and especially her capacity for friendship with other women—tentatively emerging in her teens.

Eleanor's liberation from a conventional woman's life was short-lived—higher education or a career was not considered acceptable for a woman of her class background at the turn of the century. Soon she was back home, preparing to make her social debut. For someone still as shy and insecure as she was, this occasion was approached with a certain dread, but Eleanor probably overstated her social ineptitude. Her social conscience remained strong: she joined the Junior League and began volunteering at a Lower East Side settlement house. One day her beau Franklin Roosevelt picked her up on Rivington Street, exclaiming, "My God, I didn't know people lived like that." As early as 1903, she was educating FDR about social issues, an agenda she raised to an art form in the New Deal.[11]

Eleanor had first met her distant cousin Franklin, then a student at Harvard, in 1902 at one of the endless rounds of debutante parties they both were expected to attend. He was from the Hyde Park Roosevelts, definitely the lesser branch of the family in the eyes of Eleanor's Oyster Bay clan. Born in 1882, he grew up on his family's estate on the Hudson, the only child of James Roosevelt and his much younger wife, the former Sara Delano. Widowed in 1900 at the age of forty-six, Sara proved extremely reluctant to let her college-age son go so soon after losing her husband. As Eleanor would learn repeatedly over the years, Sara was a formidable opponent.

Franklin saw something in Eleanor that she seemed blind to in herself. They talked seriously about important issues of the day, and he never tried to squelch her incipient social conscience. What she saw in him is less clear, a fact that he may have been aware of since he professed mock horror at all the congratulations he received for snaring her while no one seemed to congratulate her on winning him. If the truth be told, the young Franklin lacked the depth of personality and magnetism he showed later in life. Most people thought of him as a dandy, a mama's boy, or a "feather duster," a play on his initials by girls from his social circle who were totally unsmitten by his charms.

Franklin and Eleanor carried out a secret courtship, meeting at social occasions and writing to each other frequently. Eleanor later destroyed all his courtship letters, but her letters to him show a nineteen-year-old very much in love. When Franklin informed his mother of his plans to marry Eleanor, she was appalled, not because she didn't like Eleanor, who was a perfectly acceptable choice, but because she was not yet ready to let her son live his own life. Her strong opposition caused them to keep their engagement secret for a year. In retrospect, Sara was right to fear her son's choice, although it would take many years for Eleanor to stand up to her domineering mother-in-law.

Franklin and Eleanor were finally married on March 17, 1905, the date having been chosen so that Eleanor's Uncle Teddy, then president of the United States, could give the bride away. "Well, Franklin, there's nothing like keeping the name in the family," he joked. Living up to his daughter Alice's famous remark that "Father always wanted to be the bride at every wedding and the corpse at every funeral," Uncle Teddy stole the show.[12]

At that point Franklin was a law student at Columbia, so they delayed their honeymoon until the summer, when they set off on the obligatory (for members of their class) European tour. After several months abroad, she found she was already pregnant. Over the next decade, Eleanor was, in her words, "always just getting over having a baby or about to have one."[13] She bore six children between 1906 and 1916, of whom five survived infancy. The loss of the first Franklin, Jr., at nine months to a heart condition was a terrible blow, because it reinforced her feelings of inadequacy as a mother. Ten months later Elliott, who many thought was her favorite son, was born.

Like many women of her class background, Eleanor had little to do with the daily needs of her children, delegating such responsibility to a succession of nurses and nannies. Later she wished she had been less timid in trusting her own feelings and had learned to reach out and have fun with her children. Her children agreed. Remembered Anna, the eldest and only daughter, "She felt a tremendous sense of duty to us, but she did not understand or satisfy the need of a child for primary closeness to a parent."[14]

A big part of the problem was the presence of Sara in their lives, always meddling and undercutting Eleanor's authority. (Franklin deliberately absented himself from this sphere.) Sara was especially good at using money to win her grandchildren's affection, what one Roosevelt child called "the golden loop." Sara also mercilessly belittled Eleanor in her children's eyes, telling them, "I was your real mother, Eleanor merely bore you." Eleanor ruefully admitted, "As it turned out, Franklin's children were more my mother-in-law's children than they were mine."[15]

As the glimmerings of the autonomous and independent Allenswood Eleanor receded in the early years of her marriage, Franklin began to build his political career, a somewhat unusual choice for someone of the upper class. His model was none other than Eleanor's uncle, Theodore Roosevelt, whose career path he followed to a tee, except that he did it as a Democrat rather than a Republican. In 1910 he won election to the New York state assembly, where he first came into contact with Louis Howe, who remained a devoted political advisor until Howe's death in 1936. Next FDR angled for a position in Woodrow Wilson's administration as Assistant Secretary of the Navy, which necessitated the family's move to Washington, D.C., in 1914. In 1920, a losing year for the Democrats, he was chosen to fill the vice-presidential slot under presidential nominee James M. Cox.

In later writings and interviews Eleanor portrayed Franklin's early forays into politics as having nothing whatever to do with her. And yet as biographer Blanche Cook convincingly argues, events like his election to the state legislature awakened political ambition in Eleanor, too, although she kept it carefully under wraps. What appealed about Franklin's career choices was the opportunity they presented for her to build a more interesting and fulfilling life as a political wife than as a conventional society matron. Noted Cook, "People asked her why she did so much, and she said she did it all for Franklin. Nobody ever asked her if she enjoyed it. The fact is, from her first day in Albany she loved every minute of it."[16]

The move to Washington broadened her horizons still further. Despite the somewhat stultifying Washington social scene, she began to get involved in a range of activities that took her beyond family and household. When the United States entered the war in 1917, these volunteer activities escalated dramatically. Always happiest when she was busy and being useful, Eleanor threw herself into war work. As she later said, "the war was my emancipation and education."[17]

That statement, while perfectly true, told only part of the story: in 1918 Eleanor inadvertently discovered that her husband was having an affair with her social secretary, the attractive young Lucy Mercer. As she later confided to her friend (and future biographer) Joe Lash, "The bottom dropped out of my own particular world and I faced myself, my surroundings, my world honestly for the first time. I really grew up that year." At a family conclave Eleanor offered Franklin his freedom to marry Lucy, but divorce and remarriage would have ended his political career. In addition, Sara, who was a significant financial player in maintaining their lifestyle, was adamently opposed to divorce. So Franklin and Eleanor remained married, although her trust in him was shattered. "I have the memory of an elephant," she once told a friend. "I can forgive, but I cannot forget."[18]

As if that crisis weren't enough to test their marriage, on a trip to the Roosevelt family compound in Campobello, Maine, in 1921, Franklin Roosevelt contracted the infantile paralysis that left him paralyzed from the waist down for the rest of his life. Eleanor and Louis Howe were constantly at his side, nursing him through the initial stages of the devastating illness. Showing remarkable determination shaded by stubbornness, Roosevelt insisted he would eventually be able to walk again. Years of painful therapy brought him no nearer to this goal, but he at least mastered the illusion of walking, propelling himself forward aided by heavy braces, a cane, and the strong supporting arms of friends, his sons, or bodyguards. FDR emerged from his ordeal a stronger, more resilient person. "If you had spent two years in bed trying to wiggle your toe, after that anything would seem easy." So successful was he in overcoming his disability, and so respectful of his privacy were news photographers, that many Americans never knew that he was crippled.[19]

Franklin's illness forced changes in Eleanor's life, too. She now became his eyes, ears, and legs, shedding much of the shyness that had often hampered her in the early years of her marriage. Since she was committed to his resuming his political career rather than retiring as a semi-invalid to Hyde Park with Mama, she stepped up her public activities, although always with the same self-deprecating disclaimers: "I'm only active until you can be again" or "Much, much love to you dear and I prefer doing my politics with you."[20] But it is wrong to see her widening circle of activities in the 1920s solely as her effort to be her husband's stand-in, or even as a result of her discovery of his affair. Eleanor had already realized that she needed an independent life, and she planned to get it, somehow. Lucy Mercer and Franklin's polio just confirmed that need.

In the 1920s Eleanor Roosevelt became one of the most active and visible women in political and social reform circles, first in New York and then nationally. Women had only won the vote in 1920, but Roosevelt was typical of the ways in which women moved centrally into public life in the post-suffrage era. Her activities ranged from the League of Women Voters to the National Consumers' League to the Women's Division of the State Democratic Committee. In the process she connected with a stimulating (and to her, eye-opening) group of professional women like Esther Lape, Elizabeth Read, Caroline O'Day, and Molly Dewson, who became her friends as well as co-workers. Eleanor formed an especially close relationship with Nancy Cook and Marion Dickerman. Together the three women, along with Caroline O'Day, opened a furniture factory at Val-Kill in Hyde Park in the 1920s. Showing the link between the personal and political, the mailing address for the catalogue of Val-Kill Industries was also the headquarters of the Women's Division of the Democratic Party.

Eleanor quickly assumed a national role as a spokesperson for women's new roles in politics, giving speeches and writing articles that reached a broad audience. "Women must learn to play the game as men do," she told readers of *Redbook* in 1928. She was aware of the difficulties women faced in being taken seriously by the men, but urged them to get in there and fight. "Get into the game and stay in it. Throwing mud from the outside won't help.

Building up from the inside will." Even though she titled the chapter on the 1920s in her autobiography "private interlude," she was living a very public life, and enjoying it to the hilt.[21]

Franklin's political aspirations were very much alive, too. His comeback began with a dramatic appearance at the 1924 convention to second the nomination of New York Governor Alfred E. Smith; even though the nod went to John W. Davis after an excruciating 103 ballots, the convention was electrified by Roosevelt's "Happy Warrior" speech. (These events provide the climax of the popular movie, *Sunrise at Campobello* [1960], starring Ralph Bellamy and Greer Garson.) In 1928, when Smith became the first Roman Catholic ever to be nominated for president, Roosevelt was chosen to run for governor in New York. Smith lost, but Roosevelt won, and he was re-elected in 1930. With Louis Howe plotting every move, the stage was set for a try for the presidency in 1932.

Eleanor Roosevelt watched these developments with a growing sense of unease. She very much enjoyed the new life she was building for herself in political and reform circles, especially the women friends she was making. She feared the confinement of the official duties associated with an officeholder's wife. When Franklin took over as governor in 1929, she took the unusual step of spending only part of the week in Albany. The rest of the time she was back on her home turf in New York City, teaching at the Todhunter School, which she had bought with Cook and Dickerman, overseeing the Val-Kill operation, and working (behind the scenes) in Democratic politics.

That compromise worked well during Franklin's two terms as governor, but when Roosevelt defeated Herbert Hoover for the presidency in 1932, Eleanor feared her hard-fought independence would disappear when she moved to Washington. She never stood in the way of his presidential aspirations, not that he would have changed his plans if she had objected; she just withdrew deeper and deeper into herself. At age forty-eight she was almost stoical. "It's good to be middle-aged. Things don't matter so much. You don't take it so hard when things happen to you that you don't like." When Associated Press reporter Lorena Hickok was sent to cover Mrs. Roosevelt at the election night festivities, Hickok said to herself, "That woman is unhappy about something."[22]

Eleanor Roosevelt refused to be confined by the White House. In the process of trying to define a role for herself she changed forever the expectations of what the First Lady could be. If, as historian William Leuchtenburg has argued, all postwar presidents lived in the shadow of FDR, so too have all later First Ladies lived in Eleanor's shadow. Just after FDR's inauguration, she convened the first of the 348 women-only press conferences she held over the next twelve years; soon newspaperwomen like Bess Furman, Ruby Black, Emma Bugbee, and Genevieve Herrick became her friends as well. Lorena Hickok occupied an even closer, and more central, place in the First Lady's affections. With great pride Eleanor joined the journalism guild herself when she filed her first "My Day" column on December 31, 1935. So popular was the syndicated six-day-a-week offering that she continued it until her death.

When the first term opened, the attention of Franklin, Eleanor, and the whole country was focused on the depression that had gripped the country since the stock market crash of 1929. When Roosevelt took the oath of office, more than a quarter of the nation's workforce was out of a job; more than 9,000 banks had gone bankrupt or closed their doors, and 100,000 businesses had failed; farm income had been cut in half. During the first week after the inauguration, more than 450,000 letters poured into the White House; during the rest of that extraordinary year of 1933, Eleanor alone received 300,000 pieces of mail, and she averaged 100,000 letters a year for the rest of the decade.

Over the years Franklin and Eleanor forged a strong political partnership based on shared goals and mutual respect. "Where's Eleanor?" FDR once asked her secretary when the First Lady was off inspecting a penal institution. "She's in prison, Mr. President." He jokingly replied, "I'm not surprised, but what for?" Their styles complemented each other. Franklin was the pragmatic politician, Eleanor the idealist, the gadfly, always pushing him—and the New Deal—to do more. As Eleanor reflected after his death:

> He might have been happier with a wife who was completely uncritical. That I was never able to be, and he had to find it in other people. Nevertheless, I think I sometimes acted as a spur, even though the spurring was not always wanted or welcome. I was one of those who served his purposes.[23]

As usual she underestimated her influence: Eleanor Roosevelt served as the conscience of the New Deal.

Three areas drew her special attention—women, civil rights, and youth. Eleanor Roosevelt was at the center of a network of New Deal women who were determined to show what women could offer to government service. Aided by social worker-turned-politician Molly Dewson, who headed the Women's Division of the Democratic National Committee, Eleanor Roosevelt put the prestige of the White House at the disposal of women administrators throughout official Washington. She invited them to present their programs at her press conferences or offered the White House for conferences or meetings. She followed up their suggestions or complaints with her own pencilled in, "Will you look into this? E.R." And she got them access to the president, which Molly Dewson availed herself of on numerous occasions. "When I wanted help on some definite point, Mrs. Roosevelt gave me the opportunity to sit by the President at dinner and the matter was settled before we finished our soup."[24]

From her travels across the country, the First Lady also developed a real affinity for the problems of youth, who one writer described as "runners, delayed at the gun" because of the Depression. She was an avid supporter of programs like the Civilian Conservation Corps and the National Youth Administration, and had been instrumental in getting a small number of women added to the formerly all-male CCC. (Where was the "she-she-she"? feminists had asked.) And late in the 1930s she had tried, with mounting frustration, to work with groups like the American Youth Congress, which was challenging Roosevelt's leadership in the looming world war in ways both Roosevelts saw as Communist-inspired.

On the question of civil rights, Eleanor had to be more circumspect. Since Southern Democrats provided key votes for New Deal measures in Congress, FDR and his advisors were very sensitive to this explosive issue on which the First Lady was light years ahead of most of the American population. Yet even symbolic steps, such as placing her chair between the white and "colored" sections of a segregated meeting in the South as a protest against Jim Crow, or inviting black performers, administrators, and ordinary citizens to White House events, got enormous political mileage in the African-American community. Conversely even these small gestures earned the enmity of many citizens, Northern and Southern. Despite her generally high approval rating, Eleanor Roosevelt's public commitment to civil rights remained highly controversial.

Eleanor seems to have accepted the inevitability of a Roosevelt second term, assuming like everyone else that it would be the last. But she grew increasingly frustrated as the New Deal stalemated during the late 1930s for political and ideological reasons. Even more disturbing was the threat of war in Europe. Eleanor had been profoundly affected by World War I, and supported the League of Nations and other peace initiatives in the 1920s. She tempered her pacifism when confronted with the horrors of Nazism and Japanese totalitarianism, and by 1940 accepted that an unprecedented third term would be necessary, although like the rest of the country she waited for her husband to declare his intentions publicly. (A cartoon in the *Augusta* (Georgia) *Chronicle* showed Roosevelt in bed writing her column and saying, "But it would make such a nice scoop if you'd only tell me, Franklin.")

Breaking the two-term precedent was a harder sell to the Democratic party, and it was Eleanor's reminder to delegates at the
1940 convention that this was "no ordinary time" that saved the
day for the Roosevelt-Wallace ticket.[25]

The war years were even harder on Eleanor than the 1930s. Too
often she felt frozen out, her calls for homefront reform seen as
intrusions (or worse) by an overburdened president and staff pre-
occupied with fighting and winning a two-front war. "Mother,
can't you see you are giving Father indigestion," blurted out
Anna after one especially contentious discussion. All four of her
sons were in the military, plus her daughter's husband, and she
must have worried about the chances that all would return home
safely. All did, but it gave her an intense appreciation for the sac-
rifices that so many Americans made to win the war.[26]

The First Lady had always been an intrepid traveler, criss-
crossing the country in the 1930s on fact-finding missions and
lecture tours. Her traveling became global during World War
II, when she made three major trips abroad. In a show of solidarity with the British in 1942, she accepted the invitation of
the King and Queen of England to return the hospitality shown
them on their trip to America in 1939, just before the outbreak
of war. (Their itinerary had included a picnic at Hyde Park,
which Eleanor described in great detail for readers of "My Day,"
including Sara's horror when her daughter-in-law served hot
dogs to royalty.) Then in 1943 she made a grueling six-week
tour of the Pacific, visiting troops in Australia, New Zealand,
and Guadalcanal, and winning over dubious military officials
by the unflagging cheerfulness and good will she brought to the
soldiers. A final trip in March 1944 took her to the Caribbean
to boost the morale of troops in this often overlooked theater of
operations.

She willingly accepted these assignments from her husband,
but found them physically and emotionally draining. And she
regretted, indeed resented, that she was never allowed to accompany him to any of the major summits like Casablanca, Teheran,

or Yalta, even though his sons and daughter Anna were often invited along. Over the years she had learned to bottle up disappointments where Franklin was concerned, so she kept her feelings to herself rather than forcing the issue. "On the whole," Eleanor later wrote, "I think I lived those years very impersonally. It was almost as though I had erected someone outside myself who was the President's wife."[27]

🦌

LIKE OTHER WOMEN who achieved renown in the twentieth century, Eleanor Roosevelt's public image offered few clues to the varied dimensions of her private life. In public she was the embodiment of the woman of conscience, secure in her convictions and unflagging in her commitment to justice and fair play. But the private Eleanor diverged quite dramatically from this public icon or saint. Having drawn the lesson from her childhood and marriage that life was somewhat negative, she struggled to find a balance between her desire to be publicly useful and her need for intimacy.

Shared work, Eleanor Roosevelt believed, was "one of the most satisfactory ways of making and keeping friends."[28] As her voluminous correspondence shows (one of her sons called her "the writingest lady of our times"), Eleanor Roosevelt had an enormous capacity for friendship. Inevitably friendship led to collaboration, or vice versa. Margaret Mead, who first met Eleanor Roosevelt in 1940 at a Hyde Park picnic, remembered, "I used to welcome every opportunity to speak in her presence, because I knew if I could say something that mattered, she would take it in and make it part of something that she, better than anyone else alive, could say to the conscience of the world."[29]

Eleanor Roosevelt crossed paths with most of the major figures of the American century, many of the minor ones, and a whole cast of ordinary Americans who too became her friends. And for a small number, that friendship deepened into love, a term she used broadly as a term of endearment for those for whom she

The two most significant people in Eleanor Roosevelt's life in 1932 and 1933 were Lorena Hickok and Earl Miller, shown here in a snapshot probably taken by the First Lady on a July 1933 vacation. There are hardly any photographs of Hickok and Roosevelt together, although the two women left thousands of letters to document their relationship. There are a few more photographs with Miller, but all of their correspondence has disappeared. (Franklin D. Roosevelt Library)

cared most deeply. (Biographer Joseph Lash titled a volume of her collected letters *Love, Eleanor*). Eleanor once confided to her daughter Anna that she only liked being in close quarters with people whom she loved very much, adding, "I made the discovery long ago that very few people made a great difference to me, but that those few mattered enormously."[30]

Many of these friendships were forged out of shared interests at a specific moment in history, suggesting the satisfaction Roosevelt received from working for good causes with good people; others had a more personal cast, sometimes taking on erotic or sexual undertones. But invariably the intensity of the relationship cooled, and Eleanor moved on. This pattern recurred throughout her life, often to the distress of those left behind in her wake. Since she rarely broke off a friendship entirely, her private life was littered with those who had been drawn by her personal charisma into her orbit and then displaced from the center. The places where she lived and entertained, notably the White House family quarters and the Val-Kill cottage, often buzzed with jealousies and intricate connections between special friends past, present, and future.

For many women a spouse serves as the center or core of their emotional life, but even before the Lucy Mercer affair, it was unlikely that Franklin would ever play that role in Eleanor's life. They were just too temperamentally different: he loved to joke and horse around, she was serious and straitlaced; he loved to sail with his cronies and play cards, she hated the water and lolling about; he liked to drink, she had an understandable fear of liquor, given the havoc that alcoholism had wreaked on her family; he hated to face bad news and blithely ignored unpleasant situations, she dealt directly with family emergencies and other crises. As Eleanor told Lorena Hickok in a revealing moment in 1936, "I realize more and more that FDR's a great man, and he is nice, but as a person, I'm a stranger, and I don't want to be anything else!"[31]

An important early adult friendship was with her husband's political advisor, Louis Howe, who was one of the first to sense how much Eleanor had to contribute to politics and public life. In fact he later admitted harboring thoughts of getting her elected president after FDR had served his two terms. During the 1920 campaign, when Eleanor was bored and resentful at being stuck on the campaign train with nothing to do, he befriended her and tried to get her more involved in what was going on. Soon he became her mentor in politics, teaching her, among other things, how to speak in public: "Say what you have to say and sit down."[32] Howe was one of the few people in the complicated Roosevelt household who managed to be friendly with both Franklin and Eleanor on fairly equal terms.

If Louis Howe kept his lines of communication open to both Roosevelts, Marguerite (Missy) LeHand's loyalty belonged solely to her boss, Franklin Roosevelt. Rather than resent the role that his longtime secretary played in her husband's life, Eleanor went out of her way to make Missy feel part of the extended Roosevelt family. Missy's role was larger and more complicated than just an efficient private secretary—she was the fun-loving hostess at the cocktail hour FDR enjoyed at the end of the day; she kept the conversation going at dinner, always willing to listen to a favorite Roosevelt story no matter how many times she had heard it before. Attuned to her boss's moods, she knew when to bring people in to liven his spirits, and when to keep them away. In many ways, she functioned like a surrogate wife, and one of the Roosevelt children later made the dubious claim that his father and Missy had been lovers.[33]

Some of Eleanor's friends were appalled at how she tolerated Missy, but Missy served her purposes as well as his. Eleanor once divided the female world into the Marthas ("devoted, feminine, fun-loving, frivolous companions") and the Marys (those more interested in ideas and action). Franklin needed to have plenty of Marthas around, a role that Eleanor could never have played. Missy, on the other hand, was proud to be so central to the president's life, a remarkable success story for a working-class girl from Somerville, Massachusetts. When Missy had a stroke in

1941, it left a huge void, which Roosevelt daughter Anna increasingly filled. Tellingly, however, it was Eleanor, not her husband, who was more apt to remember the semi-invalid Missy on birthdays and holidays and it was she, not Franklin, who attended Missy's funeral in 1944.[34]

Eleanor had a more straightforward relationship with her own secretary, Malvina Thompson (always known as Tommy), who began to work for her during the 1928 campaign. This was one of the most dependable relationships that Eleanor ever had, lasting until Thompson's death in 1953, when her hand-picked successor Maureen Corr took over. For the most strenuous years of her life Eleanor Roosevelt saw Tommy practically every day; it was Tommy who typed up Eleanor's six columns a week and handled her correspondence. One reason that the First Lady found her 1943 trip to the South Pacific so draining was that her secretary did not come along for security reasons. It wasn't just her typing she missed—Tommy was a tart and caustic observer, and fiercely protective of her boss. "My boss is a very big person," she once told Lorena Hickok, "just about the biggest person in the world. Anything I can do to help her—no matter what—justifies my existence. It's enough for me."[35]

Probably the first set of really close friends that Eleanor made in the 1920s was with two same-sex couples: Esther Lape and Elizabeth Read, and Marion Dickerman and Nancy Cook. Drawn together by shared interests in politics and social reform, Eleanor was perhaps also attracted to the deep affection that bound these women together in what were often called at the time "Boston marriages." The friendship with Dickerman and Cook was especially close. It was with them that Eleanor built the Val-Kill cottage at Hyde Park in the 1920s, a welcome retreat from the formality of the big house presided over by Sara and the one true home Eleanor ever had. At first they were so much a threesome that Eleanor monogrammed doilies for the cottage with "E M N" (Eleanor, Marion, Nancy), but over the years a combination of personal, financial, and professional disagreements poisoned their personal trust, and by 1937 the friends had fallen out. Eleanor took over the Val-Kill cottage as her own, and created an apartment for Tommy as well. After Franklin's death, she used her own money to buy the cottage and surrounding 825 acres from his estate.

The termination of her relationship with Cook and Dickerman was extreme. Eleanor's more usual pattern was simply to move on, imperceptibly, to new friends and new issues, leaving old friendships intact but without the centrality (at least to the other person) they had held earlier. For example, Molly Dewson and Eleanor forged a close and extremely productive friendship in the early 1930s based on a shared commitment to getting more women into politics and government. Affectionate, almost daily letters passed between them in the 1932 campaign and in the early days of the New Deal. (Dewson was one of the few friends who called Eleanor by her given name; almost everyone else, including close friends like Joe Lash and David Gurewitsch, called her Mrs. Roosevelt. Older friends still do.)[36] But by the second term, Dewson was writing to Eleanor, "When you are shopping in New York City sometime couldn't I go along and hold your purse?" Eleanor and Molly remained friends until the end of their lives; in fact, Eleanor visited Molly and her partner Polly Porter in Castine, Maine, on her last trip to Campobello in August of 1962, just months before her death. But nothing ever matched the intensity of their friendship in the early New Deal days. Dewson was left holding the bag (literally), not quite sure what had changed. Many other colleagues and friends told similar tales.[37]

A variation on this theme at Eleanor's expense was her friendship with Harry Hopkins. A former social worker, Hopkins shared Eleanor's humanitarian commitment to social reform and worked doggedly to bring relief to as many out-of-work citizens as possible through the Works Progress Administration. In the context of the frenetic New Deal they quickly became close friends. But instead of Eleanor Roosevelt moving on, as was the usual pattern, it was Harry Hopkins who in effect dropped her, reorienting his loyalties to Franklin Roosevelt in the late 1930s and becoming one of the president's closest aides during World War II. In the divided White House, you were either Eleanor's friend or Franklin's. Eleanor never forgot the snub.

During the years when Franklin was governor, Eleanor's most important relationship was with a state trooper, Earl Miller, who had been assigned to protect the governor's wife, then forty-four years old. Miller, who was twelve years younger, cut quite a dashing figure—a former boxer, he was quite vain about his body, with good reason. Earl was a fun and relaxing companion (he encouraged her to ride and play tennis and taught her to shoot a pistol) and very protective of the woman he called "Lady" or "The Lady." Friends like Cook and Dickerman thought he treated her with just a bit too much familiarity ("manhandled" was the word they used)[38] and found it inappropriate the way he casually put his hand on her knee or his arm around her shoulder. In one suggestive scene from home movies, which have survived from the early 1930s, Earl dresses as a pirate and kidnaps a bound and blindfolded Eleanor. Near the end of his life Earl quashed rumors that they had an affair with this retort: "You don't sleep with someone you call Mrs. Roosevelt."[39]

This relationship remains the most elusive of Eleanor's adult friendships, since not a single letter survives from her to him, despite anecdotal evidence that she wrote him faithfully. Earl Miller never wrote or spoke in depth about his friendship with Eleanor, whether out of chivalrous loyalty or for some other reason. Given the near encyclopedic documentation of almost every other aspect of Eleanor's life, the silence of the archival record on Earl Miller is tantalizing.

On the other hand, there is ample documentation of Eleanor's next—in fact, simultaneous—passion for journalist Lorena Hickok, which flamed right after the 1932 election and flourished in the early days of the New Deal. The thirty-nine-year-old "Hick," as she was often called, was probably the best-known woman reporter of her day: funny, wisecracking, one of the boys, and a superb writer. Assigned by the Associated Press to cover Eleanor Roosevelt, Hick soon found herself violating Louis Howe's warning that "a reporter should never get too close to a news source." Her decision to resign from the AP in 1933 because she had gotten too close to Eleanor was a real mistake, however, because it robbed her of her rewarding and prestigious career, making her even more dependent on Eleanor emotionally. Hickok filled the void by working as a roving investigator for Harry Hopkins in the first Roosevelt term, and by doing publicity for the 1939 World's Fair and the Women's Division of the Democratic Party in the 1940s.[40]

The 3,500 letters between the two that have survived (both saved their correspondence, although Hick destroyed or edited some of the earliest letters) show the affectionate, indeed erotic way that these women wrote to each other. For example, just three days into the New Deal, Eleanor wrote to Hick just before going to bed:

> All day I thought of you, and another birthday I *will* be with you and yet tonight you sounded so far away and formal. Oh! I want to put my arms around you. I ache to hold you close. Your ring is a great comfort. I look at it and think she does love me, or I wouldn't be wearing it.[41]

The ring referred to is a sapphire and diamond pinky ring that Hick gave to Roosevelt in 1933, and that she wore until her death. Hick replied in kind:

> I've been trying today to bring back your face—to remember just *how* you looked. . . . Most clearly I remember your eyes, with the kind of teasing smile in them, and the feeling of that soft spot just northeast of the corner of your mouth against my lips. I wonder what we will do when we meet—what we will say when we meet. Well—I'm rather proud of us, aren't you? I think we have done rather well.[42]

Such passionate statements are typical of the early days of their relationship. Eleanor's ardor soon cooled, however, leaving Lorena (like so many others) hanging on for crumbs of the emotional intensity they once shared. Eleanor later tried to explain how she felt, but it likely fell on deaf ears: "I know you often have a feeling for me which for one reason or another I may not return in kind, but I feel I love you just the same and so often we entirely satisfy each other that I feel there is a fundamental basis on which our relationship stands." But, she continued, Hickok must understand "that I love other people the same way or differently, but each one has their place and one cannot compare them." And yet Eleanor remained a faithful (if increasingly distant and detached) friend to Hick, even inviting her to move into the White House during the war years when she could not afford a Washington apartment.[43]

As the second term ended, a new friend appeared in Eleanor's life: a thirty-year-old student activist named Joseph P. Lash, a leader in the American Student Union. (These student leaders were not actually students—most were well into their twenties or early thirties.) After testifying before the House Un-American Activities Committee in 1939, Lash found himself invited back for tea at the White House. "She thinks she can reform capitalists . . . by inviting them to the White House for dinner and a good talking to. . . . We had little cream puffs and were waited on by butlers," he wrote condescendingly to a friend.[44] Within a year, however, probably to his great surprise, he found himself upgraded to the status of intimate friend of Mrs. Roosevelt, invited to weekends at Val-Kill and the recipient of the nearly daily letters she showered on those to whom she was closest. And in what was becoming a ritual to mark the beginning of a special new friendship, she told him about her early life and her pain over her husband's affair with Lucy Mercer.[45]

In the midst of his deepening friendship with the First Lady, Lash had fallen in love with Trude Pratt, a fellow activist at the International Student Service who was married with three chil-

In the 1940s the most important person in Eleanor Roosevelt's life was Joe Lash, shown here in 1941 in an affectionate pose on the White House grounds with the First Lady and his future wife, Trude Pratt. Roosevelt is in mourning for her brother Hall, but Joe and Trude obviously lift her spirits. (Stock Montage, Inc.)

dren. Soon Trude was drawn into the web as well, with Eleanor Roosevelt serving as a confidante for both young lovers as Trude went through the painful decision to divorce her husband in order to marry Lash. After Lash was drafted and sent overseas, Eleanor continued the correspondence, even though she knew their letters were being intercepted and read by military authorities. A high point of her trip to the Pacific in 1943 was the chance to see Lash, who was stationed at Guadalcanal.

Lash always painted his intimate friendship with the First Lady in mother-son terms, which removed any hint of sexual impropriety. (That had not kept the FBI from once bugging her hotel room when she was meeting with Lash.) After Joe and Trude Pratt were married in 1944 in a simple ceremony with Eleanor in attendance, they remained extremely close friends, although Eleanor became somewhat less of a daily presence in their lives as Lash launched his career as a correspondent and editorial writer for the *New York Post*. A decade later Lash helped to fuel the revival of interest in her life with his Pulitzer Prize-winning *Eleanor and Franklin* (1971).

The final great emotional attachment of her life—David Gurewitsch—began when Roosevelt was serving in the United Nations. Even Joe Lash had to admit, "We all served her, but David had her heart in a way the rest of us did not." When Eleanor moved back to New York after her husband's death, she needed to find a doctor and Trude Lash recommended David, whom she had known from student days in Germany in the 1930s. Once again Eleanor not only poured out her love to this much younger and presumably inaccessible man (he was forty-five, she was sixty-three), she aided and abetted his active love life, which included an affair with journalist Martha Gellhorn and his eventual marriage to Edna Perkel in 1958. After that the Gurewitsches and Mrs. Roosevelt shared a home until her death. The young bride captured the oddity of this threesome well when she remarked matter-of-factly that she had it harder than other women: they had Marilyn Monroe for a rival, she had Eleanor Roosevelt.[46]

Due to the popularity of Lash's biographies and Blanche Wiesen Cook's recent best-selling account of Eleanor's life through 1933, considerable attention has focused on the varied dimensions of Eleanor Roosevelt's emotional life. The greatest debate has occurred over the meaning of her relationship with Lorena Hickok, beginning with the firestorm of controversy that greeted the release of their letters in 1978, ten years after Hickok's death. Since most concede that Lorena Hickok was a lesbian, these letters raised the question of whether the First Lady was a lesbian, too. For many of Eleanor's family members, former associates, and beloved followers, this was just too much to accept.

Attempts to deny or undercut the importance of the Roosevelt-Hickok relationship have taken various forms. Some have claimed that Eleanor had no knowledge of love between women, or that she was shocked by the subject, but given the large number of female couples in her circle of friends, dating as far back as Allenswood, that explanation seems pretty weak. Others have focused almost exclusively on the question of whether there was a physical dimension to their relationship to match the passion they both committed to the page, generally concluding that Eleanor would have been too much a Victorian to hop into bed with Hick.[47]

Lost in the controversy over the Roosevelt-Hickok correspondence is how similar the letters were in intensity and purpose to those that Eleanor would later write to Joe Lash and David Gurewitsch. (Since her letters to Earl Miller have disappeared, it is hard to know what language of endearment she used with him.) *They were all love letters.* Except for gender, these three men were just as "inappropriate" love objects for the First Lady as Lorena Hickok. But given the lack of uproar over public knowledge of these relationships, it seems clear that love between an upper-class lady and a state trooper, or between an older woman and a younger man, especially if these relationships are assumed to be unconsummated, is far easier to explain away than the taboos associated with love between women.

It may well be that Eleanor Roosevelt was essentially bisexual—that is, a person who was attracted to both sexes.[48] In her lifelong quest for love and friendship, she drew no artificial boundaries between men and women; at times she moved in almost totally female worlds, while at other points her primary emotional "other" was a man. As Eleanor once wrote in her journal, "No form of love is to be despised."[49]

"Something locked me up," Eleanor once confessed to Hick,

perhaps trying to explain her difficulty expressing her emotions in person.[50] But another interpretation is that she was not in fact locked up—that she found many outlets for her need to love and be loved in return. What is striking is the freedom with which she picked and chose her friends, how much she learned and took from them, and the impunity (verging at times on imperviousness) with which she outgrew them and moved on. And, of course, how she managed to do this all safely out of the public eye.

🐾

AT THE CONCLUSION of her slim volume, *It's Up to the Women*, hastily put together in 1933 to capitalize on her husband's election, Eleanor Roosevelt commented, "Perhaps we are going to see evolved in the next few years not only a social order built by the ability and brains of our men, but a social order which also represents the understanding heart of women." She was even more assertive in a 1940 article for *Good Housekeeping* assessing the positive changes that women's suffrage had brought to public life:

> . . . on the whole, during the last twenty years, government has been taking increasing cognizance of humanitarian questions, things that deal with the happiness of human beings, such as health, education, security. There is nothing, of course, to prove this is entirely because of the women's interest, and yet I think it is significant that this change has come about during the period when women have been exercising their franchise.

She concluded on a positive note that reflected her lifelong optimism about women's contributions to modern life: "It will always take all kinds of women to make up a world, and only now and then will they unite their interests. When they do, I think it is safe to say that something historically important will happen."[51]

Like many women of her generation, Eleanor Roosevelt held certain assumptions about politics, the most fundamental being that men and women brought different values, agendas, and styles to public life. "When all is said and done, women *are* different from men. They are equals in many ways, but they cannot refuse to acknowledge their differences. Not to acknowledge them weakens the case." Anticipating the gender gap of the 1980s and 1990s, Roosevelt concluded that women were often more interested in social and humanitarian outcomes whereas men saw politics as a livelihood or a game. Their styles were different too: "Women will try to find ways to cooperate where men think only of dominating." While there certainly were exceptions to these generalizations, these ideas about "difference" formed the core of the philosophy that she and many other public-spirited women brought to politics in the decades after suffrage was won.[52]

One of the main post-suffrage agendas for women was getting inside the political parties themselves, and once in, getting men to listen to them. As suffrage leader Carrie Chapman Catt told the newly formed League of Women Voters in 1920, "The only way to get things in this country is to find them on the inside of the political party. . . . You won't be so welcome there, but that is the place to be." From personal experience Eleanor Roosevelt knew that women were listened to on small things, "but when it comes to asking for important things they generally find they are up against a blank wall." One of the most frustrating moments of her political career occurred at the 1924 Democratic convention when she and her co-workers waited futilely outside the closed door of the platform committee, denied the chance to present their planks because there were no women (or like-minded men) on the committee willing to introduce them. One of Molly Dewson's proudest moments in Democratic politics was winning women guaranteed access to that committee in 1936.[53]

Post-suffrage women had a much broader definition of political power and influence than just access: they were interested in humanitarian and social reform. To implement these goals, they found multiple avenues to make their opinions known, especially through nonpartisan voluntary associations and reform groups like the National Consumers' League, the Women's Trade Union League, and the League of Women Voters. Not surprisingly, Eleanor Roosevelt was very much a part of this larger quest, first on the state level in New York in the 1920s and then on the national level during the New Deal.

One of the most troublesome issues for women in politics from the 1920s through the 1970s was the Equal Rights Amendment, which was first introduced by Alice Paul and the National Woman's Party in 1923. In some ways this might seem strange— why wouldn't former suffragists rally around a constitutional amendment seeking to outlaw all discrimination and special treatment based on sex? The stumbling block was protective labor legislation for women workers, which had the strong support of reformers like Eleanor Roosevelt.

The wording of the proposed Equal Rights Amendment threatened to throw out protective labor legislation such as limitations on maximum hours or minimum wages because they applied only to women. (The courts had allowed such laws to stand for women, but struck them down for men as an infringement on freedom of contract.) While supporters and opponents both agreed that there were many laws that discriminated against women (such as a woman losing her citizenship if she married a foreigner, or being barred from certain occupations solely because of sex), reformers urged a state-by-state approach to such discriminatory laws in order to leave labor legislation in place. Members of the National Woman's Party, on the other hand, saw all laws that singled women out for special treatment as demeaning, and they claimed that women were hurt more than helped by so-called protective legislation. The division was so deep that no compromise was possible.

As a prominent Democrat and social reformer, Eleanor Roosevelt staunchly opposed the ERA for the first two decades after women won the vote. She softened her stand slightly in the 1940s, when in response to the entreaties of pro-ERA Democratic women like Emma Guffey Miller (not coincidentally, a member of the National Woman's Party) the 1944 Democratic party platform included a plank supporting the amendment for the first time. Privately she penned a short memo to FDR saying "May be time to change," but she took no public stand. In 1951 she made a very lukewarm statement on the amendment, saying that now that women had unions to protect them it was less necessary to rely on protective legislation, but she turned down the NWP's appeal to become an outright backer.[54]

To her credit, Eleanor Roosevelt gradually modified her stance over time due to changing conditions in the labor field. In contrast, many other reformers clung to opposition to the ERA almost as an article of faith, despite the fact that laws like the Fair Labor Standards Act (1938) extended hours-and-wages protections to all workers, not just to women. As late as 1963 the ongoing opposition of reformers and union leaders convinced the Presidential Commission on the Status of Women not to endorse the amendment in its final report.

Roosevelt's stand on the Equal Rights Amendment raises the question of whether she was a feminist. This was a slippery term in the 1920s and 1930s, almost exclusively associated with members of the National Woman's Party and not commonly used by social reformers or the general public. And yet Eleanor Roosevelt used the term in her autobiography to show how far she had come on women's issues. "I cannot claim to have been a feminist in those early days," she admitted as she tried to explain her initial lack of enthusiasm for woman suffrage. Yet she caught on fast: "I became a much more ardent citizen and feminist than anyone about me in the intermediate years would have dreamed possible."[55]

In 1935 Roosevelt supplied an all-purpose definition of feminism that showed exactly what she meant by the term: "Fundamentally, the purpose of Feminism is that a woman should have an equal opportunity and Equal Rights with any other citizen of the country." Instead of demanding major changes in the prevailing gender system, she believed that women's collective success would break down discrimination and male resistance. As she told readers of the *Democratic Digest* in 1938, "It seems to me that the best way to advance the equal rights of women is for every woman to do her job in the best way possible so that gradually the prejudice against women will disappear."[56] There are more radical formulations of feminism, to be sure, but her focus on individual success worked well in the context of the 1920s and 1930s, in effect keeping the topic alive in a period without an organized feminist movement.

Journalist Ruby Black, an ardent feminist and NWP member who convinced the First Lady to speak out against a federal law that discriminated against married women, once penned a deft description of Eleanor Roosevelt's stance: "She talks like a social worker and acts like a feminist."[57] Black was right. Perhaps the strongest evidence of Roosevelt's underlying feminism was her insistence on her right to earn her own income. For Eleanor Roosevelt and many other women, married or single, economic independence was a statement about their symbolic worth as individuals.

On the face of it Eleanor Roosevelt had little objective need to earn money. She had an income from the estates of her parents, and Franklin had money of his own as well. And there was mother-in-law Sara, except that her money came with too many strings attached. And yet Eleanor never forgot the first dollars she earned on her own from a teaching job: "Each time I was actually paid I think I gained in self-confidence, in the belief that since my contribution was being recognized in the way that was ordinarily accepted, then I must be doing something of value." She felt the same about the first money she earned in the 1920s from the articles she freelanced about women in politics for national magazines.[58]

In a fairly unusual pattern for someone of her class background, Eleanor Roosevelt also became a businesswoman in the 1920s. Her first business enterprise was Val-Kill Industries, a furniture factory opened in 1927 in partnership with Nancy

Cook, Marion Dickerman, and Caroline O'Day, which produced reproductions made by local craftspeople. With those same partners, and also in 1927, Roosevelt purchased the Todhunter School in New York City, a girls' school on the Upper East Side, which merged with the Dalton School in 1939; Dickerman served as principal and Eleanor was a popular teacher. Although neither enterprise ever made much money, Eleanor clearly had a taste for entrepreneurship, something she shared with many other women who founded or ran businesses in that decade. Rather than being separate from her reform impulses in politics, Roosevelt's entry into the realm of business was part of a larger pattern of former suffragists exploring all facets of society, drawing empowerment from their new capacity as citizen-voters. The fact that all her early business undertakings were women-owned and not tied to Franklin's political career added to their attractiveness.[59]

Opportunities to make money increased dramatically once she was in the White House. What is especially surprising in light of the difficulties of recent First Ladies to express their own opinions, let alone work for pay, is how open she was about doing this. As she told her friend, AP journalist Bess Furman, she was determined to "get the money for a good cause and take the gaff." That she claimed to donate the money to good causes deflected most of the heat, despite the fact that it didn't all go to charity; a set percentage went to her agent, and she sometimes funneled money to her children during their frequent periods of financial insecurity.[60]

Examples abound of Eleanor Roosevelt's extraordinary zeal for making money during the New Deal. In 1937 the *Ladies' Home Journal* paid the phenomenal sum of $75,000 to excerpt her autobiography, *This Is My Story*. (It cannot have escaped her notice that the advance was exactly the same as the president's yearly salary.) She threw herself into strenuous yearly lecture tours, for which she received upwards of $1,000 a talk. She also broadcast frequently on the radio, which along with the lecture circuit was one of the main ways that the public at large connected with celebrities in those pre-television days; her radio appearances in

1940 alone (probably an unusual year, given the election and the looming war) earned her $156,000 in fees. Even her column had roots in her desire to earn money to give to the causes she believed in, as she explained to Hick: "400 words every day, rather a lot but I need the money."[61]

In many ways it is ironic that Eleanor Roosevelt, born into the sheltered world of the Victorian upper class, should become so publicly identified with new roles for women in American life, including business and politics. Once she did, she opened doors for other women to follow her example. And unlike younger women who seemed to feel that feminism was old-fashioned and unnecessary, Eleanor Roosevelt never lost her sense of solidarity with her sex: she remained a woman who was not ashamed or afraid to say "we." This model of public-spirited womanhood was one of her main legacies to the American century.

※

ON APRIL 12, 1945, Eleanor Roosevelt was attending the annual Thrift Shop benefit at the Sulgrave Club when she received the urgent call from the White House. Waiting until she could leave unobtrusively so as not to unduly alarm the press, she returned to the White House knowing in her heart the news that would await her. "Father slept away. He did his job to the end as he would want you to," she cabled to her four sons, all of whom were overseas. When a shaken Harry Truman asked what he could do for her, she replied, "Is there anything we can do for you? For you are the one in trouble now."[62]

As soon as Eleanor arrived in Warm Springs to supervise the funeral arrangements, cousin Laura Delano (who was a "Martha" if ever there was one) abruptly told her that Lucy Mercer Rutherford was with the president when he died. Eleanor must have felt as if she had been punched in the stomach. Franklin had promised that he would never see Lucy again, and now it turned out he had broken that pledge. Even crueler to accept, her daughter Anna had been party to the deception, acting as hostess when

Lucy visited the White House and keeping it a secret from her mother. On the night of Roosevelt's death, a bitter and hurt Eleanor angrily confronted her daughter over her role. At the time Anna feared she had lost the trust of her mother forever, but they were eventually able to rebuild their relationship.

So as Eleanor went through the ceremonial rituals of national mourning, she was dealing with far more than losing her husband of forty years. When reporters asked about her plans, she said simply, "The story is over." To certain friends she confided that she hoped to lead "a peaceful life." (This was too much for Trude Lash, who teased they should buy her a lace cap as a retirement gift.) On the other hand, the resumption of her column just four days after FDR's death was a clear statement that she planned to continue to speak out publicly: "Because I was the wife of the President certain restrictions were imposed on me. Now I am on my own and I hope to write as a newspaper woman." Off the record to her newspaper buddies, she gave a glimpse of how important this newfound freedom felt to her: "For the first time in my life I can say just what I want. For your information it is wonderful to feel free." Franklin's death was Eleanor's final liberation.[63]

Her desire to be self-supporting, which in her case meant making enough money to live on and to help her children and the various causes and charities she believed in, also shaped her postwar career priorities, especially since she turned down a government pension as FDR's widow. There were no precedents for a former First Lady to have a career after her White House years, but as usual Eleanor Roosevelt set a new standard. Soon she was earning at or above her prewar level, thanks to the continued syndication of "My Day" and her lecture tours. In addition to her ongoing radio work, she also branched into the new medium of television. She even did an occasional commercial, agreeing to plug margarine as long as she could make some statement of value of her own choosing. She reminded the television audience of world hunger.[64]

She also continued—without benefit of a ghostwriter—to write her autobiography, producing two more volumes and an abridged version of the entire opus. She found it harder to write candidly about the White House years than about her childhood and early adulthood,[65] and Bruce Gould of the *Ladies' Home Journal* found the second volume far less compelling than *This Is My Story*: "You have written this too hastily—as though you were composing it on a bicycle while pedaling your way to a fire." He failed to exercise his option, and *This I Remember* (and eventually Roosevelt's monthly column as well) went to *McCall's*, where it was just as successful as the first volume.[66]

By far the most absorbing and satisfying work of Eleanor Roosevelt's post-White House years was at the United Nations. Recognizing her prominence in Democratic circles, Harry Truman had been looking for a position to offer the former First Lady, and in December 1945 he asked her to be a member of the U.S. delegation to the first meeting of the United Nations General Assembly, to be held the next month in London. This international organization had been a dream of both Roosevelts, "the one hope for a peaceful world" in her words. After a ritual demurral, she accepted.[67]

Certain members of the delegation had been far from enthusiastic about her appointment, she later learned, but her diligence and good will won them over. Senator Arthur Vandenberg sheepishly admitted, "I want to say that I take back everything I ever said about her, and believe me, it's been plenty!" Allen Dulles apologized to her face: "I feel I must tell you that when you were appointed I thought it would be terrible and now I think your work has been fine." Noted Eleanor laconically to a friend, "So—against odds, the women inch forward."[68]

Eleanor Roosevelt's six years of service at the United Nations coincided with the height of the Cold War. Her dealings with the Soviet Union reinforced her commitment to democracy and gave her a firsthand glimpse at how power operated (or was usurped) in totalitarian countries, a lesson she never forgot. Her work on the committee devoted to humanitarian, educational, and cultural questions brought her the most satisfaction. No doubt the delegation leaders thought that Committee Three would be a safe place to park Mrs. Roosevelt, but it turned out to be one of the hottest spots, especially over the controversial issue of human rights. There Eleanor Roosevelt played a central role in one of the most lasting achievements of the international organization: the drafting of the 1948 Universal Declaration of Human Rights. Once again Roosevelt showed her commitment to feminism. When women delegates from developing nations warned her that phrases like "all men are born free and equal in dignity and rights" would be interpreted in their countries as literally only men, Roosevelt engineered the shift to the more inclusive "all human beings."

When Dwight Eisenhower was elected in 1952, Eleanor Roosevelt stepped down from the United Nations, knowing that she would not have been reappointed anyway. For the rest of her life she continued to work with the American Association for the United Nations, building support for the international organization throughout the United States and around the world. As she moved into her seventies, she became aware of the overall objective in her life: "I wanted, with all my heart, a peaceful world."[69]

One of the causes to which Roosevelt devoted the most time during the 1940s and 1950s was civil rights, the issue on which she was most hamstrung during her husband's presidency. In 1945 she joined the board of the National Association for the Advancement of Colored People (NAACP), something that would have been unthinkable while Franklin was still alive. Through that organization and others, she championed affordable housing and access to integrated schools. As the pace of civil rights activism escalated in the late 1950s, Roosevelt endorsed civil disobedience and nonviolent protests and was especially proud of the role students were playing in the movement. One morning her secretary Maurine Corr asked her why she was humming. "I had the most wonderful dream last night, Maureen. I dreamt I was marching and singing and sitting in with students in the South."[70]

She also emerged as a powerbroker in the Democratic party, although she bluntly ruled out any thought of running for office. Her sons were all jockeying to establish their own political careers (with little more success than their multiple marriages), and she wanted them to have a chance. She had generally tried to stay out of partisan politics while serving at the United Nations, but felt no such compunction in 1956, emerging as a leading backer of Senator Adlai E. Stevenson in his second try for the presidency. In this campaign she really hit the hustings, although at times she wondered whether all those motorcades and rallies made much of a difference. They certainly didn't get Stevenson elected, but that would have taken a miracle, given Eisenhower's popularity and the prosperity of the 1950s.

Eleanor Roosevelt approached the 1960 campaign with grave misgivings about the frontrunner, Senator John F. Kennedy, who in her barely disguised opinion could not hold a candle to her beloved Adlai, himself never a serious candidate. So important was Eleanor Roosevelt as a representative of the New Deal legacy that Kennedy knew he had to have her support. They met at Val-Kill one day in August, despite Eleanor's grief at learning of the death of a favorite granddaughter in a riding accident the day before. The meeting was cordial, and Kennedy had his endorsement.[71]

When Kennedy lagged in appointing women to his new administration, Roosevelt carried on her lifelong habit of pushing women for public office and presented him with a three-page list of women qualified for high executive positions. In turn Kennedy asked Roosevelt to chair the Presidential Commission on the Status of Women. Although unable to attend many of the sessions, her name gave the committee prestige as well as a strong link to past feminist efforts in the public sphere. The Presidential Commission was one of a number of factors that helped reawaken American interest in feminism as a national issue in the 1960s and 1970s. It is symbolic and fitting that Eleanor Roosevelt presided over this rebirth.

The most admired woman in the world arriving alone and unassisted at the Washington, D.C., train station in the fall of 1960. Roosevelt was then 76 years old, still carrying her own luggage and deep in thought about how much there was left to do. (Franklin D. Roosevelt Library)

"When you cease to make a contribution you begin to die," noted Eleanor in 1959 at age seventy-five. Despite the toll age and illness were taking on her, she showed no signs of retiring. "I am willing to slow down but I just don't know how," she admitted.[72] As her strength began to ebb, David Gurewitsch was put in the awkward position of being both her physician and the center of her emotional life. Her condition was diagnosed as aplastic anemia, later amended to a rare form of bone-marrow tuberculosis. In the summer and fall of 1962 she was in and out of hospitals, in great pain and practically begging to die. Swirling around her were long-standing jealousies among her children and many close friends and associates who considered themselves practically members of the family: everyone still wanted a piece of Eleanor. It was not a pleasant scene, nor was it an easy or dignified death. The end finally came on November 7, 1962, and Eleanor was buried next to her husband in the Rose Garden at Hyde Park.

Eleanor Roosevelt touched people, both symbolically and literally. During her life she probably met more Americans in person than any other official, elected or not. Even today, people of a certain age tell stories about shaking Eleanor's hand at a reception, hearing her speak, or seeing her on the street. For so many years she was a part of people's lives, and now she was gone. "She couldn't have died at 6:15," sobbed one woman. "We were eating dinner then and we were happy."[73]

Of all the tributes that poured in, few matched Adlai Stevenson's for eloquence: "She would rather light candles than curse the darkness, and her glow warmed the world." Cartoonist Bill Mauldin paid his simple respects with a procession of angels peeking around in the clouds, until one says softly, "It's her."[74] Through the force of her convictions and the strength of her charismatic personality, Eleanor Roosevelt earned the respect and admiration of her country and the world. In her footsteps have followed other courageous and independent women who, guided by her example, helped to shape the American century.

"He's giving Dorothy Thompson a piece of his mind."

T W O

"SHE RIDES IN THE SMOKING CAR": DOROTHY THOMPSON

URING HER HEYDAY in the 1930s, Dorothy Thompson was called the "First Lady of American Journalism," the most influential woman in the United States after Eleanor Roosevelt. Her syndicated column, "On the Record," reached an estimated eight to ten million readers three times a week. The horrors of fascism, Thompson's *idée fixe* as far back as 1931, inspired her most powerful and impassioned writing; her dramatic rise to national prominence went hand in hand with Adolf Hitler's awful ascent. After Americans took her advice and entered World War II, she remained influential and widely read, but never again would so many hang on her every word.[1]

Dorothy Thompson epitomized the style of personal journalism that flourished in the interwar years: "Ours is the age of the reporter," she said in a best-selling and sensational book about Hitler, and then proceeded to place herself smack in the middle of events. How she got her story—like the slightly embellished anecdote about leaving to cover a revolution in high heels and evening gown—was as much a part of the news interest as the event itself. Fellow journalist John Gunther chose the title "A Blue-Eyed Tornado" for his sympathetic 1935 profile, and it stuck: "Two things happened to Central Europe during the decade of the 20s, people in Vienna still say—the world economic crisis and Dorothy Thompson."[2]

Dorothy Thompson was part of what H. L. Mencken called "the self-exploiting, individualized star system" of news commentary. Along with Walter Winchell, Walter Lippmann, Westbrook Pegler, and Heywood Hale Broun, these columnists became celebrities, part of the daily life of the nation. ("My Day" columnist Eleanor Roosevelt was already a household name by virtue of being First Lady.) Thompson was no stranger to fame, having married novelist Sinclair Lewis in 1928, but hers became an even more broadly based celebrity than his, according to their mutual friend Vincent Sheean: Lewis was known to his readers, but Thompson was "known to the corner druggist, the taxi driver, the hairdresser and the headwaiter; people who probably had never read a book in their lives quoted her familiarly from day to day; she was as national (as much a 'star') as any baseball player or film actress." Just like a Hollywood star, she received hundreds of fan letters a day and was often featured in the papers or on the radio; as early as 1937, some even predicted a future for her in the new medium of television.[3]

Like Eleanor Roosevelt, Dorothy Thompson had her share of detractors. New Deal administrator Hugh Johnson called her "a blood-thirsty breast-beating Boadicea" and Sir Wilmot Lewis said dismissively, "She has discovered the secret of perpetual emotion." Sniffed Alice Roosevelt Longworth, "Dorothy is the only woman in history who has had her menopause in public and made it pay."[4] Even her friends and colleagues often damned her with faint praise. Fellow journalist Heywood Hale Broun compared her to the heroine of Harriet Beecher Stowe's *Uncle Tom's Cabin*: "Dorothy is greater than Eliza because not only does she cross the ice but breaks it as she goes. Moreover, she is her own bloodhound." And Walter Lippmann's comparison of Thompson to the Statue of Liberty had a definite edge to it: "Made of brass. Visible at all times to the world. Holding the light aloft, but always the same light. . . . Capable of being admired, but difficult to love."[5] As James Thurber's famous cartoon captures, nobody was neutral about Dorothy Thompson.

When *Time* put Thompson on its cover on June 13, 1939, it captioned her portrait, "She rides in the smoking car." (A lifelong chain smoker, she used cigarettes and Dexedrine to keep herself constantly "up.") It was no secret that Dorothy Thompson preferred the company of men to women. The majority of her readers were male, as were the members of the personal brain trust she tapped for her columns. After the dinner parties she loved to host, she talked with the men over cigarettes and scotch, while women guests were left to fend for themselves.

And yet Thompson was never simply one of the boys— throughout her life she had close friendships with other women. Right out of college she had worked for the woman suffrage movement and considered herself an ardent feminist. In the 1920s, like many other women of her generation, she began to find the organized women's movement out of touch with her needs, which went beyond political equality and economic independence (which she felt had already been achieved) to include the right to a satisfying personal life. When she addressed women's issues in her columns, she increasingly distanced herself from feminism, warning that women couldn't have it all and suggesting that most women would be happiest as wives and mothers. Even though she married three times and bore a son, she could never take her own advice. She worked hard to make it as a woman in a man's world, to be, in that contradictory phrase of the times, "a woman newspaperman." In many ways, her life encapsulates the possibilities, contradictions, and dilemmas of modern women.

🦌

"ODD THAT I never really knew what I wanted to 'do' with my life except live it, and not work from 9 to 5 in an office on a 'job.'

Journalism was only a means to the end—to see, to learn, if possible to *be*." The field of journalism was an apt choice for an ambitious but somewhat unfocused young woman like Dorothy Thompson. In those days being a journalist did not require a graduate degree or a lengthy apprenticeship in a city newsroom, just personal drive and ambition, a situation that worked to women's advantage. Starting with Nellie Bly and her round-the-world trip in 1889, intrepid female reporters had seized interesting professional opportunities in journalism that they would not have found in other more established areas of American life. And few reporters were more intrepid than Dorothy Thompson.[6]

Born in Lancaster, New York, on July 9, 1893, Dorothy Thompson was the eldest of three children of Peter and Margaret Thompson.[7] Her English-born father was a minister with the Methodist Episcopal Church, and his influence dominated family life and Dorothy's upbringing. "If I look back across my life," she wrote in 1957, "I am sure that the strongest, longest, and most pervasive influence in it was my father. I have never known anyone else as good, as pure in motive, or as basically human and civilized." Since ministers generally moved on to new churches every three years or so, Dorothy lived in six villages in the Buffalo area by the time she was fifteen. Her father's salary was only $1,000 a year plus a house, which meant money was tight for the family of five. Instead of resenting her family's financial situation, Dorothy was for the most part oblivious to it, only later realizing its formative influence on her character and her ability to make her own way.[8]

Many commentators later noted how much of Dorothy Thompson's political philosophy could be traced back to the core spirituality she inherited from her Methodist father. His other legacy was encouragement of her love of reading, which in turn instilled her desire to be a writer. "Books meant sheer magic," she recalled, which was lucky since there wasn't much else to do for recreation in rural New York for a girl of limited means. "There were no automobiles—none for Methodist ministers, in those days. No moving pictures. No radio. But inside the covers of books was everything, everything, that exists outside in the world today."[9]

Dorothy's childhood changed abruptly in 1901 when her mother died of the aftereffects of a botched abortion. (That was terrible enough, but Thompson's memoirs confirmed that the abortion had been induced by Mrs. Thompson's own mother.)[10] Two years later her father remarried a woman who, charitably, was totally unsuited for her role as a stepmother. One Christmas she gave Dorothy a daintily wrapped baby bottle with this note: "Merry Christmas to a cry-baby." Dorothy was so miserable that she was eventually sent to Chicago to live with two aunts and attend the Lewis Institute, a private school that offered a course of study for high school and two years of college.[11]

Like many aspiring women in the 1910s, Dorothy Thompson knew that a college education could be the opening wedge to an interesting and fulfilling life, and she dreamed of going to one of the elite Eastern women's colleges, like Smith, Bryn Mawr, or Wellesley. But those schools were far beyond her family's resources, so she attended Syracuse University, a Methodist-affiliated institution that offered special scholarship support to the children of ministers. Having entered with advanced standing as a junior, she graduated in 1914.

Syracuse was a coeducational institution, and more than half its students were women, a situation Thompson found congenial. But she quickly tired of the severe weather, forever associating the campus with the "smell of wet rubbers and fleece-lined 'arctics.' " In her two years on campus she stood out for her energy, intelligence, and lifelong propensity to dominate conversations. Needless to say, her dating experiences were less than successful. "I liked boys well enough and they did not dislike me, but they often bored me with their damp hands and callow shy advances and I frightened them off with my rather high-falutin speech. I did not care. I did not know what I wanted to do with my life but I knew that I did not want to marry until much later, and unless one desired marriage, one did not flirt around." Her goal was to find a way to support herself and help her brother and sister gain their college educations.[12]

Teaching would have been a logical next step—ever since the nineteenth century women who needed to earn a living chose that career path—but ironically Thompson flunked her state teacher's test in English. Instead she joined the woman suffrage movement as a full-time organizer for the next three years, based in Buffalo and its environs. She considered herself a suffragist as soon as she heard of the movement, and called her participation "an extraordinary experience, an education in politics, publicity, public speaking, organization and an insight into every variety of the human condition": "I do not think any movement from those days to this has been carried on with so much energy and imagination." Not coincidentally, it was also excellent preparation for her later career as a columnist. After all, stumping for suffrage involved starting arguments in public, which is precisely what Thompson did for the rest of her career.[13]

Her suffrage interlude was important to Thompson's evolving philosophy about feminism and gender roles, but its main short-term impact was to convince her that she did not like organizing, with its long hours of stuffing envelopes, passing out leaflets, and traveling on uncomfortable modes of transportation to give the same speech to hostile audiences, all for the pittance of eight dollars a week. When New York State passed its suffrage referendum in 1917, she was basically (and happily) out of a job.

Moving to New York City with a co-worker, Thompson got a fairly lucrative job, at least compared to her suffrage salary, as a copywriter for an advertising firm. When she found that unstimulating, she accepted a job in Cincinnati doing publicity work for a New York-based organization called the Social Unit, which was trying to build political consciousness in the nation's slums. Despite her father's deep Christian belief in helping the less fortunate and the Social Gospel teachings of writers like Walter Rauschenbusch, which she had absorbed at Syracuse, Thompson never felt at home in the world of social reform and social service. She soon returned to New York.

From 1914 to 1920—that is, for most of her twenties—Thompson was casting about to find an interesting way of making a living. Showing no interest in marriage or a conventional domestic life, she considered or tried many of the routes traditionally chosen by aspiring women, such as teaching and social service, as well as newer areas like politics and social reform, and found them all wanting. She already had shown a talent for writing, which she put to use to get various publicity jobs. And, although she might not have acknowledged it, she was ambitious and eager to make a name for herself: "I wanted to run away, not *from* something, but *to* something." So in July of 1920 she took $125 out of her total savings of $300 and bought a ticket to Europe. Her intention was to live by her pen: "Perhaps I can never make a go of writing, I wonder—And yet I believe in myself—why?"[14]

Her first break came on the boat over to Europe, where her traveling companions included a delegation of Americans going to a Zionist convention. When the boat docked, she had a story to sell to the International News Service. Her next scoop came quickly—what turned out to be the last interview with Irish independence leader Terence MacSwiney before he died while on a hunger strike. She was just a freelancer, however, and her savings were dwindling fast, so she took a job writing publicity for the American Red Cross at one cent a line, first in Paris and then in Vienna. "I became a very fast typist," she observed pithily.[15]

When she arrived in Vienna, she convinced the office of the *Philadelphia Public Ledger* to make her their foreign correspondent, although still on a freelance basis. Only after another scoop, this one a firsthand account of a plot to restore the Hapsburg monarchy, was she placed on salary. In 1925 she became the Central European Bureau Chief for the *Ledger* and the *New York Evening Post*, headquartered in Berlin, a first for women. At a salary of fifty dollars a week, she was responsible for *nine* countries. Still she wanted more, as she confided to a woman friend: "This isn't enough for me. It's not what I really want. I'm nothing in my own country. I want to be something there—something no other woman has been yet."[16]

A fellow journalist once pointed to "an old belief—nor is it completely unsubstantiated—that sometimes news follows good newspapermen," noting that this had happened to Dorothy Thompson on numerous occasions. During her years as a foreign correspondent in Central Europe, she often was in the middle of major breaking stories, which of course then became part of the creation of the Thompson legend as "a Richard Harding Davis in evening gown." In one story, probably apocryphal, one newspaperman says to another, "Have you heard? Dorothy Thompson got in town at noon." "Good God, what happened at one o'clock?" She considered her initial breaks as "nine-tenths attributable to a run of luck," but she noted that they gave her a reputation in the trade as someone with a remarkable "nose for news." Without belittling her reportorial skills or her ability to write vivid prose, the novelty of a woman foreign correspondent in the 1920s with a propensity to scoop her male colleagues made her as good copy as her stories.[17]

In retrospect Thompson made a brilliant career choice to concentrate her journalism in Central Europe, whose unsettled political and economic situation contained the seeds for the rise of Hitler and eventually a second world war. Whereas other foreign correspondents had their bases in London or Paris, her city of choice was Vienna, with which she had a lifelong love affair. A real-life love affair with a Hungarian Jew named Josef Bard led to her first marriage in 1923, but the relationship was troubled from the start by Bard's womanizing and their basic incompatibility. They divorced in 1927.

Often newspaperwomen were assumed to be sleeping their way to their stories, but that was never Dorothy Thompson's style. Fellow journalist George Seldes remembered, "The usual female correspondent relied a great deal on sex attraction. . . .

Dorothy was different. She was the only woman 'newspaper man' of our time." With her fluent, if somewhat idiosyncratic German, her Teutonic good looks, and her love of heavy food and drink, she set about creating her own salon, drawing interesting people into her circle and using them to educate herself and suggest sources and topics to pursue. Yet she always managed to be the center of attention at whatever gathering she was attending, and kept herself firmly focused on advancing her career. "Yes, dear," she supposedly said to an Austrian who was seeking a kiss, "but right this moment I've simply *got* to get to the bottom of this Bulgarian business."[18]

Thompson flourished in the 1920s in part because of the volatile Central European situation but also because of how open-ended news gathering still was at that time. Even foreign correspondents were a fairly recent development; many had been sent over to cover World War I and then had been asked by their papers to stay on. Being a foreign correspondent was not yet an especially prestigious post, and came with few perks: most correspondents operated their offices out of their tiny (and expensive, given European inflation) apartments. Such a situation could actually work to the benefit of women, however, who if they were good and eager could often in effect create their own jobs, even if like Thompson they had never worked in a city newsroom or had any journalistic experience before arriving.

Of course, having a good mentor helped, and Thompson found hers in Marcel Fodor, the Hungarian-born correspondent for the *Manchester Guardian*. It was Fodor who helped her with the 1926 story about a possible coup in Warsaw, which gave rise to the stories about her rushing off to cover a revolution in evening clothes. (Actually she had time to change and pack a bag before she boarded the train.) The next year she went to Russia to do a series of stories for the *New York Evening Post*, which became the basis of her first book, *The New Russia* (1928).

It was in Berlin in 1927, just after her divorce became final, that Thompson met Sinclair Lewis, the author of *Main Street*

Dorothy Thompson and Sinclair Lewis in London on their wedding day, May 14, 1928. The large number of news photographers on hand reflected the celebrity of the groom, not the bride. Soon Dorothy Thompson would be a celebrity in her own right. (AP/Wide World Photos)

(1920), *Babbitt* (1922), and then one of America's best-known novelists. She found herself strangely drawn to this charismatic yet profoundly insecure man, whom she called by his childhood name of Hal even though most of his friends called him Red. When Lewis became her second husband in 1928, he was forty-two, she thirty-four. H. L. Mencken offered this not terribly optimistic forecast for the marriage: "No telling. Red will drink and Dorothy will talk until they both go *meshuggah*. But you never know."[19]

After her marriage Thompson resigned from her newspaper chain, and prepared to return to America. In European circles, she was well known and respected but she had little reputation in the States. Marrying a celebrity like Sinclair Lewis meant the press often treated her simply as his wife. During this period she signed one letter "D.T. Housewife" and confided to her diary, "I feel that I must earn money." The couple lived in New York City and also on a 300-acre piece of land they bought in Barnard, Vermont, named "Twin Farms" for its two houses. In July of 1930 their son Michael was born; Thompson was also the stepmother to Lewis's son Wells from his first marriage.[20]

Instead of sinking into domesticity, Thompson began the process of reinventing her career. Leaving the baby with nannies or on one occasion with her friend, the writer Rose Wilder Lane, she and Lewis traveled regularly to Europe. These combined vacation and fact-finding trips gave her enough fresh material to publish long "think pieces" about the situation in Germany and Central Europe for popular magazines like the *Saturday Evening Post* and *Pictorial Review*. In 1931 she wangled a hard-to-get interview with Adolf Hitler that she expanded into a small book, *I Saw Hitler!* So linked were Thompson's and Hitler's fortunes that Sinclair Lewis was not entirely joking when he said, "If I ever divorce Dorothy, I'll name Adolf Hitler as co-respondent."[21]

The irony of this 1931 interview was that Thompson was dead wrong about Hitler, predicting that he would never amount to anything: "When I walked into Adolph [sic] Hitler's room, I was convinced that I was meeting the future dictator of Germany. In something less than fifty seconds I was quite sure that I was not. It took just about that time to measure the startling insignificance of this man who has set the world agog. . . . " Except for that monumental blooper, she produced a devastating picture of an insecure man ("I bet he crooks his little finger when he drinks a cup of tea") with an awkward figure and ridiculous mustache, "the very prototype of the little man," which she realized, ironically, was the very key to his success.[22]

Once again she was the right person in the right place at the right time. As a result of the book, she was swamped with invitations to write and lecture. On her cross-country speaking tours, there was only one subject: Hitler. Well, perhaps, two: Hitler and Dorothy Thompson. Two years later when the Nazis formally expelled Thompson from Germany, her public stature (and lecture requests, and lecture fees) rose even higher. Always an excellent public speaker, she now found herself addressing audiences of several thousand people a night.

When Dorothy Thompson and Sinclair Lewis married in 1928, they were not really a celebrity couple, since her career was not yet full-blown. By the early 1930s, they certainly were, especially when Lewis became the first American to win a Nobel Prize for Literature in 1931. (When Lewis called his wife to tell her the astonishing news, she thought it was one of his practical jokes. "Great, I just received the Order of the Garter," she replied.) Ironically, as her fame increased, his failed to thrive, adding to the tensions of a marriage already buffetted by his alcoholism and the fact that, as Thompson noted, "Mr. Lewis was simply not made for marriage." They separated in 1937 and divorced in 1941.[23]

"1935. Began Career." Thompson's pithy annotation might seem odd, given that she had already spent fifteen years as a journalist, but she felt that her career really began when she left reporting and moved into interpreting the news as a syndicated columnist. The invitation to have her own column came in 1935 from Helen Rogers Reid, co-publisher, with her husband Ogden Reid, of the *New York Herald-Tribune*, the prominent and well-respected organ of the eastern Republican establishment. Reid had been impressed by Thompson's ability to distill complex foreign issues for a predominantly female audience at a forum sponsored by the newspaper the year before. While Reid seems to have envisioned this column as appealing mainly to women, the original announcement hinted at a broader appeal: "Her column will not be a women's feature exclusively. It will be sharp analysis, sure authority and sheer good writing that will appeal to both men and women. . . . "[24]

Indeed one of the most interesting things about "On the Record," which debuted in March 1936, was that men quickly comprised the majority of Thompson's readers. Thompson was not the only woman columnist writing on foreign affairs—Anne O'Hare McCormick wrote a column for the *New York Times* on international events and became the first woman to win a Pulitzer Prize for journalism in 1937 (something that Thompson never did). But since columnists for the *Times* were not syndicated, they reached far fewer readers than did those like Thompson and Walter Lippmann, who were.

Thompson's columns combined what her biographer Peter Kurth called a "particular blend of solid reporting and naked emotion." Her style practically said, "Now . . . you . . . pay . . . attention . . . to . . . me!" One journalist estimated that an astonishing three-fifths of the words she wrote between 1938 and 1940 were about Hitler and the threat of fascism. Knowing how much worse the crimes of Nazism were than even she suspected, reading her columns today has the ironic result of making her overheated prose seem almost tame. Also remarkable from today's perspective is how Eurocentric her view of world affairs was: the equally ominous developments in Japan and the Pacific drew very little of her attention, and certainly none of her passion. Even during the war and its aftermath, she focused monolithically on Germany. For her, World War II was a one-front war.[25]

On domestic politics, her point of view was cloudier, and her voice less compelling. She never developed a distinct political philosophy, and defied categorization as liberal or conservative. She was not a great supporter of the New Deal or Franklin Roosevelt, saying, "When he is right I am for him. When he is wrong, I'm against him." The latter was more often the case, but after a highly publicized flirtation with the candidacy of Republican Wendell Willkie in 1940, she dramatically came out in support of Roosevelt's third term, mainly because of the impending war. This defection caused her column to be dropped from the staunchly Republican *Herald-Tribune* when her contract expired in early 1941, but she was quickly picked up by the Bell syndicate, which ran her column in the more liberal *New York Post*. (Columnists had to have a New York outlet if they expected to command any national prominence.) After being dumped, Thompson wrote personally to Eleanor Roosevelt to reassure her that she had not suffered financially from the change; FDR supposedly joked to her the next time they met, "Dorothy, you lost your job, but I kept mine—ha ha!"[26]

Columnists always had to have an opinion—they could never just announce "I don't know" or "I pass." The ability to produce under such pressure day in, day out was one measure of a successful columnist; the other, of course, was producing what the public was interested in reading. Both Dorothy Thompson and Eleanor Roosevelt had those twin knacks, but there the similarities ended. "My Day" was a short, fairly bland description of Roosevelt's myriad activities, presented in diary-like form without a unifying theme; only in the late 1930s did the First Lady begin, tentatively, to use her column to promote her own political agendas.[27]

On the other hand, a typical "On the Record" column was a sustained, passionate piece of writing on a single topic or a pointed, often humorous, look at the world and its foibles. A favorite stock character was "The Grouse," an acerbic breakfast companion universally believed to be modeled on Sinclair Lewis; another fictional alter ego was "Mrs. William J. Rattler, President of the Cornucopia Club," who spoke to the nation's women. Even though Eleanor Roosevelt felt that Thompson was "swayed perhaps by her own emotions, personal interests, and past experience," she saluted her for "such a gift of expression that she has a great following." In fact, Thompson's column reached twice as many readers as Roosevelt's.[28]

Getting out a column three times a week was a monumental task, requiring detailed research and access to inside sources throughout the United States and the world. Thompson's New York apartment had no fewer than nine telephones, and she used them to run up enormous phone bills at a time when calling long distance domestically (and especially internationally) was still an exotic and highly unusual act. Though she had an office at the *Herald-Tribune*, she preferred to write her columns at home in the mornings in longhand, often while still in bed. Then one of her three secretaries would do additional research and type it up. The first draft of a typical column might read, "In 1929–30 Finland spent blank percent of her total national budget on education and public health, blank percent went to defense, Sweden spent blank percent of her budget on education and social welfare, blank percent for defense. In the great states the figures are reversed. . . . " Working for Dorothy Thompson was no doubt both an education and a trial.[29]

In addition to the thrice-weekly columns, Thompson also juggled a monthly column that she began for the *Ladies' Home Journal* in 1937 (where Eleanor Roosevelt also had a column; Thompson's always ran closer to the front of the magazine than "If You Ask Me"), her extensive radio appearances, and the yearly lecture tours. Note how institutionalized and relentless this process of being a public figure was: sort of a full-time Dorothy Thompson, Inc. She may have been one of the most admired women in America after Eleanor Roosevelt, but she was also one of the most exposed. And she worked hard to keep herself in the public eye.

If you regularly listened to the radio in the 1930s or 1940s (and most Americans did), it wouldn't be too long before you encountered Dorothy Thompson holding forth on some topic. As a commentator at the time said, her radio broadcasts were "not recommended for those suffering either from complacency or cardiac disorder."
(© 1939/Time Inc.)

One way to keep in touch with her public was through lecturing. In the days before television, many people had contact with famous personages, like Will Rogers, Eleanor Roosevelt, Amelia Earhart, or Dorothy Thompson, when they visited their local Lions club, women's club, or church group on lecture tours that reached not just major metropolitan markets but America's small towns and cities. At fees ranging from $150 up to $500 at the end of the decade, these lecture tours could generate a sizeable income. Thompson also used them to keep in touch with public opinion, even though facing "shoals and shoals of women" was grueling: "It's work and it keeps one somewhat in touch with reality. With people. With, for instance, Brooklyn school teachers."[30]

By the late 1930s she also appeared regularly on the radio as a commentator, mainly for the NBC network. Radio, too, was another way that public figures forged bonds with their national audiences, as President Roosevelt's "Fireside Chats" attest; by 1939, 27.5 million American households owned a radio. Thompson's speaking style was exceptionally well adapted to radio, and as Peter Kurth noted, between 1934 and the end of World War II "she was never far from a microphone." Sinclair Lewis sighed, "I had a wife once but she vanished into the NBC building and has never been heard of since." The commentator was especially in demand during the Munich crisis of 1938 and the events leading up to the outbreak of war in Europe in August and September of 1939, when she broadcast for fifteen straight nights. So focused was she on Munich that she was oblivious to the devastating hurricane that ravaged New England, including heavy damage in Vermont. Luckily when she finally checked in with the staff at Twin Farms, her home and her eight-year-old son were fine.[31]

Despite her prominence as a public figure, the camera was not kind to Dorothy Thompson. John Gunther called her the "worst-photographed woman in America," and she always felt she came out looking like the robust singer Sophie Tucker, a.k.a. "Red Hot Mama." (They were both right.) In person she cut a far more handsome figure, with her beautiful pink complexion, blue eyes, and prematurely grey hair. With her soft skin and well proportioned bosom, she looked especially striking in evening dress. She generally opted for an elegant yet serviceable wardrobe that was somewhat reminiscent of Eleanor Roosevelt's, who also did not photograph well (although she was far less vain about it than Thompson). Too old and the wrong body type to be a flapper, at least she did not relegate herself to the dreary suits and ties favored by many career women. Even though she never really developed a signature style that made her instantly recognizable, she attracted notice. "She *became* beautiful," noted a woman who met her in 1939. "Literally, she shone with success and power."[32]

That year, 1939, saw the peak of Dorothy Thompson's popularity and influence. She received 7,000 requests for appearances, most of which she had to turn down. When Pearl Buck wanted to present her with the American Woman's Association "Woman of the Year" Award, she tried to decline: "I am convinced that I have lately received too many honors, and have consequently been publicized much more than I really like to be." (She had also just had a hysterectomy and been ordered by her doctors to cut back on her activity.)[33] *Time* magazine estimated her salary at $103,000, a phenomenal sum rivaling that of Hollywood stars in Depression America. Thompson was furious at publisher Henry Luce for publishing this figure, which she considered an invasion of her privacy. "Henry, dear, what do you earn a year?" she asked pointedly the next time she saw him.[34]

While Thompson kept up with what she saw as the concerns of ordinary Americans through lecturing and her voluminous mail, when it came to forming opinions and gathering information for her columns, she relied on a more select, almost exclusively male set of friends, sort of her own personal Brain Trust. She called herself a "first rate peripatetic brain picker": "I have taste, some energy, and a pretty good sense in spotting quality. That's why I am a good brain picker." Much of this information was gathered at the dinner parties that Thompson hosted, first at her Central Park West apartment and later at her New York townhouse on East 48th Street. Just as she had in Berlin and Vienna, she operated her own salon. She offered guests vast quantities of food and drink (good scotch especially), ashtrays for their copious cigarette ashes, and conversations in many languages, especially German. A party scene in the 1942 movie *Woman of the Year*, starring Katharine Hepburn as a woman columnist clearly based on Dorothy Thompson and Spencer Tracy as her sportswriter husband, captures (and caricatures) these United Nations-like gatherings to a tee.[35]

It was not uncommon for Thompson to greet her dinner guests with a breezy, "How *are* you? You look wonderful. You simply *must* hear my column. It's terrific—the best I've ever done. Listen!" Speaking of herself in the third person, she once pronounced herself a terrible guest: "She always talks politics and has a horrible habit of holding forth."[36] Conversations at such evenings had one center of attention—Dorothy Thompson—and one topic of conversation: what Sinclair Lewis sardonically referred to as "IT," as in, "Is Dorothy discussing IT again?" "It," of course, was the international situation (Lewis also parodied this by pronouncing it *sityashun*), and more than once it drove Lewis out of his own home.[37]

Sinclair Lewis had an absolute horror of being considered "Mr. Dorothy Thompson," and once reacted with ill humor to the rumor that his wife might run for president, "Fine. Then I can write 'My Day.' " One suspects that he would have been greatly disturbed to learn that his wife was rebuffed when she tried to charge a visit to the hairdresser to Mrs. Sinclair Lewis, but that credit was gladly extended when she mentioned she was Dorothy Thompson.[38]

On the whole, Dorothy Thompson managed to operate as a journalist without excessive attention to her sex, that is, if the repeated references to her as having the brains of a man are disregarded. (In reply, she often quoted the noted suffragist Anna Howard Shaw: "Before I acknowledge this compliment I'd like to *see* the man whose brains I have."[39]) Perhaps because of her specialty in foreign affairs, and certainly because of her demonstrated appeal to male readers as well as female, she managed to carve out a place for herself in the public eye that was fairly free of sexist stereotypes and discrimination. The goal of many post-suffrage feminists was simple: they wanted to be accepted as human beings, not just or always as women. To a remarkable degree in the 1930s and 1940s, Dorothy Thompson got that wish.

🦎

IF DOROTHY THOMPSON'S public persona was one of a successful and opinionated journalist who was accepted regardless of
her sex, her private life was far more complicated. For all the outward trappings of success, Dorothy Thompson had a tough time
getting her personal act together. She married three times: a journalist, a novelist, and a sculptor, all creative or artistic men in different media, but only the last marriage (to a man who in no way
tried to compete with her) was a success. She was a good stepmother, but had a conflicted and troubled relationship with her
son Michael. And, at times both before and during her marriages,
she had what she referred to as "sapphic" interludes where her
affections were drawn strongly to women rather than men.

While her difficulties in achieving what she considered a full
personal life were in part her own, they were also linked to the
incomplete feminist agenda that she and other women of her generation inherited: free to compete with men on the job and in the
world at large, but still caught up in traditional expectations for
love and marriage in private life. Thompson was trying to juggle
no less than what feminist Crystal Eastman called in 1927 the
"great woman question of to-day" as well as the "very essence of
feminism": "how to reconcile a woman's natural desire for love
and home and family with her equally natural desire for work of
her own. . . . "[40]

Thompson's first, and short-lived, marriage to Josef Bard coincided with trying to get her career off the ground: how better to
get to know Central Europe than to marry a Hungarian? It was
also the product of a woman in her twenties who was willing to
experiment with sex and love but not quite ready to live with a
man outside of marriage, even thousands of miles from home: "If
I were more courageous I suppose I would just live with Josef
openly, but I'm frankly *not* courageous enough,"[41] she told her
friend Rose Wilder Lane. (Thompson may have turned to men as
colleagues, but when she grappled with issues of love and sex, she
looked to women friends for advice and comfort.) The marriage's

chances for long-term success were slim, even had he not slept with many of her friends and sponged off her salary, but it was Bard who asked for a divorce.

Many women (and men) who later go on to fame and fortune make an unfortunate or inappropriate first marriage, as in the adage "Washington is full of powerful men and the women they married when they were young." Often the first union fails to survive; sometimes (as in the cases of Margaret Mead and Katharine Hepburn) these early marriages are written out of the historical record. Thompson basically moved on after her failed marriage, but not before she wrote Bard hundreds of letters, most of which were never sent, reexamining every aspect of their lives in naive and often embarrassing detail. Perhaps not surprisingly for a journalist, writing it down became Thompson's way of working through every personal crisis in her life. And then she quickly threw herself back into her work.[42]

Thompson's marriage to Sinclair Lewis offered greater rewards, and greater pain. Even though in retrospect she realized that she never felt safe in this relationship or had any illusions that it would last, she worked as hard as she could to make a go of it. Along the way she learned an enormous amount from him, especially about the craft of writing and the challenges of creativity and genius. As she noted, "No one can live with Sinclair Lewis for ten years without being educated."[43]

By far the most satisfying times they spent together were summers in Vermont. "I love that place," Dorothy told Lewis. "It is the place you promised me the day we met, and it is my home. It is, in some way, the best expression in life of both of us—beautiful, comfortable, hospitable, and unpretentious. A great many people besides ourselves have been happy there, my darling." Each summer from 1928 until the end of her life she cherished her time in Vermont to think, read, garden, entertain guests, and generally recharge herself for her hectic life the rest of the year.[44]

One of the attractions of Vermont was its no-nonsense citizenry, many of whom did casual work on the farm, always on their terms, not hers. "I would thank you not to suggest moving any perennials this year, I have plenty to do as it is," her gardener informed her when she arrived for one extended summer sojourn. (Thompson was a formidable gardener.) "Woman," said another hired man, "you think you can go through me just like you went through Russia," and then proceeded to do exactly as he pleased. The foibles of Vermonters provided almost as many good stories as Dorothy's driving, which was so atrocious that she rarely managed to get anywhere without hitting something or having some kind of vehicular mishap. Her staff rightly called her "the worst driver in history." Despite all the time and effort she poured into Twin Farms, Thompson never succeeded in making the farm pay for itself.[45]

Twin Farms was also where both parents spent the most concentrated time with their son Michael, born in 1930 at what was considered Thompson's advanced age of thirty-six. Age and career would have seemed ample justification (if anyone were so bold as to ask) for Mr. and Mrs. Sinclair Lewis not to have children, but this child was no accident, and Thompson actively tried to become pregnant again, only to miscarry. She was no fan of the process of childbirth, however, based on her experience with Michael: "Here we are in the year 1930, with every possible advancement of science upon us in every conceivable field, and yet nothing whatsoever has been done to mitigate or diminish the boredom of childbirth." After saying that she might as well be a Bulgarian peasant giving birth in a furrow, she said simply, "I protest."[46]

For the next few years, Thompson struggled with the triple responsibilities of being a mother, being married to a creative (and increasingly self-destructive) genius, and trying to keep her professional career afloat. "My brain has gone *phut* but that's due to domesticity—(which is unavoidable)," she wrote to a friend in 1930. "Show me a woman married to an artist who can succeed in her marriage without making a fulltime profession out of it. Oh, Jesus God!! . . . " In what she claimed would be seen as "heresy to feminists," she affirmed, "I'd throw the state of the nation into the ashcan for anyone I loved." But this same woman also confessed to Sinclair Lewis in 1931 that work was her salvation: "I am so much happier when I can work. I'm a working human being, habituated to work, and 'conditioned' to work." In 1937 when her marriage was on the point of collapse she turned to her writing to salvage her sanity, just as she had when she broke up with Bard: "It is so quiet, so impersonal—my work, my kind of work—and so demanding. . . . It has saved me twice in my life from utter shipwreck in emotion."[47]

Any professional woman who has children is prey to the question, or more likely, the accusation, "Was she a good mother?" (No one ever thought to question Sinclair Lewis's paternal qualities, which were nonexistent.) Dorothy Thompson certainly felt that she was a devoted mother, supervising Michael's schooling, overseeing his child-care arrangements, and caring for him when he was sick. If it seems odd that so much of Michael's care devolved to nannies and housekeepers, both in New York and Vermont (where the baby and his nurse lived in a separate house so as not to irritate his father), this pattern of child rearing was widely accepted among members of the middle and upper classes, even when both parents did not have careers. (Remember Eleanor Roosevelt's lack of daily involvement in her children's upbringing, which she later regretted.) When this arrangement worked, no one blamed the parents, but when it didn't, it was almost always the mother who bore the brunt of criticism.

Michael was a difficult and maladjusted boy who would likely have taxed the patience and love of parents far more involved in his upbringing than Thompson and Lewis, who were experiencing severe marital problems of their own. As a child he exhibited violent behavior toward playmates and caretakers, sometimes brandishing a knife or hitting them with his fists. None of the many schools he attended—from an austere military academy to the progressive Putney School in Vermont—were able to discipline his unruly nature or harness his intelligence. During his troubled adolescence he exhibited serious behavioral problems surrounding sex, fast cars, and alcohol, a precursor of a lifelong drinking problem.

Near the end of her life Thompson confided to her dear friend, the English writer Rebecca West, "If I had my life to live over I would be damned careful by whom I had a child. And I would not choose a genius or a near genius, and certainly not a drunkard." West, whose own son had turned against her by publishing a lightly fictionalized roman à clef several years earlier, shared with Thompson some thoughts about famous women and their children: "I wonder if your Mike isn't unconsciously gunning for your autobiography. Don't let him get away with it. . . . It is a feminist work we have to perform. In the past women subscribed to the legend that the mother was always wrong, and gave themselves up to the sense of guilt. We have got to refuse to go under."[48] In other words, mothers were not solely responsible for how their children turned out.

Perhaps if Michael had been a daughter, or if the Thompson-Lewis marriage had been more stable, things might have been easier. Dorothy genuinely loved Michael, her friends agreed, but she never could figure out how to build a strong, dependable relationship with him. Ironically she was much more successful as a stepmother to Lewis's son, Wells, who was eleven when she married his father. Wells was a frequent visitor to Vermont during his teens, and he developed a deep attachment to Dorothy, which she reciprocated. "I not only liked him," she later recalled, "I loved him immeasurably. He was all that I would have wished in a son." She was so devastated by his 1944 death by a German sniper that for the first and only time in her career she cancelled a scheduled radio broadcast.[49]

Back in 1921 Dorothy had confided to Rose Wilder Lane, "Some people have a 'call' to self-destruction. Something in them tells them they must have children, for instance. But nothing in me tells me I should have children. Indeed, I believe that if I had 'em they wouldn't be very nice. I have only one loud and never ceasing call, and that is to preserve the integrity of my own self." But once she married Sinclair Lewis, she suppressed or overrode her earlier doubts and plunged wholeheartedly into motherhood. Unlike women such as Katharine Hepburn and Martha Graham, who made deliberate decisions not to have children, Dorothy Thompson seems never to have seriously considered that option once she married. And yet it is hard to conclude that this aspect of her life brought her much satisfaction.[50]

Like many women who came of age during the first two decades of the twentieth century, Thompson had always welcomed a certain amount of sexual experimentation as part of her birthright as a modern, emancipated woman. "To be twenty-seven and loverless in Italy is a crime against God and man," she exclaimed melodramatically in 1921. Then she trapped herself in a marriage because she did not have the courage to live openly with a man; when he began to take lovers, however, so did she.[51]

Thompson and Sinclair Lewis had, by her account, a satisfactory sex life, at least when he wasn't so drunk that he couldn't remember what had happened. But their ties were as much intellectual as physical, as she later pointed out to him: "I wasn't even 'in love' with you in the usual sense of the term. I didn't, anyhow, have an overwhelming physical desire to sleep with you. That was nice enough, too. Very nice. But you said to me once, half whimsically, half apologetically, 'I exist mostly above the neck.' Well, I understood that. So do I."[52]

Throughout her life, and even as her first two marriages were disintegrating, Dorothy Thompson took lovers and had affairs. But at certain other points, sometimes even in the midst of a successful heterosexual relationship, Thompson was strongly, and sexually, drawn to women. As a young girl, she had had crushes on other women, and during her suffrage organizing days she had been deeply attracted to Gertrude Franchot Tone, an older woman of thirty-seven. (Lesbianism and intense relationships between women are a strong theme in Sinclair Lewis's 1933 book about the suffrage campaign, *Ann Vickers*, which drew heavily on conversations with Thompson about her suffrage activity. The portrait of these relationships is not a flattering one.) There is also mention of a brief affair with another woman in Europe around 1925 or 1926, what she described as being "thrown back into a semi-homosexual state of adolescence by Budapest eroticism."[53]

The most intense emotional attachment that Thompson formed was to the German novelist Christa Winsloe, the author of the classic schoolgirl-crush text that was later made into the movie *Maedchen in Uniform*. At this point (1932) Thompson had been married for four years, had given birth to Michael, and was trying to get pregnant again. Since she seemed to think her earlier bouts of homosexuality had been "overcome" (her word), the intensity of her feelings took her by surprise, but she made no effort to conceal or disguise them.[54]

"So it has happened to me again, after all these years," she confided to her diary: "the soft, quite natural kiss on my throat, the quite unconscious (seemingly) even open kiss on my breast, as she stood below me on the stairs. . . . What in God's name does one call this sensibility if it be not love?" And yet Thompson continued to see love between women as something different than love between a man and a woman: "There's something weak in it and, even, ridiculous. To love a woman is somehow ridiculous. *Mir auch passt es nicht. Ich bin doch heterosexuel* [Anyway it doesn't suit me. I am heterosexual]."[55] Her feelings for Sinclair Lewis were intact: "I don't love Hal any less. Rather more." When Christa, Dorothy, and her son Michael set up housekeeping together in Portofino on a holiday, Dorothy wrote long, full letters to her husband. "We are having a lovely time here together—she's the most sympathetic woman I have met in years and years. As for your last admonition to me—do you remember it?—have no fears, I ain't thata way."[56]

"I ain't thata way." Was Dorothy Thompson correct to claim that she was basically heterosexual, despite the strong undercurrent of "sapphic interludes" in her emotional makeup? Like

Eleanor Roosevelt, Dorothy Thompson did not feel it necessary to hide this aspect of her personal life from posterity, because when she left her papers to Syracuse University, including her diaries explicitly describing these incidents and Christa Winsloe's letters, she placed no restrictions on their use. Perhaps she felt free from any stigma or taint of deviance because she did not consider herself a lesbian, despite the fact that she had affairs with women.

Another reading of her openness and unconventionality is to suggest how unstable or fluctuating the categories of homosexual and heterosexual were during Thompson's formative years of sexual experimentation. By the 1920s the work of sexologists such as Freud, Krafft-Ebing, and Havelock Ellis was just beginning to alter the American understanding of the role of sexuality in modern life. Being normal increasingly meant being actively heterosexual, which in turn caused relationships between women to be seen in a more negative light. It also reinforced the tendency to see these relationships in more explicitly sexual terms than ever before. Once love between women came to be seen as more about sex than about sisterhood, it became easier to label it perverse, distorted, or unnatural. This process was well underway by the 1920s and 1930s, and intensified in the postwar years.[57]

In this increasingly polarized view of sexuality, Thompson was being asked to define herself as either/or; faced with that choice she labeled herself heterosexual. And yet one suspects that this was a somewhat false, or arbitrary, choice for her, as it likely was for Eleanor Roosevelt. Thompson and Roosevelt had both shown the capacity to love men and women, either sequentially or simultaneously, although Thompson being younger may have been more willing to admit a sexual dimension to these attractions. They were both essentially bisexual.[58]

In any event, the affair with Christa Winsloe seems to have been the last time that Dorothy Thompson fell deeply in love with another woman. When her marriage to Lewis ended, Thompson did not lack for male company: she had plenty of suitors, and not a few lovers. As she approached fifty, she would not

Dorothy Thompson liked to boast that the sofa in her Turtle Bay townhouse had room for "five of the most distinguished bottoms in New York." Given her style of entertaining, those bottoms would likely be hers and those of four men. (Ralph Crane, Black Star)

necessarily have expected to find a new husband. Yet she did.

Sculptor Maxim Kopf, Thompson asserted, was "the man I should have married in the first place." A refugee from Hitler's Europe, where he spent five months in a concentration camp, Kopf married Thompson in 1943 at Twin Farms in Vermont. They had by all accounts a successful and mutually satisfying marriage that lasted until Kopf's death in 1958. "When we make love the whole house shakes," Thompson told more than one startled recipient of her confidences. Maxim was a warm and gregarious man, a good stepfather to Michael, who was only thirteen when his mother remarried. Maxim never tried to dominate or control Thompson's life—he saw his role as her companion and helpmeet, rather than competitor. By the time they met, Thompson was already a star, her public persona and style securely in place. She had nothing to prove. She could choose wisely, for once, whom to love. No, it wouldn't have worked to marry him the first time around, but for the third husband, he was the charm.[59]

🦋

AT FIRST GLANCE Dorothy Thompson might have seemed a likely poster child for modern feminism—college graduate, suffrage veteran, famous career woman, wife, and mother. The fact that such a liberated and successful woman failed to identify with the women's movement speaks volumes about the fortunes of feminism in the post-suffrage era, specifically about how it failed to win the allegiance of the very women who were living out its promises and struggling with its incomplete agendas in their daily lives. Instead of seeing herself in the vanguard of new roles for women, when Thompson spoke out on issues of importance to women she fell back on traditional gender definitions. For other women, that is, never for herself.

Dorothy Thompson came of age and to political consciousness at a specific moment in the history of American feminism. Suffrage and political equality for women were on the verge of being won, and she herself participated passionately in the final stages of the battle. But now, women like her seemed to be saying, it was time for women to move forward as individuals, to succeed on their own merits, rather than as part of a self-consciously feminist movement. As journalist Dorothy Dunbar Bromley noted in a biting 1927 satire, " 'Feminism' has become a term of opprobrium to the modern young woman. For the word suggests either the old school of fighting feminists who wore flat heels and had very little feminine charm, or the current species who antagonize men with their constant clamor about maiden names, equal rights, woman's place in the world, and many another cause . . . *ad infinitum*."[60]

Dorothy Thompson is a perfect example of the generation gap that surfaced in the women's movement in the 1920s. (Eleanor Roosevelt, born in 1884, straddled the generational divide, but was closer in spirit to the older woman-identified suffragists than Thompson's modern female friends.) If feminists were seen as old battle-axes with no sex appeal, or as younger ideologues still throwing hand grenades even though the worst of the battle was over, then no wonder women like Dorothy Thompson (and Margaret Mead, and Martha Graham, and to a lesser degree, Katharine Hepburn) wanted nothing to do with them. In 1926 Thompson showed how skittish she was about what an older generation of women had called with great pride "the cause": "Women, conscious of themselves as 'the sex,' are a bore. Large bodies of women aggressively being women. . . are infinitely wearisome when not somberly terrifying." That was not exactly showing respect for her elders.[61]

One of the things that Thompson held against the older women's-rights activists was their supposed antagonism to men. No matter that many of the old-style feminists were more pro-woman than anti-man, to young women seeking acceptance in the heterosocial world of the 1920s, sex antagonism was anathema. She had never been a militant feminist, Thompson said, while adding in the same breath, "I like men too much." This widely shared sentiment (in the 1920s, and even today) that being a feminist meant being anti-male was—and is—one of the main fault lines of modern feminism.[62]

Another aspect of this generation gap was that women coming of age in the 1910s and 1920s found it annoying to be singled out for their accomplishments specifically as women—they wanted to be treated as individuals first, and only incidentally as women. Thompson was devastating on this point in a 1926 article she wrote for *The Nation*, challenging the very assignment (in which she was asked to describe the difficulties she had faced as one of the first women foreign correspondents) as lending itself to "the specious feminism of the women's magazines, which persists in finding cause for jubilation every time a woman becomes, for the first time, an iceman, a road surveyor, or a senator. Actually, this playing up of women is a disservice and an anachronism, in a day when no one any longer questions their general intelligence." She concluded tellingly, "This see-what-the-little-darling-had-done-now attitude ought to be outlawed."[63]

Yet in different moods Thompson was far less hostile to the goals of modern feminism. She supported divorce and birth control as part of her belief that modern women should be free to control their lives; she kept her own name at a time when such a decision was seen as a clear feminist statement, even though she probably could have commanded fees twice as high writing as Mrs. Sinclair Lewis in the early years of her marriage. Like Eleanor Roosevelt, she spoke out for married women's right to earn money during the Depression, bucking the popular trend that wanted to send women back home and give their jobs to men. This stance was part of Thompson's broader conviction about the centrality of work to human existence, especially for women: "Work is *not* merely a job; work is *not* merely a means to earning money or supplementing a man's income. Work is an essential of life itself, as necessary as bread and love. . . . "[64]

In the 1930s Thompson took a more international view of the role of feminism in the modern world, or rather, the absence of a need for a feminist movement. She opened a 1934 *New York Herald-Tribune* conference on women and current problems with this striking statement: "If we look around the world today we are forced to observe that the feminist movement, which reached its apex during the war and immediately afterward, is as dead as last week's newspaper." As she continued her argument, it was not as bleak, or as anti-feminist, as that initially sounded. Thompson's point, after noting that the status of women was actually regressing in certain countries (she was thinking of Germany), was that the cry for equal opportunities and women's emancipation had little resonance in the post-suffrage world. The answer to society's problems lay "not in the conditions of women but in the condition of society as a whole." In turn, "the status of women is changing because the world is changing."[65]

The deteriorating world situation was one reason why feminism seemed less relevant in the 1920s and 1930s; another, according to Thompson, was the inherent limitations and flaws in feminist ideology itself. A provocative *Ladies' Home Journal* article in 1939 titled, "If I Had a Daughter," sounded an early warning about the difficulty of "having it all." Asserting that only one woman in a thousand could have a demanding profession, enjoy sexual and economic freedom, and at the same time have a happy and productive marriage, she announced:

> With only the exceptions that prove the rule, women are happy when they are happily and securely married and when they have several healthy and loving children. If I had a daughter I would warn her, with warmth and gravity, not to bite off more than she can chew. . . . If I had a daughter I would tell her that she has to choose.[66]

When such sentiments come from a woman who once considered herself an ardent feminist, something has shifted.

Obviously Thompson was questioning the very goals and standards that she thought feminism stood for: "Perhaps in the competition to enter the world of men, women have too eagerly accepted the standards and values of men, losing confidence in their own intuitive knowledge of life, and in the values deriving from their unique experience of life." By the 1940s and 1950s she proposed a very different definition of women's emancipation than from her suffrage days: women need to "realize that the object of their emancipation is not to make them more like men, but more powerfully womanly, and therefore of greater use to men and society. . . . "[67]

Perhaps not surprisingly, sentiments like those made Dorothy Thompson one of Betty Friedan's targets in her 1963 classic, *The Feminine Mystique*, although Friedan did not skewer her as savagely as she did Margaret Mead. Thompson's 1951 paean to domesticity called "Occupation: Housewife" set Friedan off. Thompson's piece revolved around the supposed feelings of inferiority of a friend who when asked to fill in the question, "occupation," was only able to answer, "housewife." "When I write it I realize that here I am, a middle-aged woman, with a university education, and I've never made *anything* out of my life." Thompson bursts into laughter, reassuring her friend that there is no single word to cover the dozen occupations and services she performs in her roles as wife and mother, which she then proceeds to list in glowing detail. Thompson's final words to her friend are: "You are one of the most successful women I know."[68]

It is hard not to think, quoting from *Hamlet*, "The lady doth protest too much, methinks." Focusing only on the difficulties of trying to have it all rather than its admittedly imperfect rewards, Dorothy Thompson was deeply reluctant to set herself up as any kind of role model for women: "It happens that I have led most of my life in the thick of problems of the outside world. It has been an interesting life, and I should not like to have changed it. But I should hate to see most women so exteriorize their lives as I have done. I have an ever-increasing respect for those women who stick to their knitting. . . . " Or as she said in one of her last *Ladies' Home Journal* columns, "Combining a demanding career and a family is so difficult for a woman to manage that from personal and often bitter experience I would like to see fewer women attempt it."[69]

Dorothy Thompson was not the first, or the last, successful woman to say in effect, "Do as I say, not as I do." But if Thompson admired women who stuck to their knitting, many of those very women looked up to Thompson precisely because she symbolized the expanding possibilities open to women in the modern world. *Time* captured her impact in its 1939 cover story. Women saw

Dorothy Thompson could always hold her own—and then some—with men. Here she participates in Columbia Pictures's "Roundtable of the Screen" with fellow journalists Linton Wells, William L. Shirer, and Wythe Williams. (Culver Pictures)

Thompson as "the typical modern American woman they think they would like to be: emancipated, articulate and successful, living in the thick of one of the most exciting periods of history and interpreting it to millions." Journalist Charles Fisher's 1944 profile made a similar point: "The ladies of the hinterlands . . . think of her as the type of unfettered womanhood of which they sometimes dreamed over the dinner dishes."[70]

Even though Thompson never set herself up as a role model for women, she could not prevent scores of admirers from appropriating her life in that way. A young journalism major at the University of Georgia in the late 1930s could aspire to have the kind of exciting and important life she led. A fan from Syracuse could write her idol, "I am really proud that we belong to the same sex. I feel that as long as we have folks like you behind us pushing we'll get there eventually."[71]

That men read Dorothy Thompson so intently also seems to have brought a certain vicarious satisfaction to many women, confirmation that women did have brains and opinions worth listening to. A suburban woman who often came into New York on the train developed the habit of seeing what her fellow travelers were reading. "Do you know who most of the people *are* who are reading Dorothy Thompson's column?" she excitedly asked a friend. "Men!"[72]

🐎

"I NEVER WROTE to be popular. It cost me a lot."[73] Many of her friends thought that Thompson should give up writing "On the Record" when she was dropped by the *New York Post* in 1947 and thus lost her outlet in the key New York market. But as grueling as the column was, she still craved the exposure, the income, and the heady feeling that people were reading, and arguing, about her ideas three times a week. It is hard to resign voluntarily from the upper echelons of power and influence, and Dorothy Thompson was no exception—she doggedly kept at the column until 1958. Unfortunately for her, commentators could easily be demoted or summarily dumped by an indifferent or hostile public. After years of leading a large and adoring readership in the direction she was going, Thompson suddenly looked over her shoulder at a much diminished following.

"1949—Began Decline"[74] reads a stark annotation in her papers, but actually the decline in Thompson's popularity began earlier. In the aftermath of World War II, she was one of the few voices asking for tolerance toward the German people (as distinct from their Nazi leaders), a stance that cost her popular support. Then she lost a huge chunk of her constituency when she became a vocal opponent of Zionism, alienating many of her Jewish readers and putting her out of step with America's staunchly pro-Israel foreign policy. (Columns sympathetic to the Arabs had caused the liberal *New York Post*, which had a large Jewish readership, to drop her column.) This turn of events was ironic, of course, given that Thompson had probably spoken out on the Holocaust and the refugee issue more consistently than any other political commentator in the 1930s and 1940s. To Thompson personally, it was a harsh blow even to be considered anti-Semitic, but she never considering backing down from her stand.

Dorothy Thompson never really found a replacement for Adolf Hitler. After the war she attempted to mobilize women to press for disarmament through W.O.M.A.N. (World Organization of the Mothers of All Nations). Eleanor Roosevelt warned her that W.O.M.A.N. was being used as a propaganda tool by the Communists, and by 1952 Thompson withdrew her support. Next she turned her attention to the crisis in public education, and for a while mounted a crusade to upgrade the status of domestic service. She remained generally silent, however, on the great issue of the 1950s, civil rights. "Politically she was like a great ship left stranded on the beach after the tide has gone out," commented one of her friends.[75]

As her career wound down, Thompson occasionally sounded bitter and alienated when she reflected on the journalism profession and her standing in it: "The means swallowed the end and the search for freedom became a (voluntary) slavery. I find today that the 'success' I had means nothing to me whatever. I wonder *exactly* what went wrong."[76] And yet at other times she seemed to have made her peace with these changes, as this 1952 *Ladies' Home Journal* column suggests: "All my life I have had what one might call an unhappy love affair with the world—its charms and achievements; its wars, revolutions, injustices. Now I know that the world got along without me for a long time and will do so again. Once I was very eager to reform my fellow men and their institutions. Now I am more concerned to understand them."[77]

The decline in her reputation was not entirely her fault: journalism itself was changing in ways that increasingly left her behind. In retrospect, the highly-charged personal journalism she typified peaked around the time of World War II; in the shifting priorities of postwar America, columnists such as Thompson,

Walter Lippmann, and Walter Winchell found it more difficult to maintain their followings. (Winchell, for example, had lapsed into total obscurity by the time of his death in 1972.) Newspaper readers were just as likely to turn to editorial pages as to columnists for opinions; television offered new competition with its news departments and hard-hitting documentaries like Edward R. Murrow's "See It Now." Dorothy Thompson had retooled her career once before, when she returned to America as Sinclair Lewis's wife in 1928. It would have been far more difficult to reinvent herself a second time, especially as she approached sixty and her fourth decade in public life.

For years Thompson had had the idea of writing a reflective and philosophical look at the world, but with the thrice-weekly column, her *Ladies' Home Journal* pieces, and other demands on her time, she never seemed to have the energy to devote to the book, especially during her summers in Vermont, when entertaining guests and weeding the perennial borders seemed more appealing than chaining herself to one of the dozen typewriters scattered around Twin Farms. When she gave up "On the Record" in 1958, she succumbed to the trap that often afflicts prominent people when they leave public life: she decided to write her memoirs. After all, she had lived through, indeed been part of, some of the great moments of the twentieth century. New York agents and publishers all assured her that her book, especially if it was a "life and times" and not just a "life," would be a guaranteed best-seller.

Based on the surviving draft (she never got past her childhood and college years), it seems unlikely that this would have been a critical or commercial success. Her descriptions of her youth are almost mechanical, as if she hoped by setting down details she would trigger a larger perspective. There was also the question of audience: assuming the book took three to four years to complete, it would have appeared in the early 1960s. How compelling would her stories of gallivanting around Europe and standing up to Hitler have seemed to a postwar America obsessed with the

Cold War? How would her moralistic callings for simpler values, a remnant of her Methodist childhood, have gone over in the heady consumerism and affluence of postwar America? And how would the story of a *woman* journalist and political commentator have been received in the period of the late 1950s and early 1960s, when feminism fell to its nadir? Ironically, while Thompson was struggling with her autobiography, she produced what many considered one of her finest pieces of writing: a profile of Sinclair Lewis for the *Atlantic Monthly* following a visit to his birthplace in Sauk Center, Minnesota, nine years after his death.[78]

In these years Thompson was not in especially good health, slowed by heart problems and other ailments. It may be that all those years of hard drinking, heavy eating, chain smoking, and a lifelong habit of popping Dexedrine took their toll. She continued to try to build a better relationship with her son Michael, whose troubled childhood and adolescence were followed by an almost equally troubled adult life. (He became an actor and died of cancer in 1975.) Even though she struggled as a parent, she was by all accounts a wonderful grandmother to Michael's two sons and a good mother-in-law to his first wife Bernadette. And the last years of her life were enriched by her warm and loving relationship with Maxim and by the many friends who shared their life in New York and Vermont.

Kopf's sudden death in 1958 devastated Thompson, dealing her a blow from which she never fully recovered. She was only sixty-four, but she seemed much older. Now she knew it was time to retire. She wrote moving farewell columns for "On the Record" and the *Ladies' Home Journal*, which triggered an avalanche of letters from lifelong readers who could not imagine opening a newspaper or magazine and not finding her there. She turned desultorily to her memoirs, but never regained her old drive. When she died of a heart attack in 1961 (alone, in a hotel room in Portugal, where she was visiting her grandsons and their mother), she was sixty-seven years old.

Her obituaries evoked her passionate crusade against Hitler

and called her the greatest woman journalist of her time, but by 1961 Dorothy Thompson's grip on the public was long past. Given the fleeting nature of celebrity and fame in twentieth-century American life, it is remarkable that she dominated public opinion for several decades, with the period from 1935 to 1947 representing the peak of her influence. In those years she was a daily part of millions of American lives through her column, radio broadcasts, speeches, lectures, and other writings. Her combination of emotion and intellect was well suited to the tenor of public life in the late 1930s, as Americans began to confront the possibility that there might be some things so evil as to force the nation to war again. She led the way, and when her following diminished, she made her peace with that, too.

In a joint biography called *Dorothy and Red*, Vincent Sheean noted, "The characteristic of 'stardom' in American life is that it glitters tremendously while it glitters, but is obliterated when its day is gone."[79] Sinclair Lewis left a body of novels, which are a respected part of twentieth-century literature; Dorothy Thompson, like most journalists, did not leave behind such an enduring opus. Reading her columns sixty years later is an eerie experience: much of the passion and emotion that animated her daily life and her journalism seems flat, lifeless, transient. Her columns were what people were talking about *that day*—they were topical, which was precisely why they were popular. Thompson's style of journalism does not age well.

And yet her contributions to the American century are undeniable. Dorothy Thompson stood up to Hitler and profoundly influenced the debate over American participation in World War II. She served as a role model for countless young women contemplating careers in foreign affairs or journalism, and she made ordinary housewives feel part of national and international events, flattering them as no male columnist could by assuming they were intelligent enough to wrestle with events happening beyond the four walls of their kitchens. Her star may not have glittered forever, but while it did, it shone like a meteor.

"Young men, you've now reached the age when it is essential that you know the rites and rituals, the customs and taboos of our island, Rather than go into them in detail, however, I'm simply going to present each of you with a copy of this excellent book by Margaret Mead."

T H R E E

COMING OF AGE WITH MARGARET MEAD

UTH BENEDICT ONCE said of Margaret Mead, "She isn't planning to be the best anthropologist, but she *is* planning to be the most famous." Long before her death in 1978, Mead had fulfilled that prophecy. More than any other person, this "self-appointed materfamilias to the world" popularized the field of anthropology in modern American culture and in the process made herself practically a household name. Wherever she went—and she traveled constantly until the very end—she was instantly recognizable by her trademark forked walking stick, which her biographer Jane Howard called "one of the most inspired decisions of her career." Looking like a bishop or a shepherd (or as one wag noted, "Big Bo-Peep"), the thumbstick confirmed her celebrity status. "Any time I want to disguise myself, I'll throw it away," but of course she never did.[1]

Margaret Mead's career took off on its meteoric rise while she was still in her twenties with the 1928 publication of *Coming of Age in Samoa*, which went on to become the best-selling anthropology book of all time. Even today it is common on a city bus or subway to see a student deeply engrossed in this engaging, almost novelistic tale. That book, and Margaret Mead's example, encouraged many young people to choose anthropology as a career. And for general readers, it confirmed the association of Mead with the topic of sex, especially of the Pacific Island variety, as *New Yorker* cartoons over the years loved to play up.

"I am here to receive. . . . *Teach* me something." Even though Margaret Mead was not a terribly original thinker, she was an excellent synthesizer and she never stopped learning. When she traveled she preferred to stay in private homes rather than hotels, requesting not the sterile guest room but one of the children's rooms so she could see what was on kids' minds. Unlike many celebrities, she talked with you, not at you, her tongue unconsciously flickering in and out while she spoke. Like Dorothy Thompson, she excelled at networking and was a first-rate picker of brains, always carrying a small notebook to record ideas and information she gleaned. But she was also the kind of person you could talk to when your marriage was in trouble, or the night before your Ph.D. orals. Wear a nice dress, she called to remind one nervous graduate student, who never forgot the gesture.[2]

Margaret Mead, a third-generation professional woman, managed to combine marriage (three, in fact), motherhood, and career with aplomb. The secret of a successful marriage was to marry someone whose interests were the same as yours: "I always did that and all my marriages were a great success," she said with tongue only partly in cheek. For many women, she was the symbol of a truly liberated lifestyle, or in writer Gail Sheehy's memorable phrase, "a general among the foot soldiers of modern feminism." In 1963 Betty Friedan called her the "symbol of the woman thinker in America." But Mead had a somewhat testy relationship with the younger women who rediscovered feminism in the 1960s and 1970s. Her prolific writings on women and gender sent a mixed message: she supported the full realization of women's talents and capabilities, but also glorified traditional female roles. Yet on balance she was far more friend than foe of modern feminism.[3]

Margaret Mead was far from universally beloved. "Everybody talks about Margaret Mead but nobody does anything about her," mumbled a disgruntled male colleague. Not until 1973 was she elected to the National Academy of Sciences. Many considered her overexposed, an international busybody; fellow anthropologists were sometimes appalled at her popularizations and sound bite generalizations. Others dismissed her as an uppity woman: "Margaret, have you found a culture yet where the men had the babies," ran a one-sentence review of a 1935 book. But like Eleanor Roosevelt, she seemed to grow in stature until people were just glad to have her around; people recognized her greatness, without quite being able to explain it.[4] Starting out as a young anthropologist with something to say to America in the 1920s, she deeply embedded herself in popular culture and thought for the next five decades.

🔅

MARGARET MEAD ALWAYS felt fortunate that the women she knew best growing up—her mother and her paternal grandmother—demonstrated that a woman could have a career and raise a family at the same time. "I was lucky because I myself did not have to design a lifestyle that combined work and homemaking. My grandmother and mother had both been professional women, and I grew up believing that it was natural for women to use their brains *and* to have children." The first baby born in a new modern hospital, she was also breast-fed, a combination of the old and the new that defined her approach to anthropology and culture. "For me, being brought up to become a woman who could live responsibly in the contemporary world and learning to be an anthropologist, conscious of the culture in which I lived, were almost the same thing."[5]

Margaret Mead was born on December 16, 1901, in Philadelphia; she never fudged the date to make herself seem younger, perhaps because she was so young when she first became famous. She was the eldest of five children, four of whom were girls. Sibling rivalries were hard to avoid in a family where the first-born announced at a tender age, "I'm going to be famous some day, and I'm going to be known by my own name." After listening to Margaret lecture some years later, her sister Priscilla commented, "I was hoping that for once someone would ask my sister a question she didn't know the answer to." Her wish was not granted.[6]

Most of Margaret's early schooling was at home, at the hands of her beloved grandmother Martha Ramsey Mead, a pioneer in child psychology who was "the most decisive influence in my life." When Mead began trying to translate her anthropological training into insights of interest to the general public, she always envisioned her grandmother as her audience, "the one person whom I wanted most to understand what my work was about and the one it would be hardest to convince that I had chosen well in becoming an anthropologist."[7]

Equally important were the models of her parents, Edward Sherwood Mead, a professor of economics at the University of Pennsylvania, and Emily Fogg Mead, a sociologist who was completing her Ph.D. when Margaret was a child. She derived different legacies from each parent. "I had my father's mind, but he had his mother's mind. Fortunately, his mother lived with us and so I early realized that intellectual abilities of the kind I shared with my father and grandmother were not sex-linked." In turn her mother and her circle of well-educated friends "gave me a sense of the wide range of choices open to a woman who wanted to be a person and make a contribution to the world, but they also showed me that a gift by itself was not enough. You had to work hard to turn a gift into some kind of accomplishment."[8]

Although her mother was "filled with passionate resentment about the condition of women," coming of age in the 1920s Margaret seemed to feel that the gender issue was settled and that a modern woman could freely choose the direction of her life. Even as Mead rejected the public side of feminism, however, she never questioned its private dimension, especially the desire for personal autonomy and self-fulfillment. As historian Rosalind Rosenberg pointed out, the main difference between the mother's and daughter's feminism "was that the daughter's struggle was far more self-consciously personal than her mother's ever dared to be."[9]

Unlike other late nineteenth- and early-twentieth-century women who had to fight their families for the right to higher education, Mead always assumed she would go to college and likely take an advanced degree. But instead of going to Wellesley, which her mother had attended, she enrolled at her father's alma mater, DePauw University in Greencastle, Indiana. DePauw, a Methodist-affiliated institution, was a less than ideal choice for this spirited and somewhat snobbish young woman. Arriving on campus with the wrong clothes, the wrong attitude, and an Eastern accent in a sea of Midwesterners, Mead experienced the "first and only real experience of discrimination" in her life when she was snubbed by her classmates and blackballed by a sorority.[10]

Perhaps her undisputed drive and ambition could eventually have triumphed over the hostile DePauw campus, but after her freshman year she convinced her parents to let her transfer to Barnard College, where she graduated Phi Beta Kappa in 1923. Mead possessed an urban temperament that needed to be around bustling activity and interesting people, and she found Barnard's urban campus far more to her liking. Later when one of her *Redbook* readers asked where she would most like to live, she gave this succinct answer: "Where I do live—New York City."[11]

Mead quickly linked up with a talented and free-spirited group of Barnard women. This was 1920, at a time when women's emancipation, the flapper, bobbed hair, and sexual experimentation were all the rage, especially in a place like New York. The word "free" crops up repeatedly in Mead's memories of this period. "We belonged to a generation of women who felt extraordinarily free—free from the demand to marry unless we chose to do so, free to postpone marriage while we did other things, free from the need to bargain and hedge that had burdened and restricted women of earlier generations." Mead thrived in this atmosphere, strengthened by the deep friendships she made with women like Leonie Adams, whose poetry had already been published while she was an undergraduate. One friend who knew Margaret at this time remembered her as "a missile waiting to be directed—she was going to be *something*."[12]

Despite all this talk of freedom and emancipation, Mead was engaged to be married throughout her Barnard years. Many of her friends had only the shadowiest sense of her fiancé, Luther Cressman, who was at that point studying for the ministry. (He later shifted to archaeology.) In fact, they had become engaged when Margaret was a mere sixteen years old, allowing her to bypass the usual adolescent struggles with popularity with the opposite sex. "I never had to live through that period of being rejected by a man," Mead later recalled. "If you had a man, you weren't continually thinking about them." Cressman recalled that their long engagement gave him "the opportunity to observe her devotion to the ideals of equality of the sexes (not similarity) and that women could do anything men could and as well. The idea would become almost an obsession with her."[13]

Barnard gave Mead her introduction to anthropology. What a fortuitous link. During her senior year she took a class with Franz Boas and his teaching assistant, Ruth Benedict, a somewhat older woman who had recently completed her Ph.D. under Boas's direction. Something clicked, and Mead determined to do graduate study in this new field at Columbia. When she did not win the one fellowship for a graduating Barnard senior, Benedict personally presented Mead with a "First Award No Red Tape Fellowship" of $300, which allowed her to enroll in graduate school.[14]

This was just one of the many acts of personal and professional kindness that Ruth Benedict bestowed on the young Mead, who started out as a sort of surrogate daughter (Benedict, married and fifteen years older, had no children), then quickly became a colleague, and much more. "By electing anthropology as a career, I was also electing a closer relationship to Ruth," Mead later wrote. Theirs was the most profound friendship of each other's life, unbroken until Benedict's death at age sixty-one in 1948. "When she died, I had read everything she had ever written and she had read everything I had ever written. No one else had, and no one else has."[15]

After marrying Cressman in September of 1923 (who was not amused to be described in her autobiography as her "student husband," which implied a less than permanent commitment), Mead began her graduate work at Columbia. Her masters thesis was on intelligence testing among Italian immigrants, a topic inspired by her mother's dissertation research on Italian families in New Jersey. In 1925 she completed her own Ph.D. thesis, *An Inquiry into the Question of Cultural Stability in Polynesia*, a dry and quite lackluster piece of scholarship drawn entirely from secondary sources. She defended the thesis that year, but did not officially receive her Ph.D. until 1929, after the dissertation was published, which was customary at that time.

Having finished the dissertation, Margaret was eager to go into the field. Although much anthropological work focused on American Indians, her horizons went beyond America. A favorite quote from graduate school days captured her sense of urgency: "The last man on Raratonga who knows anything about the past will probably die today. I must hurry." She set her sights on the South Seas.[16]

"Slow down, Margaret," Franz Boas and Ruth Benedict must have said, to no avail. Despite her tender age (she was only twenty-four when she defended her thesis) and her marital status (Cressman conveniently arranged for a year's fellowship at the General Theological Seminary in England), she was determined to go. Feeling that it would be more destructive to try to stop her than to let her go, her mentors agreed, despite grave concerns about her health, her ability to handle the psychological rigors of field work alone, and her vulnerability as an unattached young white woman in a foreign land.[17]

Years later Mead penned a description of the qualifications a woman needed for a career in field anthropology, and it obviously grew out of her nine-month sojourn in Samoa, the first of the five extended field trips she undertook between 1925 and 1939:

> She should like people. She should be able to stand people in crowds; she should not shrink from physical contact with persons of another race and a different standard of personal hygiene; she should not have a squeamish stomach, an over-sensitive nose or a strong tendency to recoil before the bare facts of birth, sex and death. She should like children, and she should have had experience in handling small babies and in making friends with very young children. She should like women and be able to identify herself with her sex, as a sex, in a way that the modern American educated woman is hardly ever called upon to do. She should like the raw stuff of life, its sights and smells and sounds.[18]

In other words, she had better be adaptable.

But what was Mead to study? Before she left New York, "Papa Franz" (as Boas was called by his female students) had suggested that she study the question of "how the young girls react to the restraints of custom": "We find very often among ourselves during the period of adolescence a strong rebellious spirit that may be expressed in sullenness or in sudden outbursts. . . . I am not at all clear in my mind in how far similar conditions may occur in primitive society and in how far the desire for independence may be simply due to our own modern conditions and to a more strongly developed individualism."[19] Mead immediately accepted the assignment.

She also accepted Boas's suggestion of American Samoa as her research site, a place that met his criterion that American ships must dock there regularly. With financial support from the National Research Council and from her father, who paid for her

Margaret Mead never told her Samoan hosts that she was married, and the 24-year-old anthropologist could easily have passed for an adolescent. Here she is in Samoan dress with Fa'amotu, the daughter of a local chief with whom she stayed at the beginning of her research trip. (Collections of the Library of Congress)

expensive round-the-world travel ticket,[20] Mead arrived at Pago Pago, American Samoa, in the fall of 1925. Soon after she arrived, the island was hit by a hurricane, causing her mother to remark petulantly, "I suppose you knew there was going to be a hurricane. There is one every ten years, you say, and you chose this year on purpose."[21] Her first task was to learn the Samoan language. After what seems in retrospect a very short period of six weeks, she announced she had made sufficient progress to begin her field work on the remote island of Tau.

At five-foot-two and ninety-eight pounds, with short bobbed hair, the twenty-four-year-old Mead did not look that far removed from her subjects, female adolescents, especially since she chose not to divulge the fact that she was a married woman. Her research agenda was open-ended. Boas told her to sit around and listen even when it seemed like a waste of time, so she made up a methodology as she went along. (Another researcher once wrote in frustration from the field, "How anyone knows who is anybody's mother's brother, only God and Malinowski know.") Mead also had to cope with the loneliness of not having anyone to share her daily experiences with and the homesickness of being so far removed from friends and family. Never again would she do field work alone.[22]

On the long boat trip back to Europe in the summer of 1926, where she was to reunite with her husband, Mead met Reo Fortune, a twenty-four-year-old New Zealander on his way to do graduate study in psychology at Cambridge University in England. As they talked passionately about their work, they began to fall in love. By the time Mead reached Europe, she sensed that her marriage to Cressman was over, although she and Fortune did not marry until 1928. (Mead's first marriage was effectively excised from the public record, not to be reacknowledged until the publication of her autobiography, *Blackberry Winter*, in 1972. "We had neither a book nor a baby together," she later explained. As far as the public knew, Fortune was her first husband, Gregory Bateson her second.) In the meantime she and

Cressman returned to New York City, where she took up a position in 1926 as an assistant curator of ethnology at the American Museum of Natural History, her professional base for the next fifty years.[23]

Margaret Mead was already developing a national reputation, and not just among her anthropological peers. In early 1928, even before the publication of *Coming of Age in Samoa*, Mead received the news that she had been elected to the recently formed Society of Women Geographers, with which she maintained a lifelong association. This group had been organized in 1925 by four friends—Gertrude Emerson Sen, Marguerite Harrison, Blair Niles, and Gertrude Mathews Shelby—to bring together women interested in geography, world exploration, anthropology, and related fields, along the lines of the Explorers Club, which did not admit women until 1981. Membership was open only to those who had done "distinctive work whereby they have added to the world's store of knowledge concerning the countries on which they have specialized, and have published in magazines or in book form, a record of their work." Other members included Eleanor Roosevelt, Mary Beard, Fannie Hurst, Margaret Bourke-White, and mountain climber Annie Peck. In 1942 the Society presented Mead with their Gold Medal; the only previous recipient had been Amelia Earhart after her 1932 solo flight across the Atlantic.[24]

Unlike many anthropologists, who wait years, if ever, to write up their field notes, Mead was always punctual about publishing her results before she undertook another trip into the field. Some of her research was published as monographs with appeal only to fellow academics, but from the start Mead was determined to bring her work to a wider audience. Working deliberately and self-consciously, she turned her research on Samoan adolescence into a hugely successful popular book.

The thesis of *Coming of Age in Samoa* is strikingly similar to the charge she had been given by Franz Boas to investigate: that in primitive societies adolescence was not necessarily a time of stress and strain, but rather an orderly development of more mature interests and activities. In Samoa young girls had casual love affairs and were in no hurry to marry because this was the most carefree time of their lives; their familiarity with sex meant that sexual experiences were not charged with conflict or recrimination. Even though Mead protested that only sixty-eight of the book's 297 pages dealt with sex, the sections on casual love affairs, masturbation, night-crawling (a kind of surrogate rape), and the overall impression of a society where sex was natural and pleasurable shocked and titillated readers. This was 1928, and America was still very much the small-town world that Sinclair Lewis had described in *Main Street*. Decades later students were still furtively turning to Mead's book for these very same sections.[25]

One of the distinctive features of the book was Mead's style of writing, which was jargon-free, fluid, and as languorous as the subject matter. Mead had a simple retort—"I wrote it in English"—but that masks how unusual it was, then and now, to have a piece of academic research stir a wider audience. Mead's descriptions of the beautiful and (at her hands) peaceful Samoan society started with a composite "A Day in Samoa" containing sentences like this: "As the dawn begins to fall among the soft brown roofs and the slender palm trees stand out against a colourless, gleaming sea, lovers slip home from trysts beneath the palm trees or in the shadow of beached canoes, that the light may find each sleeper in his appointed place." Unlike her prose in later books, which was often lackluster or hurried, these sentences shine. Mead uses the first person sparingly, but it is clear that she too is part of the story. Like Dorothy Thompson's personal journalism, this "I was there" style is found in much of her anthropological writing.[26]

Without question the key to the book's success was the addition, at the suggestion of publisher William Morrow, of several sections explicitly comparing the Samoan experience with America. The narrative unfolds in such a way that it was impossible not to draw constant comparisons between American teenagers, whose adolescence was supposedly fraught with tension and generational angst, and their Samoan counterparts. Mead undertook these additions with reluctance, as she confessed to Professor William Ogburn of the University of Chicago: "The beginning and the end I wrote under pressure, as you know I think no one under forty should be sporting about with general ideas." (Mead was all of twenty-six at the time.) In the end, she told Morrow that he had been absolutely right.[27]

William Morrow was a new publishing firm in the 1920s, and they pushed this book hard. (In contrast, the more established Harper and Brothers had turned it down.) Morrow created a seductive cover featuring palm trees and a young couple seemingly coming from or going to a tryst. The publisher collected blurbs from outstanding cultural and scientific authorities such as Havelock Ellis ("Not only a fascinating book to read but most instructive and valuable"), Dr. Bronislaw Malinowski of the University of London ("An absolutely first-rate piece of descriptive anthropology . . . an outstanding achievement"), and George Dorsey, author of *Why We Behave Like Human Beings* ("An extraordinary, illuminating book. I wonder if we shall ever be as sensible about sex as the Samoans are?"). The publisher budgeted the then substantial sum of $1,500 for advertising and promotion. In 1928 and 1929 Mead made $5,000 from royalties, quite a coup for an academic book. It was also double her annual salary at the museum, providing a nice nest egg for future field work.[28]

The popular reviews were overwhelmingly positive, with only a few commentators objecting to the somewhat impressionistic data or the sweeping comparisons between Samoan and American adolescence. The *New York Times* called it "warmly human yet never sentimental, frank with the clean, clear frankness of the scientist, unbiased in its judgment, richly readable in its style." Freda Kirchwey wrote in *The Nation*, "Most of us probably will read Miss Mead's impressive study and then continue as before to cling to our difficulties and our delights, with occasional impulses of escape to the expansive simplicity of the South Seas." The academic reviews were also generally positive, although they expressed more skepticism about the explicit present-mindedness of the comparisons and challenged some of the methodological assumptions.[29]

Ironically Margaret Mead was out of the country when this favorable publicity was pouring in, on a year-long field trip to New Guinea with her new husband, Reo Fortune; because of the slowness of the mails it was months before she knew she had a best-seller. When they returned from the field in September 1929, Mead once again quickly wrote up her results for a popular audience, which Morrow published in 1930 as *Growing Up in New Guinea*. This book was the first anthropological study of young children's growth in primitive society, and the first to look at the educational methods of a people (in the publisher's blurb) "whose lives are still entirely unspoiled by civilization."[30]

While it received very good popular and scholarly reviews (the *New Republic* thought it was even more interesting than *Coming of Age in Samoa*), it did not do nearly as well as her earlier book. The onset of the Depression, which decimated book sales (and so much else), was doubtless a factor, as was the fact that this book was not about the hot topic of sex. In any case, of the trilogy of books published from her field work in these years (*Coming of Age in Samoa* [1928], *Growing Up in New Guinea* [1930], and *Sex and Temperament in Three Primitive Societies* [1935]), Mead always considered the New Guinea book the "clumsiest" of the three.[31]

Margaret Mead in these early years was an active and persistent player in the building of her reputation. From the start, as evidenced by her willingness to add the contemporary slant to the Samoa book, she had been willing to adapt in order to win readers. Being away from the country for extended periods on field trips kept her from landing a regular lecture contract, but she worked hard to keep her name before the public and find a popular audience for her work.

Given the ongoing Depression, and the cut in salary she took at the museum because of it, the extra income from her books must have been welcome, but this drive for recognition was about more than money. During her lifetime Mead could have become a very wealthy woman from her writing and lecturing, but she typically channeled her royalties and fees into her research projects rather than keeping the money for herself. All her life she lived modestly, collecting friends rather than wealth or possessions. She never owned a car or learned to drive. "To some success is your name in neon lights," she once said. "Or it's the accumulation of money. To me success is the freedom to pursue your own goals."[32]

In the 1920s and 1930s a woman anthropologist who journeyed to such exotic places as Samoa or New Guinea was news, with or without a best-selling book. For example, Mead's return from the field in 1933 was the lead blurb in the *Literary Digest*'s popular feature "They Stand Out from the Crowd." Widely syndicated photographs of Mead, with her short, bobbed hair, bangs, and eager expression (she removed her glasses for these shots), reinforced the perception of youth—she looked like a college student. Never the least bit interested in exercise or physical activity, later in life she grew heavier. She kept the bobbed hair and bangs, but the look was more no-nonsense than flapper. As her age and physique expanded, she was most often described as grandmotherly, quite a contrast to her earlier image.[33]

Margaret Mead did not rely on her friends and colleagues to send her news stories and syndicated photographs: in 1930 she engaged a clipping service. While many of these clippings were reviews, they also included the kind of human interest story that ran under titles like "Woman Scientist Is Also Samoan Dancer," "The Youngest Anthropologist Studies Youth," or "Philadelphia Girl Plans Cannibal Sojourn."[34]

As early as 1930, Mead was working with a literary agency to place her ethnographic studies with magazines reaching a broad readership. She had already discovered that lecturing about her field work to general audiences was excellent preparation for this kind of popularizing, but she was also a willing pupil for advice like this her agent passed along in 1930: "Sit down at the type-writer whenever you get a chance and just write the stuff out as if you were telling it to whatever audience most inspires you. Put in a lot of stories, conversation and personal descriptions. Don't forget to record your own emotions. Tell all the funny things that happened. In brief, forget for a little while that you are a scientist and reel off all the stories and personal experiences that you so carefully kept out of your book—the juicy bits that you tell your family and friends."[35]

With her agent's help, Mead published fairly widely in such mainstream magazines as *The Forum, The Nation, Scribners', The New Republic, The American Mercury*, and *Parents Magazine*, as well as in the *New York Times*. She even tapped the young adult market by contributing a chapter to *All True! The Record of Actual Adventures That Have Happened to Ten Women of Today* (1931). Despite occasional rejections, from the start Margaret Mead had, or learned, the knack of writing for a popular audience, and she continued to display this talent throughout her prolific career.[36]

But it would be wrong to see the anthropologist merely as a popularizer, especially in the 1930s. She continued her field work at a prodigious pace, returning to New Guinea with Fortune for more research in the fall of 1931. This time she planned to study sex roles, and the research she did would form the basis of her 1935 *Sex and Temperament in Three Primitive Societies*. This field trip was one of the most stressful parts of her life, "the closest I've ever come to madness." In addition to being stymied theoretically, she was experiencing strained personal relations with her husband, who was moody, possessively jealous, and held patriarchal views about women—in other words, not the ideal research partner and certainly not the ideal mate for an independent character like Margaret Mead.[37]

In the summer of 1932 Fortune and Mead linked up in the field with Cambridge-trained biologist Gregory Bateson. All three were starved for conversation and companionship, but it gradually became clear that there was something more going on between Bateson and Mead. One night, fearing an attack on their quarters, they took turns standing guard. Fortune awoke to hear Margaret and Gregory talking, and in a memorably understated phrase from *Blackberry Winter*, Mead commented, "There is much to be said for the suggestion that the true oedipal situation is not the primal scene but parents talking to each other in words the child does not understand." In this intense triangular situation Bateson and Mead were falling in love, but, she hastened to add, "this was kept firmly under control while all three of us tried to translate the intensity of our feelings into better and more perceptive field work." Mead's second (and least successful) marriage was essentially over when they returned from the field, and in 1936, while on their way to Bali, Gregory Bateson and Margaret Mead were married. They were much closer in age (she was thirty-four, he thirty-one) than in height: at six-foot-five-inches Bateson towered over his petite wife.[38]

Mead later called the early years of her marriage to Bateson, which were spent doing field work together in Bali, "the perfect intellectual and emotional working partnership," adding, "I think it is a good thing to have had such a model, once, of what anthropological field work can be like, even if the model includes the kind of extra intensity in which a lifetime is condensed into a few short years." One of their innovations was the use of still and moving photography: planning to take 2,000 photographs, they ended up taking 25,000 instead. According to Mead, it would be twenty-five years before this approach to documenting a culture was fully appreciated by the anthropology profession.[39]

By 1938 it was becoming distressingly clear that war might soon come to the Pacific, which would mean a cessation of field work. Mead and Bateson returned to New York, and several months later, she learned that she was pregnant at age thirty-eight. Their daughter Mary Catherine Bateson (Cathy) was born on December 8, 1939. Gregory was not present, having returned to England after the outbreak of the war, but he saw his daughter when she was six weeks old.

Of Mead's three marriages, the one to Gregory Bateson was by far the most success-ful and satisfying. This portrait captures the tenderness of the early years of their relationship. (Collections of the Library of Congress)

Pearl Harbor occurred nine days before Mead's fortieth birth-day. For Mead, Bateson, and so many others, World War II marked a distinct break in their lives, both personally and pro-fessionally. Because of the war and because of her daughter, Mead undertook no field work again until 1953, and never again with the intensity of her early years.[40] During the war Bateson returned to England to serve in the war effort, and Mead worked in Wash-ington with the National Research Council, where she wrote a popular treatise about wartime America called *And Keep Your Powder Dry* (1942). Although their marriage survived the wartime separations, in the immediate postwar years they grew apart intellectually and (on his part) emotionally, and in 1950 they divorced.

Margaret Mead is so closely associated with the field of anthropology that it is worth pausing to consider how unconventional her career actually was. To be sure, she made a point of attending the yearly conferences of the American Anthropological Association ("Have you no interest in observing the ritual behavior in your own culture," she chastised a colleague who complained they were dull), and she even happened to die on the first day of the 1978 convention, thereby overshadowing the proceedings. She was enormously generous to young and old colleagues in anthropology and related fields, and probably did more than any other scientist to attract young people to the discipline. "My name can open doors," she told them all. "If you ever need or want to use it, do. Don't hesitate."[41] She never doubted her choice to cast her lot with anthropology.

From the start she charted her own way, choosing "not to compete with men in male fields, but instead to concentrate on the kinds of work that are better done by women," such as studying women and children. Even though she taught, mainly at Columbia, she was largely removed from the conventional academic establishment and its dreary academic politics and bureaucratic battles. She remained an adjunct professor at Columbia for many years, turning down offers of full professorships in 1958 and 1963 because they came too late and by then her plate was too full.[42]

Instead, her institutional base was the American Museum of Natural History, but even there she was not given full professional recognition, remaining an Associate Curator until 1964. She was never really part of the (male) museum world either, noting that she was more likely to meet the other curators at the men's night of the Society of Women Geographers (where many of their wives, professional women in their own right, were active) than in the corridors of the museum. On the other hand, her hard-to-find office, tucked up in one of the museum turrets with lovely views of the city from its prime Central Park West location, kept her handily out of the purview of that male world, a situation that suited her just fine. More than anything else, this hidden tower office, which students, colleagues, and journalists struggled to locate over the years, was the prime symbol of her independent professional life.

Given the pervasive discrimination against women in academe and the professions, even in a field like anthropology, which was fairly kind to women, Mead may have made these choices because she knew that a traditional academic career would have been closed to her except at a women's college, or perhaps at a fairly supportive place like Columbia. (Even at Columbia, Ruth Benedict was only made a full professor in 1948, the year of her death.) On the other hand, perhaps these choices were a creative alternative to avoid being tied down, which in turn allowed her to develop her unique role as a go-between for the seven societies she studied and American culture. It probably was a bit of both.

In the end, like Dorothy Thompson, Mead was able to create her own career path, one that allowed her to do what she wanted with the minimum of institutional demands and the maximum of public exposure. She was marginalized in subtle ways by academe, but she worked the margins to her benefit. To accomplish this took an enormous amount of discipline, self-esteem, and chutzpa, but as one of her professors had noticed as far back as 1927, "I don't know Margaret, You just got drive!"[43]

❦

A *New York Times* editorial after Mead's death noted that she had "married and shed three husbands without taking their names or subordinating her work to theirs."[44] To many people that fact seemed outrageous enough, but it was only one aspect of her incredibly complicated personal life. For Margaret Mead also had deep, intense, sexual relationships with women throughout her life, her love affair with Ruth Benedict being the most significant. Just as Eleanor Roosevelt and Dorothy Thompson managed to lead unconventional personal lives while carrying on their well-respected professional careers, so too did Margaret Mead. In all three cases these aspects of their lives became public knowledge only after they died.

In a 1975 column for *Redbook* entitled "Bisexuality: A New Awareness," inspired in part by Nigel Nicholson's recent book about the unconventional marriage of his parents, Harold Nicholson and Vita Sackville-West, Mead argued that the time had come to recognize bisexuality as a normal form of human behavior. Using her social scientist's mantle to point to "the well-documented, normal human capacity to love members of both sexes," she posited that "a very large number of human beings—probably a majority—are bisexual in their potential capacity for love." The tone of the article was engaged but impersonal—the reader would have no way of knowing whether this subject meant more to Mead than, say, her columns on the generation gap, public education, or legalizing marijuana. But no doubt her friends and some of her colleagues could read between the lines to see that Mead was talking about herself.[45]

Her daughter was one of the first to speak publicly about this facet of her mother's life. In her 1984 memoir, *With a Daughter's Eye,* Bateson identified a "double pattern," in which her mother sustained deep, often parallel relationships with one man and one woman. A friend put a slightly different twist on it: Mead "fell in love with women's souls and men's bodies. She was spiritually homosexual, psychologically bisexual, and physically heterosexual. She had affairs with both men and women—though never with two men or two women at the same time; in an eccentric way she had a very stern morality. . . . "[46]

While Mead had crushes on women, especially in college, it was her deepening relationship with Ruth Benedict at Columbia that unlocked this aspect of her psyche. Indeed, as her daughter realized, Benedict became the model: "The intimacy to which Margaret and Ruth progressed after Margaret's completion of her degree became the model for one axis of her life while the other was defined in relation to the men she loved and married." This affair with Benedict coexisted alongside her marriage to Luther Cressman. According to Benedict's biographer, Mead and Benedict were lovers during a visit to the Grand Canyon while Mead was on her way to Samoa in 1925, and the affair continued when they met again in Europe the next summer on Mead's way back. By then, Cressman had been replaced by Reo Fortune, with no impact on the Mead-Benedict relationship.[47]

Dorothy Thompson separated her feelings for women from what she considered her essentially heterosexual nature, but Margaret Mead saw no reason to limit herself to one kind of love at a time. "I've never known the kind of union that made me want to exclude other people," she once said. While Mead seemed reasonably free from guilt or stigma about her love for women, she never explicitly discussed this part of her life with her daughter, and once even upbraided Cathy for an adolescent lesbian affair that might have damaged her mother's reputation had it become known.[48]

Confounding Freud's theory of penis envy, the young Margaret was glad she had not been born a boy because it meant someday she could bear children of her own. The adult Margaret Mead approached the question of having children in a very calculating, almost instrumental manner. (One can imagine her transported to the 1980s or 1990s and deciding to have a child as a single parent.) In 1926 Mead was told that she had a tipped uterus, which would make it very difficult to carry any pregnancy to term. Taking this "as a kind of omen about my future life," Margaret began to plot her career accordingly, perhaps following the lead of Ruth Benedict who once said, "I don't have children, so I might as well have Hottentots."[49]

"I had married Luther with the hope of rearing a household of children in a country parish," Mead recounted with something less than total candor. "But now he was giving up the ministry and I was told that I could not have a child. I believed he would make a wonderful father, but this was no longer a possibility— for us." By this point, Margaret wanted out of her marriage to Cressman for a variety of reasons, mainly that she had outgrown him and was ready to proceed with her plans to marry Reo Fortune. She coldly stated her reasoning: Fortune would not make a good father, because he was too demanding and jealous, but a childless marriage to him could offer "a life of shared field work and intellectual endeavor." She chose the latter.[50]

The balance changed once they were ensconced in the hostile Mundugumor culture in New Guinea, a culture she especially hated for its attitude toward children. Men wanted daughters and women wanted sons, and babies of the wrong sex "were tossed into the river, still alive, wrapped in a bark sheath": "I reacted so strongly against the set of the culture that it was here that I decided that I would have a child no matter how many miscarriages it meant." She convinced Fortune that one child would not change their lives that much, but she failed to get pregnant. Once she married Bateson, whom she considered far more suitable father material, she still had difficulty conceiving. Finally in 1939 their daughter was born.[51]

Mead claims that if she could not have had children, she would have faced that with regret but not with remorse. Yet given the absolute joy she took in children—her own daughter, the children of her friends, and children everywhere—it surely would have been a great loss for her. Mary Catherine Bateson was a wanted, and much loved child; when she later wrote of her upbringing and her relationships with her parents, she did so with great affection and respect for how she was raised. And when Cathy had a daughter, Vanni, in 1969, Margaret Mead received as much pleasure from her new status as grandmother as from any honorary degree or professional award.

Mary Catherine Bateson probably had what was in her own words the "best-documented childhood" in America, starting with a film of her birth in the delivery room. This was 1939—in so many ways Mead was ahead of her time. Having been a breast-fed baby herself and having had so much experience with that tradition in the field, she was determined to breast-feed her baby from birth, adjusting the feeding schedule to the baby's needs rather than the clock. Since this was counter to standard hospital procedure at the time, Mead enlisted a young pediatrician named Benjamin Spock, whom she liked because he had been psychoanalyzed, to be on hand during the delivery. (Gregory Bateson was in England because of the war, but in those days fathers were automatically barred from the delivery room anyway.) To win over hospital nurses skeptical about her unusual views of childbirth, Mead screened "First Days in the Life of a New Guinea Baby," the documentary film she and Bateson had just completed based on their field research.[52]

One of Mead's main priorities in providing a home for her daughter was to avoid the isolated nuclear family and instead offer a multi-generational mix of adults, children, hired helpers, and other assorted friends and relatives. "The bold and generous way she defined the word 'family' survives as the most enduring of her legacies," concluded Jane Howard. During the war Mead and her daughter lived in a cooperative household with social scientist Lawrence Frank and his wife Mary, who had an infant son plus five older children from his previous marriages; this situation worked well while Mead commuted to Washington for her war work. And summers were spent communally in Holderness, New Hampshire. Another continuity was provided by Marie Eichelberger, Mead's former Barnard classmate and devoted lifelong friend, who became Cathy's "Aunt Marie."[53]

Mead and Bateson were devoted to their daughter, but in the end these two brilliant yet quite different individuals were unable to sustain their marriage. "Gregory's interest was in systems, and Margaret's was in pattern," was how friend and fellow anthropologist Lola Romanucci-Ross summed up their differences. Mead's bland statement in her autobiography ("My years as a collaborating wife, trying to combine intensive field work and an intense personal life, also came to an end") masks the pain that this split, which was instigated by him, caused her. Gregory was one of the two loves of her life, a place of honor shared with Ruth Benedict. Bateson, who remarried twice and whose intellectual interests expanded beyond anthropology to embrace ecology, cybernetics, and Zen Buddhism, remembered that Mead basically wore him out: "I couldn't keep up, and she couldn't stop. She was like a tugboat. She could sit down and write three thousand words by eleven o'clock in the morning and spend the rest of the day working at the museum." He was not the first, or the last, to be overwhelmed by her energetic, almost frenetic zest for life.[54]

Even though Mead did not marry again, she sustained a rich emotional life, which included (according to her daughter) a long-term love affair with a man and deep relationships with women. She maintained her ongoing "private friendship" with her Barnard classmate, Marie Eichelberger. And in the 1940s Mead began collaborating with a younger colleague, Rhoda Metraux, and eventually shared a home with her, living with her longer than with anyone else in her life.[55]

And then there were her friends, an intricate, constantly expanding network of colleagues, godchildren, relatives, ex-husbands and their families, and so forth. Paralleling Eleanor Roosevelt's lifelong capacity for new friendships, Mead boasted that she made at least one new friend of importance every two to three months, without losing any of her old ones. It would have been impossible to map the intricate interconnections of this friendship web, and there were many parts that were kept secret, perhaps deliberately. Noted her former student William Mitchell, "Of course nobody knew all of what she was doing. Already, she was all over the place. Whoever you were, however important she made you feel, you only saw a little piece, a teeny fragment of the iceberg."[56]

Mead herself was aware of how divided, almost compartmentalized her life was. In a letter drafted in 1955 "To Those I Love" in case of sudden accidental death, she wrote: "I have become increasingly conscious of the extent to which my life is segmented, each piece shared with a separate person, even where within the time and space of that segment." She ended with this statement:

Margaret Mead's radiant delight in children is evident in her interaction with her granddaughter, Vanni, but it extended to children everywhere. Her favorite age? Eleven. (© Ken Heyman. All Rights Reserved.)

> It has not been by my choice of concealment that anyone of you have been left in ignorance of some part of my life which would seem, I know of great importance. Nor has it been from lack of trust—in any person—on my part, but only from the exigencies of the mid-twentieth century when each of us—at least those of us who are my age—seems fated for a life which is no longer sharable.[57]

With Mead's customary exponential growth in friendships, imagine how much more complex these webs of feelings and friendships had become two decades later at her death.

Yet, more successfully than most, Margaret Mead created a personal and professional life that worked for her. Her daughter noted how Mead "moved generously through a diversity of relationships," accepting the fragmentation as a price of professional autonomy. And yet she avoided prolonged intimacy, never letting anyone come too close, even Ruth Benedict. Toward the end of her life she became even more of that tugboat that had driven her third husband out of their marriage—she could not slow down. At times it seemed as if she was almost afraid of being alone with herself, terrified of having an unstructured hour or two with nothing to do and nobody with whom to talk. Solitude or reflection held no attraction for Margaret Mead. The woman her daughter called "a one person conference" always had to have somebody else around.[58]

༖

NO MATTER WHAT culture Margaret Mead studied, remembered Gregory Bateson at her memorial service, "she could always somehow keep track of the babies." One of the most distinctive features of Mead's long career was her focus on topics not usually seen as important, specifically childhood, adolescence, sex roles, women, and family life. Partly a strategic choice for advancing her career but mainly because these were the anthropological questions that interested her, she carved out an area of expertise where being a woman would be an asset, not a hindrance.[59]

Margaret Mead was well ahead of her time in her attention to the complexities of gender. One of her most interesting books was *Sex and Temperament in Three Primitive Societies*, published in 1935. The core of the book was a treatment of the three very different cultures she and Reo Fortune had studied in New Guinea: the gentle, mountain-dwelling Arapesh; the cannibalistic, river-dwelling Mundugumor; and the headhunting, lake-dwelling Tchambuli. (Actually, there is a fourth tribe—her own—which Mead analyzes in concluding chapters similar to *Coming of Age in Samoa*.) Her goal was to discover to what degree temperamental differences were innate and to what extent they were culturally determined. With only slight exaggeration, *The Nation* summarized the findings as "a voyage which takes you, first, to a land where everybody is womanly; then to a land where everybody is manly; and finally, to one where the men are womanly and the women manly."[60]

Mead drew a more scholarly conclusion about the malleability of human nature: "If those temperamental attitudes which we have traditionally regarded as feminine—such as passivity, responsiveness, and a willingness to cherish children—can so easily be set up as the masculine pattern in one tribe, and in another be outlawed for the majority of women as well as for the majority of men, we no longer have any basis for regarding such aspects of behavior as sex-linked." Showing the unmistakable influence of Ruth Benedict, whose *Patterns of Culture* was published the year before, Mead concluded with a plea for a "recognition of genuine individual gifts as they occurred in either sex." Such a message could be especially liberating for women, because it held out the possibility that there was nothing intrinsic about Western gender definitions that confined women to the home and sent men off into the world. In Depression America, with its lack of an organized feminist movement, this was a strong, albeit covert, statement.[61]

While Mead never argued there were no differences between the sexes, *Sex and Temperament*'s discussion of the enormous variability in definitions of maleness and femaleness leaned heavily toward cultural relativism. And yet when Mead returned to the subject of gender roles fourteen years later in *Male and Female: A Study of the Sexes in a Changing World* (1949), her tone and focus had shifted. To be sure, she never went back on her insight that many aspects of American life, including sex and gender roles, were culturally shaped and that American culture needed to guarantee women fuller participation in social and cultural life. But now she seemed to place more weight on primary sex differences linked to reproductive functions and biology.

There are several possible explanations for the shift. *Male and Female* was more explicitly geared to a popular audience and had fewer scholarly pretensions than *Sex and Temperament*: anthropologist Peggy Reeves Sanday noted its style "placed it more properly on drugstore racks than on the scholar's shelf." Mead rarely strayed too far from the era's dominant values and wrote what her audience would read; *Male and Female* was nicely in tune with postwar American culture's emphasis on domesticity, consumption, and traditional gender roles. Finally, in between the two books Mead had given birth to her daughter and achieved the vaunted status of mother: once a woman "has borne a child," she wrote, "her full sex membership, her ability to conceive and carry and bear another human being, is assured and can never be taken away from her." Mead brought her maternal perspective and a new respect for biology to the book.[62]

Male and Female is impossible to reduce to a single argument, which no doubt helps explain the contradictory reactions it receives from readers and scholars. Employing a somewhat clunky organization, Mead offered insights from the seven cultures she had studied followed by extensive comments on contemporary American life. The general argument suggests some kind of universal sexual asymmetry, but much of the evidence supports an alternative interpretation about the fluidity of such roles. In other words, there was fuel for those who wanted women to keep close to their biological roles but also for those who wanted women to be allowed fuller participation in society. Still, the balance had decidedly tipped toward psychological and biological imperatives over cultural.

Male and Female shared some of the characteristics of Simone de Beauvoir's even more massive *The Second Sex*, published in France in 1949 but not available in an English translation until 1953. The main similarity concerned Mead's finding that in every human society that had been studied, male achievement was always valued more highly than female: "Men may cook, or weave or dress dolls or hunt humming-birds, but if such activities are appropriate occupations of men, then the whole society, men and women alike, votes them as important. When the same occupations are performed by women, they are regarded as less important." This insight (which Mead chose not to pursue and whose implications would later be identified as patriarchy by radical feminists) was in line with Beauvoir's thesis that men were human, but women were the second sex, the "other."[63]

But there the similarities end. Beauvoir's text was a grim and pessimistic catalogue of the myriad disadvantages of being a woman and none of the joys. (Dorothy Thompson bemoaned the book's "total lack of humor.")[64] Beauvoir rooted women's discrimination entirely in culture (women are made, not born), so downplaying biology that she did not even allow for maternal feelings. Mead, on the other hand, embraced women's biological roles and portrayed them as a source of strength, not oppression: "Women will see the world in different ways than men—and by so doing help the human race see itself more completely."[65]

The generally evenhanded reception that *Male and Female* received from readers and reviewers alike in 1949 is in striking contrast to the polemical attack on Mead that Betty Friedan launched in *The Feminine Mystique*. In a chapter called "The Functional Freeze, the Feminine Protest, and Margaret Mead," Friedan labeled *Male and Female* "the cornerstone of the feminine mystique" and Mead "the professional spokesman of femininity." Friedan had done her homework, because she quoted extensively from *Sex and Temperament*, with its documentation of the fluidity of sex roles. Friedan saw a missed opportunity: "From such anthropological observations, she might have passed on to the popular culture a truly revolutionary vision of women finally free to realize their full capabilities in a society which replaced arbitrary sexual definitions with a recognition of genuine individual gifts as they occur in either sex." Instead, Friedan noted, the feminine mystique took from Mead "not her vision of woman's great untested human potential, but this glorification of the female sexual function . . . a world where women, by merely being women and bearing children, will earn the same respect accorded men for their creative achievements."[66]

Despite her harsh critique of Mead's writings, Friedan was simultaneously drawn to the example of Mead's highly liberated life, another example of the gulf that often exists between person and persona. "Margaret Mead has lived a life of open challenge, and lived it proudly, if sometimes self-consciously, as a woman." When Mead died in 1978, Friedan came to the memorial service to pay her respects to a woman whom she now recognized as one of the most important women in twentieth-century America, and one who had also had a large impact on the history of American feminism.[67]

The year 1963 saw not only the publication of Betty Friedan's *The Feminine Mystique*, but also the release of the final report of the Presidential Commission on the Status of Women, appointed by President Kennedy in 1961 and chaired until her death by Eleanor Roosevelt. Both these events played major roles in the revival of feminism. When Scribner's published a commercial edition of the commission findings in 1965, Margaret Mead, not Betty Friedan, was asked to write the introduction and epilogue because of her reputation as an expert on women's lives in contemporary America.

Unlike Eleanor Roosevelt, who died before the movement really got going, Margaret Mead would live the rest of her life in a climate energized—and polarized—by feminist questions. Mead was no stranger to feminism. It was just that, like Dorothy Thompson, she thought it had all been settled back in the 1920s and 1930s. "We women are doing pretty well," she announced in 1976. "We're almost back to where we were in the twenties." Mead placed feminism in a long historical continuum, tracing it back to her mother and grandmother's generations: "My mother was a suffragette, and I grew up with the idea that the battle for women's rights had already been won." But the progress of the 1920s and 1930s was replaced by the postwar retreat into domesticity "and it went for naught" until women were ready to try again in the 1960s and 1970s.[68]

There was also a sense that she, Margaret Mead, did not need feminism. "I'm a third-generation professional woman and I'm absolutely free of any imprinting about dust under the bed," she told a Radcliffe audience forthrightly. Does that mean that when you left home to come to Cambridge, you didn't care what your apartment looked like, challenged a questioner? "It certainly does," replied Mead. "That's exactly what it means. . . . Seeing your mother dealing with that dust under the bed is very, very difficult to get away from." Feminist organizations like the National Organization for Women, founded in 1966, would never claim her allegiance. Confirming her lifelong approach to politics and social change, she never dwelt on women's grievances or discrimination, stressing instead the individual contributions women could make: "I've never spoken against anything. If you speak out, you just mobilize hostility. . . . I always speak positively."[69]

Many of her pronouncements infuriated feminists, and heartened those who hoped that women's lib would simply go away. For example, a headline in the *New York Times* in 1971 stated, "Dr. Mead, Lifelong Feminist, Says 'Nonsense' of Many in Women's Lib 'Gets Us Nowhere.' " Addressing a conference on women and the church, Mead challenged, "What in thunder is gained in reversing 'God is He' into 'God is She' except irritating people?" (She similarly deplored terms like herstory and chairperson, addressing a woman who introduced her to an audience as "Madame Chair Thing," only half in jest.) Mead often used adjectives like "angry" and "strident" to describe the second-wave feminists, deploring their "bitterness, rancor, and self-centeredness." (Mead was far from alone in these sentiments.) One of the few things she found to commend in the new women's protest groups was "the rediscovery that women can think and work together and find common ground for action."[70]

Like Dorothy Thompson several decades earlier, Mead was especially bothered by unrealistic expectations about the ease of combining career and family. Critiquing a special 1964 issue of the *Ladies' Home Journal* called "Woman, The Fourth Dimension" as "over glamourized and misleading," she felt such media coverage would make ordinary women think of themselves as failures:

> Only the exceptionally energetic and creative woman, with healthy children, with good health herself, with a sympathetic husband and with a preference for life lived at the pace of a chain

store check-out counter can manage such a life. By carefully avoiding the question of the millions of women, unmarried, divorced or widowed, who work under no such circumstances as these, you give the impression that a job—like a new kind of hair do, or girdle—will make all women, more lovable, better mothers, more attractive to men, and more youthful. This seems to me as unrealistic and overemphasized an approach as the one to which it is counterpointed—the togetherness emphasis of the 50's.[71]

Sharing a cab once with television commentator Barbara Walters, Mead said to her, "If the woman's movement has done any harm, it's to make it seem as if it all were easy. It *isn't* all easy!" A dumbfounded Walters could only stutter in reply, "You? The most independent woman in the world? *You* have such thoughts as these?"[72]

Twenty years before cracks appeared in the popular facade of the superwoman, Mead was telling women they couldn't have it all. Sounding very much like Dorothy Thompson in her *Ladies' Home Journal* columns, Mead offered an alternate vision, one that accepted difference rather than trying to erase it: "We will not achieve equality by making women into substitute men. What we need most to work out are new and diverse ways in which men and women can share easily in the responsibility for the children they want to have and the life they lead together."[73]

But even Mead was changing with the times, as witnessed by her belated support of the Equal Rights Amendment. Like many other women in public life, she had long opposed the ERA because of its impact on protective labor legislation. Once the amendment passed Congress and was sent to the states for ratification in 1972, the parameters of the public debate shifted. As early as February 1973 she withdrew her objections to the ERA. And yet she had hardly become an enthusiastic convert, as this letter to the National Organization for Women in 1974 shows: "Although I still think that there were very valid reasons for the opposition to the way the Equal Rights Amendment was phrased, I now find it necessary to support it, if only because of the nature of the opposition which has so distorted the issues involved." A public statement released by Mead's office the next year took a more positive tone, stating, "ERA is in line with the needs of the world in 1975," and linking the amendment to America's international standing: "The United States can hardly stand up among the nations of the world as the land of the free while arguing over the passage of the Equal Rights Amendment. ERA must be passed; we can not do otherwise."[74]

Mead's placing of the ERA in a world context may have been linked to her strong support of the International Decade of Women (1975–1985). Mead was a highly visible presence at the National Women's Conference held in Houston in 1977 as part of the initiative, just a year before her death. Thousands of delegates took time off from convention duties to serenade her with "Happy Birthday." Mead gave a powerful speech at the plenary session on peace and disarmament, eloquently calling for women "to go on believing in life, when there was almost no hope . . . that if we will act unitedly, forget every other consideration on earth, as we do when our children are at stake, we may be able to turn this world around and produce a world in which our children and other people's children will be safe."[75] By then she was once again back in the fold of feminism, not that she had ever really left.

🐾

WHEN SHE WAS about ten, Cathy Bateson complained that it was hard to have a "half-famous" mother "because when I assume that people know who you are, so often they don't." (Cathy's definition of famous: "Being in crossword puzzles.") If Margaret Mead wasn't 100 percent famous in 1950, she soon became so ubiquitous that one colleague called her "a brand name." With her medley of scholarly and popular activities, Mead in her fifties and sixties was her own best example of what she once called "post-menopausal zest."[76]

Mead's turret office at the American Museum of Natural History was always over-flowing with books, correspondence, works in progress, and a bevy of assistants try-ing valiantly to keep up. Note the absence of artifacts or mementoes from her many research trips. There was no room, of course, but Mead was never a collector—that is, of anything but people. (Neg. No. 338668 Courtesy Dept. of Library Services Amer-ican Museum of Natural History)

Even though her professional work increasingly took a back seat to her popularizing, Margaret Mead continued to exert a profound influence on anthropology. Her wartime work in Washington fed into an ambitious project at Columbia called the Institute for Intercultural Studies, which aimed to study the national characters of contemporary cultures worldwide. Only when it became clear that there was little demand for the Institute's research did Mead make the pragmatic decision to abandon this line of scholarship, which she and many others had greatly enjoyed because of its interdisciplinary nature, then rare in academe. In addition to her ongoing affiliation with Columbia, Mead was a visiting professor at institutions such as New York University, Yale, the University of Cincinnati Medical School, and the Menninger Foundation. Either personally or by reputation, she continued to have an impact on each rising generation of anthropologists.

From this point on, however, Mead was primarily interested in interpreting and understanding her own culture. Unlike the 1920s and 1930s when her reputation was built mainly on pathbreaking books such as *Coming of Age in Samoa* or *Sex and Temperament*, now she was more likely to reach people through other forums, including the new medium of television. Even though she did not have her own television show like Eleanor Roosevelt, Mead was a frequent guest on talk shows, including Johnny Carson's "Tonight Show" where her ability to offer pithy (if never terribly memorable) sound bites on contemporary culture went over big with late-night audiences. In fact, so frequent were her media appearances that Mead joined the American Federation of Television and Radio Artists, probably the only anthropologist on the roster.

Mead saturated postwar American culture through two other routes: prolific magazine articles and extensive speaking tours. Mead had been reaching out to audiences through mainstream magazines since the 1920s, but she found a far larger audience in the postwar period. While she still wrote for the *Nation*, the *New*

Republic, and the *New York Times*, she was far more likely to show up in magazines specifically geared to women, such as *Parents'*, *Woman's Day*, *McCall's*, *Family Circle*, and *Redbook*, where she had her own column starting in 1962. The *Redbook* pieces were closer in spirit to Eleanor Roosevelt's "My Day" and "If You Ask Me" than Dorothy Thompson's "On the Record", but whenever Mead said something controversial or thought-provoking, such as advocating trial marriages for couples before they decided to have children or questioning the prohibition of marijuana, her ideas were picked up by the wire services and reprinted widely. This outspokenness was part of her appeal, but it was also fodder to those who dismissed her as a foolish old lady with a thumbstick and too-liberal ideas.

Lectures, conferences, and speaking engagements also kept Mead very much in the public eye. Rarely speaking from a pre- pared text, she established a magical rapport with her audiences. She literally drew strength from them—"I'm so exhausted. If only I could give a lecture!" she once exclaimed—and probably learned as much from listeners as they did from her. She often asked audiences to write down questions that she had not had time to answer as a way of gauging what was on people's minds. This became more important when her increasing deafness made it difficult for her to take questions from the floor.[77]

A side benefit of lecturing was the chance to keep up with her extended networks of friends and family. If there was a town in America where Margaret Mead didn't know someone, she was always ready to make a new acquaintance. Mead hardly limited herself to the United States, becoming an intrepid international traveler in the postwar years. Such globe-trotting gave her the chance for more frequent visits with her daughter, who lived for extended periods in the Philippines and Iran after her marriage to Armenian-born engineer Barkev Kassarjian, whom she met while studying at Harvard.

To handle all her invitations, galley proofs, travel arrange- ments, and television appearances, to say nothing of her extensive correspondence and ongoing professional projects, Mead relied on a team of assistants who overflowed from her turret office at the American Museum of Natural History. Almost always women, and usually aspiring anthropologists, these research assistants helped keep track of the increasingly complicated professional life of the woman they universally referred to as "MM." Given that her personal and professional lives were basically inseparable by this point, these assistants also found themselves chauffeuring Mead to the airport, picking up her dry cleaning, or filling the prescriptions for Dexedrine that she (like Dorothy Thompson) used to keep herself going. Recalled one, "If she'd been a man, I'd have had grounds for a lawsuit," but of course it was such an education working for "MM" that few ever complained.[78]

Everything that had characterized Margaret Mead since the 1920s became even more so toward the end of her life—more conferences, more books, more friends, more travel, occasional controversy, and even more adulation. As Jane Howard observed, "Margaret Mead, who had hungered all her life for acclaim, companionship, and a full schedule, got all three, in the last dozen years of her life, to a measure that even she must have found a little befuddling." One result was that Mead increasingly fell victim to a "diva" mentality that assumed her needs took top priority and that everyone was put on earth to be at her service. She was now leading a very public, and very fragmented life, and she spread herself too thin—the lectures were a little more slapped together, the prose (and ideas) of the articles more pedestrian. But she refused to slow down, finding any moment of unscheduled time an affront. "I expect to die, but I don't plan to retire."[79]

In 1972 Mead published *Blackberry Winter*, a memoir covering her life through the birth of her daughter in 1939, supplemented by thoughts about becoming a grandmother. Her sense of timing was superb, because the resurgence of feminism had created a huge market for women's biography and autobiography. Reviewer Caroline Bird called it "a grandmother's tale for a time that needs grandmothers very badly." But others found the memoir conceited and felt that Mead had been unwilling or unable to reveal much about her inner self. No sequel was contemplated. Psychic Jean Houston, a founder of the human potential movement who became quite close to Mead in her final years, felt that another volume "would have taken too much discretion. Hers was the most complex life imaginable. She had so many fingers in so many pies, and was behind the scenes on so many levels, that her public image was just the tip of the iceberg."[80]

Given her broad familiarity with birth and death processes in eight cultures, one might have expected from Margaret Mead one of those triumphant natural deaths, at home surrounded by her family and loved ones, unencumbered by advanced medical technology. That was not the way it happened. On some level, Margaret Mead was in denial about dying, not even admitting to friends and the public that she had cancer until a week before her death. And when she died on November 15, 1978, it was in a New York City hospital, not at home.

Perhaps denial is too strong a term. It was not that Margaret Mead was afraid of dying, it was just that she had too much left to do. She had had such fun celebrating her seventy-fifth birthday during the nation's bicentennial that she was probably looking forward to greeting the twenty-first century on her 100th in 2001. She felt betrayed by the onset of pancreatic cancer, the same cancer that had killed her brother. "My body isn't going to last as long as I thought it would," she told a friend glumly.[81]

Unlike Eleanor Roosevelt, whose stature has continued to grow since her death, or Dorothy Thompson, who mostly faded from view following an accomplished life, after her death Margaret Mead was the subject of a devastatingly hostile attack that says as much about her standing in popular culture as it does about disputes within the anthropological profession. In 1983, Australian professor Derek Freeman published *Margaret Mead and Samoa: The Making and Unmaking of an Anthropological Myth*, a book that was deeply critical of Mead's research. The *New York Times* put the book's findings on its front page a full two months before its official publication date, and its publisher, the Harvard University Press, rushed to capitalize on the publicity surrounding Freeman's highly personal attack on Mead. "I rather suppose that I may have written a book that will create the greatest denouement in the history of anthropology so far, not excepting Piltdown Man!" spoke Freeman immodestly.[82]

Once the controversy degenerated into a media event, any serious attention to the issues was eclipsed by the sensationalism surrounding the attack. This highly public debate was awkward for anthropologists, who were suddenly called on by journalists for sound bites on whether Freeman or Mead was "right" about Samoa. Any attempts to introduce complexity into the debate (because many anthropologists did consider Mead's research somewhat impressionistic, but still felt her findings were essentially correct) were lost in the media pressure to take sides either supporting or debunking the great or not-great Margaret Mead.[83]

When anthropologists and other social scientists finally had a chance to read the book, most were unconvinced. Anthropologists were appalled by Freeman's mistaken identification of what he called "The Boasian Paradigm"—"the notion that human behavior can be explained in purely cultural terms," a huge generalization that neither Boas nor disciples like Mead or Benedict ever subscribed to. The book was actually as much an attack on Boas and cultural relativism as it was on Mead.[84]

So why take on Mead, who had only recently died and did not have a chance to respond to the criticisms? And why did the press promote this attack so feverishly in the 1980s? More than one anthropologist wondered if there was an underlying antifeminist agenda. The Equal Rights Amendment had just been defeated and America was entering what journalist Susan Faludi later identified as a backlash against feminism. Anthropologist Lenora Foerstel, who in 1953 accompanied Mead on one of her numerous field trips to New Guinea, thought the lesson of the whole controversy was simple: "we can't tolerate a monumental female figure."[85]

On the other hand, perhaps the attack struck home so deeply because Mead and her book on Samoa were important to the general public in ways that anthropologists had not realized. As scholars and lay people rushed to Mead's defense, they showed that Americans could tolerate, indeed practically canonize, a monumental female figure. Lowell Holmes, an anthropologist at Wichita State University who did a reevaluation of Mead's Samoan research that confirmed many, but not all, of Mead's findings, noted, "It is amazing how people identify with Margaret Mead. . . . I find an element of resentment of a foreigner attacking 'our Margaret.' America loved this woman."[86]

In the end the public seemed to care less about disputes over Samoan character between two anthropologists than about standing up in support of an American icon who had long ago earned their trust and respect for giving them commonsense advice about issues of contemporary life. Derek Freeman assumed that his attack would permanently tarnish Mead's reputation, but two decades after her death, she seems secure in her standing, both as an anthropologist and as a genuinely respected figure in twentieth-century public life. And high school students still pore over the details of Polynesian sexuality while riding to classes on New York City subways, and probably will for years to come.

"Oh, she's been acting that way all day. Someone told her she looks like Katherine Hepburn."

F O U R

LIVING LIKE A MAN: KATHARINE HEPBURN

*T*HE VOICE IS inimitably Katharine Hepburn: "I put on pants fifty years ago and declared a sort of middle road. I have not lived as a woman. I have lived as a man. I've done what I damn well wanted to and I've made enough money to support myself and I ain't afraid of being alone."[1] Perhaps more than any other Hollywood actress, indeed more than almost any other figure in twentieth-century popular culture, Katharine Hepburn is the embodiment of the independent woman. Well-born, well-educated, and dressed in pants long before they became fashionable, she projected an image of confident and uncompromising individuality that was rare for women then or now. "I'm a personality as well as an actress. Show me an actress who isn't a personality and you'll show a woman who isn't a star." By the last decades of her life, a mythic status had grown up around her: "I'm like the Statue of Liberty to a lot of people. When you've been around so long, people identify their whole lives with you."[2]

Hepburn's sense of timing, like her personal style and dress, was impeccable. The 1930s truly were Hollywood's Golden Age, and a golden age for women in the film industry. "I came along at a point in the movie industry when nothing like me had ever existed—with a loud voice and a very definite personality and a rather belligerent look." Those qualities hardly guaranteed an easy climb to stardom, however. The careers of few stars have had as many ups and downs as Hepburn's: "My career has wavered around, stumbled, fallen, picked itself up, crawled back and jumped. You're not talking about somebody who just sat on the throne." Hepburn strongly empathized with Coco Chanel, whom she played in a Broadway musical that opened in 1969: "We're two females who have never been intimidated by the world, who never shifted our styles to conform to public opinion." Katharine Hepburn could never, ever have played a dumb broad. As *Pictorial Review* observed presciently just two years after she first arrived in Hollywood, "What Miss Hepburn has, however, is the personality from which celebrities are made."[3]

The career and persona of Katharine Hepburn have always had special resonance for women. Columnist Anna Quindlen, who once crossed a New York street so as not to meet her idol face to face ("I know everything I need to know about Katharine Hepburn, *my* Katharine Hepburn, from the movies"), recalled how she and so many other women wanted to be the Katharine Hepburn characters they saw on the screen: "Perhaps it's because Hepburn was the only woman we saw regularly who was full of herself, full of how terrific it was to be a woman. . . Hepburn made confidence palpable, vivid, above all female." Most women were socialized to be selfless, cheerfully putting the needs of others before their own, but Katharine Hepburn was "unapologetically self-centered." Identifying one key to Hepburn's ongoing appeal, Quindlen wrote, "Growing up, self-center was a good place to start when you weren't sure you had a self at all."[4]

Other Hollywood stars had loyal followings, but Hepburn's allure was about more than fans. People were interested in Katharine Hepburn as a person—or what they thought she was like as a person—and they identified with her. They also invested in her many of their hopes and dreams, for themselves and for women in general. "She was one of my models too," remembered author Nancy Friday. "Unmarried, childless, flat-chested—she is the antithesis of what mother and society want for us. And yet my mother adores her, and men too seem to sense something heroic in her. She transcends looks, style, or whatever particular circumstances the script writer places her in; through force of character, by making it on her own, by never giving up and keeping her integrity intact, she wins us all. She is an image of the separate person."[5]

Just as Hepburn distanced herself from her legend, so too did she caution against using her life as a model. "The reason people have affection for me now is that I think a lot of people—a lot of women, anyway—believe that the sort of life I've lived would be a nice life to live. They think it's free and that I've done it all. But it hasn't been free, and I really haven't done it all. They don't understand, for example, that maybe they have five children, and I don't have any." She concluded forthrightly, "When you come right down to it, I haven't lived life as a woman after all."[6]

But she has lived as a woman—just a different kind of woman. Among other things, Hepburn made it okay to say no to marriage and children, and to do so affirmatively without sacrificing the chance for a full and satisfying life. Even though most women don't make that choice themselves, part of Hepburn's ongoing appeal is the safety valve that such an option provides, to say nothing of the glorious example she provided of how a truly liberated life might play out, warts and all. As Elaine May once observed to Garson Kanin, "She really is about the only person who gives you the feeling that maybe it *could* be a woman's world."[7]

🎔

"THE HEPBURNS OF Hartford, Connecticut, must be numbered among America's most remarkable families, each an individualist, and none more so than Katharine Hepburn," ran a piece of MGM publicity drivel from 1943. From the very start of Hepburn's career, the studios fixated on her family and privileged upbringing as a key to explaining her unique style. In her early years in Hollywood, fan magazines inflated the Hepburns' middle-class status into upper-class, with the actress often being described as an heiress. Hollywood was wrong about the heiress part, but right on the mark when it came to family. "The single most important thing anyone needs to know about me is that I am totally, completely the product of two damn fascinating individuals who happened to be my parents." Even after she became a movie star, she never really left home.[8]

Katharine Houghton Hepburn was born on May 12, 1907, the second of six children and the oldest girl. (No surprise—she shaved two years off her age when she headed to Hollywood, claiming 1909.)[9] Her father was Virginia-born Thomas Norval Hepburn, a prominent Hartford urologist who had trained at Johns Hopkins School of Medicine. Her mother was Katharine Houghton Hepburn, a member of the family that founded the Corning Glass Works, and an 1899 graduate of Bryn Mawr.

Had she not mothered one of America's most famous actresses, Mrs. Hepburn would still be remembered as typical of the early twentieth-century college-educated matrons who tackled Progressive-era social issues, such as votes for women and social hygiene, and then continued to fight for reform in the 1920s and 1930s. Katharine Houghton Hepburn's name was most associated with the cause of birth control, and she emerged as one of Margaret Sanger's chief lieutenants in the 1930s. In 1934, just after her daughter had a hit with *Little Women*, she testified before the House Judiciary Committee in support of the legalization of birth control information. "Hepburn's Ma Begs OK of Birth Control" ran one headline. Never concerned that her mother's outspokenness might hurt her career, the daughter who shared her mother's name said simply, "My mother is important. I am not."[10]

The Hepburn household was unusual for the interesting people who came through its doors and the high level (and volume)
of talk. The first question to a guest was often, "How do you
stand politically?" and woe to him or her who was deemed dull
or boring, the ultimate insult in this highly verbal and competitive family. (Margaret Mead felt exactly the same way.) The fact
that many of these brilliant visitors were women, friends of her
mother, was not lost on the young Kate. "My mother always
brought me up to believe that women were never to be under-
dogs . . . and she taught me from a very early age that we were
not necessarily the weaker sex." The English suffragist Sylvia
Pankhurst used to stay with them, Charlotte Perkins Gilman
stopped in, and Margaret Sanger was a frequent guest. Another
regular visitor was Sinclair Lewis, then living in Hartford with
his first wife Grace.[11]

Closer to home, Kate's aunt Edith Houghton Hooker was a
vivid and appealing role model. A reform-minded physician and
classmate of Tom Hepburn's at Johns Hopkins (which is how her
sister met her future husband), she was also a lifelong feminist,
part inspiration for Hepburn's portrayal of Jo March in *Little
Women*. One of Kate's lines as Jo on screen, "I like strong words
that mean something," could just as easily have been uttered, and
probably was, by her outspoken Aunt Edith.

Like Margaret Mead and Dorothy Thompson, the young Kate
never felt the oppression of sex at home, absorbing in her childhood the message that women were the intellectual equals of
men. This model of female empowerment gleaned from her
mother and her mother's progressive friends stayed with her for
the rest of her life. "They are the *real* independent women. I knew
so many absolutely fascinating women when I was growing up,
women who had *real* daring, who did all the legwork for the stuff
that's being done now. . . . All this talk about women always
strikes me as funny because it never occurred to me that they
were in any way inferior to men."[12]

Called Kath, Kathy, Kate, and Redtop (for her bright red hair), for a time she wondered if she was the wrong sex, cutting her hair short like a boy's and calling herself Jimmy. Her tomboy exploits foreshadowed a lifetime of athleticism in sports, including golf, tennis, and swimming. ("If there's a heaven, and if that's where I end up, and if I'm a tennis champion—then I'll be happy.") Despite her mother's active reform career and her father's medical practice, the dominant images Kate remembered from her childhood were of a mother who was always sitting by the fire when the children got home from school, and a father who always came home for tea. "Apart from the freckles and the red hair that all my schoolfriends mocked, mine was a marvelous and secure childhood. . . . I was listened to and loved."[13]

Kate was especially close to her older brother, Tom, born in 1905. (Hepburn biographer Barbara Leaming noted that the six children came in pairs: Tom and Kathy, Dick and Bob, Marion and Peggy. Family planning at its most deliberate.) As the eldest son, Tom was held to very high standards by his father, but had what seemed a fairly normal adolescence. And yet in 1921, while on a family trip to New York, the sixteen-year-old was found hanging by a rope in the third-floor room of a family friend; his sister Katharine found the body. While all signs pointed to suicide, the family insisted that it was merely a prank gone awry. There was in fact a strong history of suicide on both sides of the family (Mrs. Hepburn's father had committed suicide, as had an uncle, and Dr. Hepburn's brother had recently taken his life), but the family would allow no discussion of the possibility that Tom had deliberately ended his life. For all their freedom of expression and thought, the Hepburns exhibited a striking lack of emotional candor. The subject simply was never mentioned. In a bizarre twist, Kathy adopted Tom's birthday of November 8th as her own, and her family dutifully celebrated on that day rather than her correct May 12 birthdate from then on.

Hepburn had a difficult time in school after her brother's death, so her parents decided to have her tutored at home, with the goal being college at her mother's alma mater, Bryn Mawr. By the 1920s higher education for women no longer represented the daring statement of women's emancipation it once had. Contrasting herself with her "brilliant" mother, a leading member of the class of 1899, Hepburn, class of 1928, considered herself "just mediocre," relieved to have gotten through "by the skin of my teeth." Even if she did not excel academically, and felt painfully self-conscious among her accomplished classmates, the Bryn Mawr philosophy of "You Can Do It" embodied by longtime president M. Carey Thomas affected her enormously, just as it had her mother. "Bryn Mawr was my springboard into adult life." Most importantly, Bryn Mawr taught her to work hard and persevere, a lesson she found of "tremendous help" when she was fired from nearly every job she landed in the early part of her acting career.[14]

On graduation, she decided not to follow her father into medicine and turned instead to the stage. Dr. Hepburn was initially appalled at his daughter's choice: "Your mother's work was in the public interest. This is nothing but your own vanity." Even more biting, and probably closer to the mark, "You just want to show off and get paid for it." Eventually he relented; her mother was supportive from the start, delighted with her daughter "for being sort of a free soul." "If you always do what interests you," Kate quoted her mother, "then at least one person is pleased."[15]

The choice of an acting career shaped Katharine Hepburn's ideas about feminism and women's equality in subtle ways. Had she pursued a career in medicine, she would have faced blatant sex discrimination: In the 1930s, for example, most hospitals refused to permit women medical graduates to serve as interns, the gateway to prestigious medical careers. The theater and Hollywood, on the other hand, seemed to provide unlimited opportunities for both sexes. "In the theatre there is complete equality between men and women," Hepburn observed in a 1942 statement supporting the Equal Rights Amendment. "If that has worked well for the theatre, why not for all walks of life." Despite the ups and downs of her career, Katharine Hepburn always claimed that she was never held back by her sex. "It never occurred to me that I was an inferior sex. I was a different sex."[16]

Acting was a somewhat curious choice for this young college graduate, even though she had dabbled in Bryn Mawr theatricals. No one ever accused her of being overendowed with natural talent. Her personality was so overwhelming that she practically blew everybody else off the stage. What she did have, however, was drive and ambition, and she was determined to power her way onto center stage. As she once confessed to Garson Kanin, "When I started out, I didn't have any great desire to be an actress or to learn how to act. I just wanted to be famous."[17]

For the next several years, Hepburn tried to launch her acting career on the stage, but she either quit or was fired from many of the parts that she landed and hardly a success in the few minor roles she managed to hold on to. Her breakthrough finally came in 1932 in a Broadway play called "The Warrior's Husband." Dressed as the Amazon warrior Antiope in sleek tights, which showed off her fabulous legs, she hurtled herself onto the stage carrying a stag slung over her shoulder, which she then deposited at the feet of the Amazon queen. "Get me a bowl of water, will you," she roared to the Queen's attendants. "I'm in a terrific sweat!" That bravura performance won her a Hollywood contract, and her movie career was launched. "They didn't like me until I got into a leg show" was her somewhat snobbish reaction.[18]

As she prepared to take on Hollywood, few of the studio moguls or indeed many of her theater friends knew that she was a married woman. "Was I ever married? I really can't remember. It certainly wasn't for very long," went a typical flippant response. In fact, just several months after her Bryn Mawr graduation, she had married twenty-nine-year-old Ludlow Ogden Smith, affectionately called Luddy, whom she had met through friends at college. He was from a Main Line Philadelphia family, and had been educated at the University of Grenoble; although he had a degree in industrial engineering, he listed his occupation as insurance broker. His career was not a high priority, however, and he turned out to be wonderfully accommodating to his decidedly nontraditional wife. When she realized she could never live a suburban lifestyle, they moved into the city. When she toured with plays, he conveniently found other things to keep him busy. While she sought the limelight, he stayed in the background. In fact, she was walking all over him. Her family adored him, however, and for years after their 1934 divorce, he was a frequent visitor at the Hepburn summer cottage Fenwick, at Old Saybrook on the Connecticut shore.[19]

While Hepburn was willing to try marriage, at least briefly, she decided very early on that she was not cut out for motherhood. "There came a time in my life when I had to face the issue of motherhood squarely. I was quite young. It was a matter of being the best actress I could be or becoming a mother. But not both; I don't think I could do justice to both. . . . I made the decision not to have children many, many years ago. And I don't regret it. I also chose not to make a career of medicine. And I don't regret that either."[20] At base was her deep respect for what her parents had contributed to her upbringing, and her realization that she was unable, or unwilling, to follow their model. " 'Kath, are you going to be willing to take that much trouble with your own children?' " she'd ask herself. "Well, obviously, I never dared find out."[21]

It is interesting to compare the different lessons that Margaret Mead and Katharine Hepburn drew from their upbringings, and specifically from their mothers' examples. Both had mothers who combined marriage, large families, and interesting work; Katharine Houghton Hepburn and Emily Fogg Mead were feminists who gave their daughters a clear sense that women were not men's inferiors and had much to contribute to the world at large. Mead remembered a mother (and a grandmother) who success-

fully juggled marriage, career, and children, while Hepburn valorized a mother who fit her reform activities around her family
responsibilities, always making sure to be home for tea. Unlike
Emily Fogg Mead, who moved her family from Philadelphia to
Hackensack,' New Jersey, to pursue her dissertation research,
Katharine Houghton Hepburn always demurred when suffrage
leaders or later Margaret Sanger tried to lure her to Washington
to work full-time for the cause, knowing that her husband would
never stand for such disruption of their family life. But still, Mrs.
Hepburn was a busy and talented reformer who also had six children. If her daughter had wanted to remember her childhood differently, she too could have inherited a positive model for
combining domestic and public responsibilities.

In the end it came down less to family models than to the fact
that Margaret Mead wanted to have children, and Katharine
Hepburn decided she did not. And yet it is intriguing to imagine what would have happened if she had had a child after all—
Katharine Houghton Hepburn III. Of course it is possible that
this daughter, like many children of celebrities, Hollywood or
otherwise, would have resented her mother's career and success
and later written a tell-all book about how ignored and maltreat-
ed she was as a child. But that is not the only scenario. Perhaps
the next Katharine Houghton Hepburn would have inherited the
political activism and gender consciousness of her grandmother
and the drive for independence and personal autonomy of her
mother. That would have been quite a package.

When Hepburn headed off to Hollywood in 1932, her husband was nowhere in evidence, but a friend named Laura Harding was. (In Laura's honor, Hepburn suggested that the Dorothy
Thompson-like character in *Woman of the Year* be called Tess
Harding.) Harding came from a wealthy New Jersey family and
had been educated at Miss Porter's finishing school. The unex-
pected death of her banker father, J. Horace Harding, chairman
of the board of the American Express Company, left the young
debutante with an inheritance estimated at $7 million in 1929.

Hollywood stars spend a lot of time waiting around. Here Hepburn passes the time on the set of Bringing Up Baby *with her knitting, her perfectly coiffed hair and camera-ready makeup in sharp contrast to her dungarees and mocassins. (Photofest)*

Harding, like Hepburn, studied with the well-known acting coach Frances Robinson-Duff, but she was really only dabbling at an acting career; the two women met while doing summer stock in the Berkshires and quickly became fast friends. With no need to support herself and in no hurry to marry (she never did), Harding was happy to tag along on Kate's escapades. Hepburn, in turn, learned an enormous amount from Harding about upper-class sophistication, studying her mannerisms and style almost as if she were a part: if Hollywood publicity portrayed Hepburn as an heiress, Laura was the model. She was also Kate's inspiration and her personal support system: "Laura Harding—what strength she gave me. I thought she was wonderful and she convinced me that *I* was."[22]

It was the prominent role that Laura Harding played in Hepburn's early career in Hollywood, along with Hepburn's penchant for wearing pants, that gave rise to rumors that Hepburn was a lesbian. In Hollywood the assumption was if you weren't sleeping with men, then you must be sleeping with women. When Hepburn said things like, "Keep away from her—she's my woman," or Laura identified herself on the phone with, "Oh, tell her it's her husband," the Hollywood gossip mill assumed the two women were a couple, even though Hepburn later claimed she had no idea that's how they were perceived.[23]

Hepburn's tendencies, however, were definitely heterosexual. Even before her divorce became final, Hepburn was dating her agent, Leland Hayward; later she was linked romantically with Howard Hughes, John Ford, and, of course, Spencer Tracy. These affairs fed her lifelong distrust of the media. Realizing that "I was leading the kind of personal life that would be sort of titillating to the public . . . I would go to absolutely *endless* trouble to fix it so that the reporters knew nothing."[24] In fact, the first that many in Hollywood knew about her marriage to Luddy was when the wire services picked up the news of her quickie Mexican divorce.

While Hepburn continued her close friendship with Laura Harding for the rest of her life, and from the 1950s on lived with her companion Phyllis Wilbourn, who came to work for her after serving as actress Constance Collier's secretary, the rumors of lesbianism seem more linked to Hollywood's inability to deal with her eccentricity and forthrightness than to any real reflection of her sexual orientation. In the 1930s even the fact of a woman living alone was considered suspicious or threatening; a woman who hung out with another woman, and was not seen in public with men, was even more suspect. It is interesting, however, that while women like Margaret Mead, Dorothy Thompson, and Eleanor Roosevelt had deep relationships with other women and got away with it, Katharine Hepburn, who seemingly did not, was accused of deviant behavior. By the 1930s, being a lesbian had become a stigma, something to be hidden or covered up, despite the large number of gay men and women in the industry.[25]

Hollywood was supportive to Hepburn in other ways, however. Stage acting always held a certain terror for Hepburn, but she immediately warmed to film. For one thing, as an early riser, she loved the daytime hours on the set, finding them far more congenial to her internal time clock than the late hours required for theater work. But it was more than that—she felt at home in front of the camera. "When I tested for the movies, it was immediately a warm experience—exciting but not scary. Why this is so I do not know. I just find the medium sympathetic—friendly." She never held out any illusions that acting was an especially difficult or noble art, noting that Shirley Temple had been doing it perfectly adequately since the age of four. But she brought a special intensity to the craft, which prompted director Frank Capra to call her a "rare professional-amateur": "Acting is her hobby, her living, her love. She is wedded to her vocation as a nun is to hers, and as competitive in acting as Sonya Henie was in skating. No clock-watching, no humbug, no sham temperament. If Katharine Hepburn made up her mind to become a runner, she'd be the first woman to break the four-minute mile."[26]

When Hepburn first arrived in Hollywood in 1932, she behaved so strangely that she must have been extremely insecure or extremely immature or both. She was only twenty-five years old, overly eager to make an impression, any impression, and fairly insensitive to the needs of others, a trait that characterized her whole life. Instead of trying to fit in and learn the ropes, she cultivated an aura of eccentricity that bordered on downright rudeness. She appeared on the set dressed in a ragged old pair of dungarees (this was long before jeans become acceptable wear outside of farms), with a pet monkey on her shoulder. She squat-

ted on the curb to read her fan mail. She turned down all invitations to parties or other social occasions. As soon as she finished
a film, she rushed back East to Connecticut to her family. She
later rationalized that such behavior was necessary to be taken
seriously: "when I was sweet and cooperative and willing, no one
paid any attention. When I got sour and difficult I had them all
eating out of my hand. It still works." Yes, but at the cost of
being known as "La Hepburn" or "Katharine of Arrogance."[27]

So focused was she on her career that she was totally oblivious
to the Great Depression all around her. "I kept thinking, 'What
is wrong with everyone?' I was in Hollywood making money and
lucky lucky lucky." From the start her father took charge of her
financial affairs, ensuring that she prospered even when the country did not.[28]

The movie industry, far more than any other profession,
requires its practitioners to expose their private lives (selectively,
at least, and in homogenized form) to an inquisitive public, but
Hepburn refused to participate in this game. When asked questions by reporters, she would often make up flippant replies, such
as saying that she had five children, three of whom were colored.
She rarely gave autographs. "How dare you refuse?" one angry fan
confronted her. "We made you what you are today." "Like hell
you did!" she replied and stomped off. She never had a press
agent, turned down all invitations for appearances, and rarely
went out in public. She snubbed her nose at all the rules of Hollywood. It was not that she did not crave celebrity or success—
she was just determined to do it her own way. Her strategy
worked: her independent streak and disdain for reporters were
dutifully reported, thus ensuring she still got plenty of publicity
anyway.[29]

Part of Hepburn's dilemma was the difficulty that female stars
faced in creating an image that worked with their audiences but
also was consistent with their own personalities. Without a clear
persona or type it was practically impossible to build fan loyalty.
Whereas an aspiring male actor could pick from a fairly wide

range of types, the options for actresses were more limited. Even though Hollywood in the 1930s had large roles for women as actresses, directors, screenwriters, and other behind-the-scenes roles, there were still limits to how far women could stray from dominant notions of feminine behavior.[30]

This was how Hepburn chose to present herself: "I had a lot of energy and looked as if I was (and I *was*) hard to get—wasn't mad about the male sex—perfectly independent, never had any intention of getting married, wanted to paddle my own canoe, didn't want anyone to pay my way."[31] No wonder the studios didn't know what to do with her.

Hepburn's early filmography was a mishmash of roles: John Barrymore's upper-class daughter in *A Bill of Divorcement* (1932), an Amelia Earhart-type aviator in *Christopher Strong* (1933), Jo March in *Little Women* (1933), and an Appalachian mountain girl in *Spitfire* (1934). Perhaps her best early part, and the one for which she won her first Oscar, was as the aspiring actress Eva Lovelace in *Morning Glory* (1933) with Douglas Fairbanks, Jr., and Adolphe Menjou. With the exception of the popular *Little Women*, thirties audiences were not especially interested in Hepburn in costume dramas, despite RKO's repeated casting of her in such roles. Director Pandro Berman put his finger on the problem when he noticed that Hepburn wasn't a movie star of the ilk of Joan Crawford or Norma Shearer who were "able to drag an audience in by their own efforts. She was a hit only in hit pictures: she couldn't save a flop. And she also invariably chose the wrong vehicles."[32]

British film historian Andrew Britton provided an apt summary of Hepburn's film career: "No other star has emerged with greater rapidity or with more ecstatic acclaim. No other star, either, has become so unpopular so quickly for so long a time." By the late 1930s, despite films such as *Stage Door* (1937), *Bringing Up Baby* (1938), and *Holiday* (1938), which are now among her most critically acclaimed efforts, she had been labeled "Box Office Poison" by the Independent Theatre Owners' Association because of a string of movies that were commercial and popular failures. Although Joan Crawford, Greta Garbo, and Marlene Dietrich (all actresses who, like Hepburn, often portrayed independent or defiant characters) were also singled out, the charge stuck especially to Hepburn. When RKO wanted to demote her to a "B" film called *Mrs. Carey's Chickens*, Hepburn bought out her contract and returned to her family in Connecticut for an extended stay.[33]

No one who saw her gardening at Fenwick, swimming in the Long Island Sound, or golfing would have had the slightest hint of a star whose career was in trouble. Her trait of taking and leaving Hollywood (she never bought a home there, always rented, because she never planned to stay) stood her in good stead, as did her father's astute money management, which allowed her to be choosy about her projects. Because of this forced vacation from Hollywood, Hepburn was at Fenwick in September of 1938 when a major hurricane moved up the East Coast (the same storm that damaged Dorothy Thompson's Twin Farms), and literally removed the house from its foundation and sent it floating out to sea. All that remained was some of the family silver, buried in the sand, and a bathtub. The family quickly determined to rebuild, and the new Fenwick became just as much the center for the extended Hepburn clan as the old.

Hepburn realized that she needed a comeback vehicle. She had hoped desperately to play Scarlett O'Hara in the movie version of *Gone with the Wind*, but studio executive David Selnick supposedly nixed the idea because he couldn't see Rhett Butler chasing after Katharine Hepburn for ten years. She chose to return to the stage in a vehicle that was explicitly written with her in mind— the role of Tracy Lord in Phillip Barry's play, *The Philadelphia Story*. (Barry also wrote *Holiday*, which she understudied in 1930 and then starred in in the 1938 film version.) Showing excellent business sense, she acquired the screen rights to what became a hit play, which she then sold to MGM. Cary Grant and Jimmy Stewart replaced Joseph Cotten and Van Heflin from the stage

Katharine Hepburn and Spencer Tracy were both major Hollywood stars, but they did not meet until they made Woman of the Year *in 1941, the first of their nine films together. Hepburn once compared Tracy's acting to a baked potato—very basic, skins and all, "cooked and ready to eat." No one would ever compare Hepburn to a baked potato. (Photofest)*

version, but Hepburn kept the part of Tracy Lord for herself. "When Katharine Hepburn sets out to play Katharine Hepburn," wrote *Life* in 1940, "nobody is her equal." Under the expert direction of George Cukor, she found herself once again at the front ranks of actresses. Her days of unpopularity over, she now entered a new phase in her career.[34]

Hepburn once noted about her years in Hollywood, "Well, it's just a question of survival. If you survive long enough you're revered, rather like an old building. The great trick is to get over the middle period. That's the tricky bit."[35] Hepburn's middle period, 1941 to 1967, might aptly be called "The Spencer Tracy Years." The two first met when they were cast opposite each other in *Woman of the Year*, and they went on to make eight more pictures together, ending with *Guess Who's Coming to Dinner* (1967), finished just three weeks before Tracy's death. They also conducted a longstanding affair, which was widely known in Hollywood but in those very different times it was never gossiped about in print. While Hepburn made films on her own in this period, notably *The African Queen* (1951) with Humphrey Bogart, much of her personal and professional energy went into her relationship with Spencer Tracy.

"I fear I may be a little too tall for you, Mr. Tracy." "Don't worry," shot back producer Joe Mankiewicz. "He'll cut you down to size."[36] So, at least according to Hollywood legend, went the first meeting between these two stars on the set of *Woman of the Year*. She had long admired his work, and had wanted to cast him in *The Philadelphia Story* but he was tied up on other projects. He, on the other hand, had doubts about working with her: "How can I do a picture with a woman who has dirt under her fingernails and who is of ambiguous sexuality and always wears pants?" (Hepburn later realized Tracy thought she was a lesbian.) At the time they began their relationship, she was thirty-four and he forty-one, although he seemed older since his health had been seriously impaired by years of heavy drinking.[37]

Spencer Tracy was also married, very much so, and unwilling to seek a divorce. His Catholicism was only part of the reason. The Tracys' oldest son Johnnie had been diagnosed as deaf at age ten months. To help deaf and hard-of-hearing children and their families, his wife Louise Treadwell Tracy founded and ran the John Tracy Clinic, which became a nationally recognized center for education and advocacy; in the process she became practically a saint in the Southern California film community. In return for her status as Mrs. Spencer Tracy and her fulfilling work at the clinic, she looked the other way at her husband's numerous affairs, which long predated his relationship with Hepburn. When Louise Tracy finally met Hepburn after her husband's

death, she betrayed an amazing streak of self-deception by telling
Kate, "But you see, I thought you were only a rumour. . . . "[38]

Hepburn always said she was not interested in marriage (conveniently erasing Luddy, just as Margaret Mead erased Luther
Cressman), and she did not want to have children, so her somewhat unusual situation with Tracy suited her just fine. They
never shared a home, and never went out together in public.
When they traveled, they always stayed at separate hotels. Once
in London when he was staying at Claridge's and she at the Con-
naught, Tracy received a summons from the assistant manager.
Instead of objecting to her frequent visits, as he had feared, the
hotel staff merely complained about Miss Hepburn walking
through the lobby in "trousers." Kate continued to visit Claridge's, but came and went through the service entrance.[39]

This was not an easy, or an equal, relationship: she subsumed
her needs to his, regularly putting her career on hold for months
to take care of him and nurse him back from his episodes of alcoholic excess. Periodically he would stop drinking entirely, then
disappear on a bender for days or weeks at a time. Of course when
they were working together on a film, she could keep an eye on
him. But if she went off on location (like when she went to Africa
to make *The African Queen*), he often resumed his pattern of self-
destructive behavior.

Hepburn was not an introspective person, and her family had
hardly trained her to be forthright about facing emotional issues,
as witnessed by their collective denial of Tom's suicide. She later
admitted that she never really understood the demons that
plagued Spencer Tracy: "Who was he? I never really knew. He
had locked the door to the inside room. I had no idea, even
whether he himself had the key." Nor did they ever talk about
their relationship or their feelings for each other. "I can only say
I think if he hadn't liked me he wouldn't have hung around. As
simple as that."[40]

Certain Hepburn biographers have painted Tracy as a villain, out to humiliate and dominate his partner. Calling Tracy "a reasonable facsimile of Dad," her brother Bob was not the first to notice similarities in how Kate deferred to Tracy just as her mother had deferred to Dr. Hepburn.[41] Yet the choice to take care of Tracy, to put his needs first, was freely undertaken by Hepburn. After her parents, this was the most important relationship in her adult life, and an excellent example of how her off-screen behavior was far more traditional than the independent persona she created for the screen. The relationship with Tracy allowed her to move beyond her customary self-absorption to love and be loved in return, all without ever having publicly to put on an apron. And yet she always maintained a certain separateness, never merging or subsuming her personality into his, and never totally abandoning her acting career, something that she was financially secure enough to do.[42]

Now that their long affair is so widely known, there is a tendency to review her entire career through the lens of this three-decade long relationship. It is very difficult today, for example, to watch *Adam's Rib* (1948), where they play married lawyers on opposite sides of a case, or their last film together, *Guess Who's Coming to Dinner* (1967), without bringing to the movies the knowledge of their personal relationship. Yet at the time, their affair was not public knowledge, in part out of journalists' respect for Mrs. Tracy's stature in the community but also out of deference to the two stars. Drama critic Sheridan Morley even compared the press's treatment of Hepburn with that accorded Eleanor Roosevelt: "It wasn't that she, any more than Eleanor Roosevelt, could always be sure of a good press or even a successful year; but there was something about the way she was treated publicly, something about the space she was given to lead her own very private life, something about the respect she was gradually accorded, which was very royal indeed."[43]

As more details about their relationship leaked to the public after Tracy's death in 1967 (especially Garson Kanin's *Tracy and Hepburn: An Intimate Memoir*, published to Hepburn's horror in

1971), people began to see Hepburn as the real Spencer Tracy widow, not Louise. Biographer Anne Edwards wrote melodramatically, "Tracy would belong to her in death as he never had in life."[44] Despite its undercurrent of the devastating impact of alcoholism, the tandem of Hepburn and Tracy became transformed, homogenized almost, into a straight love story, which in turn became part of the Hepburn mystique.

That was how Hepburn got through those tricky middle years. With Tracy's death (she was then sixty years old), she was poised for an even more public role, which co-star Nick Nolte summed up in 1987: "She's a legend, but once you get beyond that she's just a cranky old broad who can sometimes be a whole lot of fun."[45]

※

SHE CALLS HERSELF the "original bag lady," but to many others, Katharine Hepburn has come to represent the essence of classic style. Confessed *New York Times* style reporter Mary Cantwell, "In childhood I lived in a world where all the girls wanted to look like Katharine Hepburn, and in middle age I still do." For ease, comfort, and practicality, in midlife she adopted a uniform and stuck to it: beige pants, tailored shirt or turtleneck, loose sweater or overblouse, comfortable shoes, a tattered cap. Sometimes the clothes were new, more often patched and mended. On a less confident woman her "Civil War rags," as she called them, would seem grotesque, but people simply accepted her style as vintage Hepburn. Like so much else about her persona, it seemed to click with her public's expectations of how an independent and self-reliant Hollywood star would choose to dress.[46]

Katharine Hepburn had always worn her strangeness, her odd physicality as a badge of elegance. As a Bryn Mawr freshman she was snubbed as "a self-conscious beauty" but that failed to temper such personal eccentricities as showering in cold water several times a day, scrubbing her face until it shone, and shunning most makeup. Once she reached Hollywood, the studios tried to make her into a glamorous creature (at least when they could get her to pose for publicity shots), but despite her gorgeous cheekbones, she was far from a traditional beauty, as she herself realized: "Now that I am Saint Katharine it is fashionable to say that I am a beauty with a well proportioned face. But when I was beginning they thought I was just a freak with a lot of freckles." In all her early movies and stills, the freckles disappear under heavy makeup.[47]

The freckles weren't featured, but her red hair was, even in black and white films. Cary Grant calls her "Red" in *The Philadelphia Story*, a reference to her hair color, which would immediately have been picked up by her fans. Thirties films were populated with peroxide blondes like Mae West, Jean Harlow, and Carole Lombard, but the redhead was a popular type, too. Redheads stood for spirit, brashness, temper, all qualities that meshed with the developing Hepburn persona. Although studio hairdressers found attractive ways to style her fairly thin hair in a long, soft bob, Hollywood never tampered with her hair color. Red she remained, well into her eighties.

Hepburn also had a beautiful slim body, perfect for athleticism and physical movement—and the camera. "Not much meat on her, but what there is is cherce," says Spencer Tracy in *Pat and Mike*. She adored sports, and it showed. She could eat anything that she wanted, including pounds of chocolate and huge steaks, and never gain weight. Only five-foot-seven, she seemed taller. Costumes draped especially well over her lithe figure. Obviously there were many body types in Hollywood, with more seductive and fuller-breasted females also in demand. But in the thirties many actresses were not buxom—"mammary madness" belongs to the fifties. By then a middle-aged Hepburn was usually playing spinsters, so being a "crazy, psalm-singing skinny old maid" as Humphrey Bogart called her in *The African Queen* did not hurt her appeal.[48]

Certain movie stars were associated with a specific aspect of their physical appearance: Groucho Marx's mustache and cigar, Carole Lombard's peroxided hair, Mae West's ample figure, Joan Crawford's shoes.[49] With Hepburn, it was pants. "Louella," she told the gossip columnist Louella Parsons, "there are certain privileges and rights one must reserve to oneself. I reserve the right to wear pants." Lauren Bacall remembered a press conference to promote *The African Queen* (she was married to co-star Humphrey Bogart) "for which I got myself all done up in a Balenciaga suit and Katharine Hepburn stole the show in her pants." Not only did Hepburn wear pants in public, she used pants as a prop to establish her characters on screen. Luckily Hepburn had the perfect long-legged, slim-hipped body to look good in them. Since very few women's stores sold slacks off the rack, Hepburn had pants and suits made to order by tailors in California and London.[50]

Like so many Hollywood stars, indeed almost all celebrities, Hepburn turned her somewhat unusual appearance into a look that worked for her. Her fans came to expect a certain upper-class elegance coupled with a comfortable athleticism. As she realized in 1986, "My good fortune and length of life is due to the fact that I am really an example of someone who was born at the right time for their *shape*, for their *attitude*, for their *mentality*, for their *looks*, and for their *sound*."[51]

But what about Hepburn as an actor? Ever since Dorothy Parker's 1933 quip ("Miss Hepburn ran the gamut of emotion from A to B,"), it has been acceptable to belittle her acting ability. Robert Benchley once said dismissively, "She is not a great actress, certainly, but she has a certain distinction which might with training possibly take the place of great acting in an emergency." Hepburn realized that she came on strong, both on screen and off: "I can just open my mouth and it irritates some people. You know, my personality is a sort of challenge. It just says, 'What the hell are you gonna do about this?' " (A *Saturday Evening Post* article in 1940 quoted a detractor, "If she were cast

as Little Red Riding Hood, she'd end up by eating the wolf.")
Despite the different roles she played, her screen presence did not
vary greatly: "I think I'm always the same. . . . There are certain
dominant qualities in your personality, and if you play them they
come over with a real zing."[52]

To learn more about Dorothy Thompson, turn to her newspaper columns or radio broadcasts; for Margaret Mead, her articles
and books; for Eleanor Roosevelt, look to the world. Katharine
Hepburn's films are the documents for understanding her life and
appeal. It is not just a question of Katharine Hepburn playing
Katharine Hepburn—that is far too simplistic. Nor are her varied screen and stage roles easily reduced to the Hepburn persona
of a strong and independent woman. But her filmography does
offer some tantalizing hints about her priorities as a star, her
impact on audiences, and the implications of her screen persona
for the experience of American women.

Drama critic Brendan Gill once noted about the generic early
Hepburn heroines, "They would make love after marriage and
then only with a certain fastidious reluctance, nostrils flaring." In
fact, not all Hepburn characters waited to make love until after
marriage. *Christopher Strong* (1932), her second film and one with
explicitly feminist undertones, concerned the love affair between
a married British aristocrat played by a stodgy Colin Clive and a
much younger female aviator, Lady Cynthia Darrington, played
by Hepburn. The opening costume ball scene introduces Hepburn in a form fitting gold lamé outfit with helmet that makes
her look like a moth; thereafter she strides through scenes wearing jodhpurs and a leather flying cap. Dismayed at the impact
their extramarital affair might have on family and friends, the
lovers decide to separate, and she sets off on a round-the-world
trip. But they cannot keep apart, and Cynthia becomes pregnant.
While attempting to break the world altitude record in her
plane, she deliberately removes her oxygen mask, knowing that
this will cause her to lose control of the plane and crash. As biog-

rapher Barbara Leaming pointed out, this suicide scene, which was eerily reminiscent of how her brother Tom slowly strangled himself, must have been excruciating to play.[53]

The film was directed by Dorothy Arzner, one of the few successful women directors in Hollywood, and the screenplay was by Zoe Akins. Although director and lead star respected each other (they both liked to wear pants), they did not exactly hit it off; after several weeks on the set they were still "Miss Arzner" and "Miss Hepburn." Later Hepburn recalled Arzner, who always dressed in men's clothing, had short, slicked back hair, and was reputed to be a lesbian, in this way: "She just did what she wanted, working along quietly, and nobody thought a damn about it. Of course, looking back, it seems queer as the dickens, but not so then. Ladies just did a lot of things without talking about them."[54] Of course, given her own eccentric behavior and dress, Hepburn could have been describing herself.

Christopher Strong, almost certainly modeled on celebrity aviator Amelia Earhart, was Hepburn's first role as a fierce, independent, career-minded modern woman. "You gave us courage for everything," a woman tells the Darrington character after one of her record-breaking flights. But the movie, even under Arzner's direction, is scarcely an unequivocal endorsement of feminism or women's freedom. With suicide presented as the only viable option after an affair with a married man and an unwanted pregnancy, the film serves up a fairly explicit warning to transgressive women. Yet until the ending, the aviator character leads a dashing, exciting life. Thus could a Katharine Hepburn character triumph over whatever plot exigencies the studios demanded.[55]

Another characteristic of Hepburn's early films was what Andrew Britton called a certain "gender ambiguity," which she shared with such stars as Greta Garbo, Marlene Dietrich, Bette Davis, Joan Crawford, and Barbara Stanwyck: "This is not to say, of course, that the star-as-*person* was gay or bisexual, but that certain dominant traits of the *persona* are strikingly out of true with

Katharine Hepburn with her drama coach, Frances Robinson-Duff, in 1935. Hepburn's pants and athletic stride were quite a contrast to the almost Victorian dress and demeanor of the older woman. Note too Hepburn's very short haircut acquired for her part as a boy in Sylvia Scarlett, *then in production. (UPI/Corbis-Bettman)*

dominant social norms of 'femininity.' " Even when Hepburn played conventional heterosexual roles, there was something quite unsettling, indeed disturbing about how aberrant her sex-

uality and gender could be. She was almost too strong to be confined in conventional gender roles. Put another way, her presence
alone in a movie could subvert or challenge gender definitions.[56]

The most infamous example of Hepburn's gender ambiguity is
the 1935 film *Sylvia Scarlett*, where she plays a boy for most of the
movie, kisses another woman while she is cross-dressed, and
arouses a male Bohemian artist more as a young man than as a
woman. "I don't know what it is that gives me a queer feeling
when I look at you," says the confused artist, which means something quite different when the audience knows "he" is a "she."
Given her penchant for pants and men's suits, Hepburn thought
it would be fun to dress as a boy and cut her hair short. (She
caused quite a stir driving around Los Angeles in an open con-
vertible with her boy haircut and lipstick—people thought she
was a man in drag.) "The dynamic Miss Hepburn is the hand-
somest boy of the season," announced the *New York Herald-
Tribune*, and *Time* concurred, "*Sylvia Scarlett* reveals the interesting fact that Katharine Hepburn is better looking as a boy than
as a woman." Critics panned the film, and audiences hated it.
When Hepburn saw the movie again in the 1980s, she found it
"revolting," but by then it had become a cult classic.[57]

While many of Hepburn's films like *Stage Door* (1937) and
Bringing Up Baby (1938) deal with what we would now identify
broadly as gender politics, one unusual feature of her filmography
is the number of films that deal with explicitly feminist themes.
Bette Davis, on the other hand, an equally strong female screen
presence, never played feminists. In addition to *Christopher Strong*
and *Little Women*, *A Woman Rebels* (1937) concerns a defiant young
woman named Pamela Thistlewaite who has an out-of-wedlock
child and then goes on to become a crusading editor of a women's
magazine in Victorian England. Even the unlikely World War II
morale-booster, *Dragon Seed* (1944), based on Pearl Buck's novel
with a screenplay by Marguerite Roberts and Jane Murfin, had a
strong feminist subplot as a heroic Chinese woman Jade (Hepburn) challenges the traditional role of women in society to take

on (and poison) legions of the invading Japanese army.[58]

Two other Hepburn films explicitly dealing with feminism and women's rights, *Woman of the Year* (1942) and *Adam's Rib* (1948), were set in contemporary America and thus more accessible to domestic audiences. Hepburn made *Woman of the Year* for Metro-Goldwyn-Mayer under the direction of George Stevens; the husband-and-wife team of Garson Kanin and Ruth Gordon wrote the script. She played Tess Harding, a brilliant foreign affairs columnist who knows prime ministers and diplomats from all over the world, reads *Huck Finn* going down the Yangtze, gives parties where guests speak seven languages, and meets deadlines with the help of a male secretary. Somewhat improbably she falls in love with and marries Sam Craig, a sportswriter for her newspaper. Deeply involved in the fight against fascism, Harding agrees without much thought to adopt a young refugee child from Europe. Selected "Woman of the Year" by a prominent women's organization, she plans to leave the child home alone while she and Sam go to the awards ceremony. He stays home in a huff to babysit, proclaiming "The woman of the year isn't a woman at all." Chastened in the end, she determines to be more of the wife her husband wants.

The Tess Harding character was clearly modeled on Dorothy Thompson, with a dash of Clare Booth Luce thrown in. Hepburn owned a townhouse in New York City at 244 East 49th Street, just one block from Dorothy Thompson's, but there is no evidence that they ever met. In a 1939 "On the Record" column, Thompson had once assembled a mythical dinner party of twenty interesting people, which included Katharine Hepburn "because of a modest earnestness in the midst of so much good looks."[59] After seeing the virulent portrait in *Woman of the Year* (which the columnist called "a sickening travesty and thoroughly unconvincing"),[60] Thompson no doubt retracted the invitation retroactively. One wonders too what Hepburn's mother, who coached the actress on the content and delivery of the speech she delivered at the awards banquet, thought of the film's negative portrayal of a feminist-minded career woman and the women's rights movement that valorized her.

The film's final indignity is the extended last scene where Harding tries to make breakfast for her husband and shows herself totally unfamiliar with anything resembling a kitchen. (The Business and Professional Women's magazine, *Independent Woman*, noted acidly, "Any business or professional woman who displayed such incompetence as she did in the kitchen scene would hardly have been the woman of the month, or even of the moment, in any job save perhaps that of check girl! Indeed, even as check girl, she'd get fired.") This excruciating humiliation of the Harding character is far out of proportion to what her husband seems to want: "I don't want to be married to Tess Harding anymore than I want to be married to Mrs. Sam Craig. Why can't you be Mrs. Tess Harding Craig?" Maybe they will rebuild their marriage along more equal lines, but audiences are left with a bitter aftertaste.[61]

The way in which a strong, overtly feminist career woman like Tess Harding had to receive her comeuppance ("For once strident Katharine Hepburn is properly subdued," ran one review, conveniently collapsing the actress and her persona) was in many ways foreshadowed in *The Philadelphia Story*. Though lacking the career aspects, *The Philadelphia Story* has a similar plot line of knocking the haughty and arrogant Hepburn character off her pedestal and humanizing her, which means making her conform more with dominant notions of femininity, among other things. *Woman of the Year* in turn has parallels to another Garson Kanin-Ruth Gordon collaboration, *Adam's Rib* (1948), where Hepburn and Tracy, under George Cukor's direction, play lawyers on opposing sides of a case of a wife (played by Judy Holliday) who has shot and wounded her husband for having an affair.[62]

On the surface, Adam and Amanda Bonner seem to have the perfect companionate marriage—dual careers, a fantastic New

York apartment complete with maid, a farm in Connecticut with dogs and a barn, witty dinner parties, and famous friends. But in the courtroom scenes, it becomes clear that Amanda Bonner has gone too far in trying to strike a blow for women's equality. She calls a string of witnesses to show what women have accomplished in all walks of life, including research chemistry and the building trades, but what could have been a strong statement in support of women's equality turns sour when a vaudeville performer chosen to demonstrate women's strength physically lifts opposing counsel Adam Bonner over her head, humiliating him. Now the uppity woman will have to pay: her marriage in trouble, a tearful reconciliation, and her capitulation. Yes, she admits, respect for the law is more important than making a point about women's inequality in the modern world. And yes, there really are differences between the sexes.

Katharine Hepburn once analyzed the appeal of her movies with Spencer Tracy by painting them as the ideal film couple: "We balanced each other's natures. We were perfect representatives of the American male and female."[63] While their liberated repartee often contained moments of true equality, there was a downside: Tracy damped her spirit, neutralized her unorthodoxy, ultimately put Hepburn in her place. Their on-screen pairing often lacked spontaneity or spark, as film critic Molly Haskell noticed: "However much we may love thorough-bred Hepburn and bearlike Tracy in the films they made together, there is, occasionally, something a little too clever and self-congratulatory about the perfect fit of their relationship."[64] Spencer Tracy is widely recognized as one of Hollywood's consummate film actors, an actor's actor, but he did not do his best work with her. Nor did she do her best work paired with him.

The next to last of the Hepburn-Tracy "battle of the sexes" movies was *Pat and Mike* (1952), where Hepburn played a physical ed teacher named Pat Pemberton and Tracy played a sports promoter named Mike Conovan who agrees to manage her professional sports career. (His main property is a dumb fighter named Davie Hucko, played by Aldo Ray.) Once again there is snappy dialogue (Tracy describes the perfect relationship as "five-oh, five-oh" and reprises his "I'm old fashioned! I like *two* sexes" line from *Adam's Rib*), but this movie seems to be just going through the paces. Its one redeeming quality, and this is a big one, is the chance to see Hepburn (then forty-five and still in superb physical condition) excel at various sports, including golf and tennis, against real-life athletes like Babe Didrikson Zaharias, Helen Dettweiler, Betty Hicks, Gussie Moran, and Alice Marble. Hepburn characters had played sports on screen before, notably the opening golf scene in *Bringing Up Baby*, but never had her athleticism been so central to the plot.

One reason *Pat and Mike* seemed stale was that it was released several months after *The African Queen*, and Pat Pemberton just couldn't hold a candle to Rose Sayer. Concluded Barbara Leaming, "This film, more than any other, is responsible for the enduring power of the Hepburn image. This is how we think of Kate: a strong, life-loving, indomitable woman, graced with vulnerability and a child's sense of wonder." Shot mainly on location in the Belgian Congo, Hepburn's first color picture allowed audiences to see her red hair, freckles, and ash-grey eyes. Hepburn only admitted to being forty-two at that point (she was actually forty-four), but she played Rose as if she were fifty-five. When she had trouble getting into the part, director John Huston gave her a superb piece of direction, telling her to base her character "on Eleanor Roosevelt when she visited the hospitals of wounded soldiers, always with a smile on her face."[65] It worked.

The African Queen appeared in 1951, just eleven years after Hepburn's glamorous and sensual portrayal of Tracy Lord in *The Philadelphia Story*. (That decade represents the difference between "Put me in your pocket, Mike," as she and Jimmy Stewart head off for a romantic, champagne-induced midnight swim, and Rose Sayer's sexually repressed but still suggestive "I never dreamed a

mere physical experience could be so exhilarating," after successfully negotiating the rapids with Humphrey Bogart.) In eleven
years she aged twenty-five on-screen, which of course says something about the difficulty women stars face in getting good roles
as they grow older. Except for *Desk Set* (1957), where she played
the head reference librarian for a television network battling an
early computer engineer played by Spencer Tracy (a classic case of
labor versus capital as well as women versus men), she no longer
was cast in the independent career woman roles of her youth. In
her last picture with Tracy, *Guess Who's Coming to Dinner?*, she
functions solely as a wife and mother—any independent existence
on the part of her character has been written out of the plot.

In the 1950s the typical Katharine Hepburn role was a spinster or old maid. Film historian Jeanine Basinger pointed out that
Hepburn was now playing exaggerated versions of her younger
self: "Once independent of men by choice, Katharine Hepburn
began to play a woman who has been left a spinster." It had
always proven difficult to marry off a Hepburn character—think
of *The Philadelphia Story*—but this spinster pattern is quite striking. In *Summertime* (1955), Hepburn plays a middle-aged secretary on a trip to Venice whom Rossano Brazzi introduces to love
against the lush Italian backdrop. In *The Rainmaker* (1956) Burt
Lancaster awakens an old maid's sexuality ("Can a woman take
lessons in being a woman?"), and makes it rain on her drought-
plagued farm, before moving on. Of a somewhat different ilk was
The Iron Petticoat (1956), a blatant rehash of Melvyn Douglas and
Greta Garbo's 1939 classic, *Ninotchka*. Somewhat incongruously
paired with Bob Hope, Hepburn plays a Russian pilot who
defects to the West and succumbs to the lures of capitalism and
love. Garbo did it much better.[66]

Hepburn's film output dropped off sharply in the 1950s and
early 1960s, as she took frequent breaks from film and stage to
devote herself to an increasingly ill Spencer Tracy. With roles
such as Mrs. Venable in Gore Vidal's adaptation of Tennessee
Williams's *Suddenly Last Summer* (1959) and Mary Tyrone in a

1962 movie version of Eugene O'Neill's *Long Day's Journey into Night*, Hepburn, who was then in her fifties, for the first time in her film career played mothers, albeit old and highly dysfunctional ones. The only previous films in which she had children on screen were *Woman of the Year*, where she briefly adopts an orphan, and the melodrama *Sea of Grass* (1947). In the 1940s Hepburn characters were often married (*Undercurrent* [1946] and *State of the Union* [1948]) or widowed (*Without Love* [1945] and *Keeper of the Flame* [1942]), but still childless. Katharine Hepburn as mother was a role only for very late in her career, when her strident independent persona had long since receded.

After Spencer Tracy's death, Hepburn continued to receive major dramatic opportunities, including *The Lion in Winter* (1968) with Peter O'Toole, *The Madwoman of Chaillot* (1969) with Charles Boyer, and *Trojan Women* (1971), costarring Vanessa Redgrave and Genevieve Bujold. She also continued to perform on stage, starring in her first musical, *Coco*, in 1969, and appearing on Broadway in *A Matter of Gravity* (1976) and *West Side Waltz* (1981). In 1975 she reprised her spinster role to team up with John Wayne in the unlikely, but highly successful western, *Rooster Cogburn*. In 1981, she won her fourth Oscar playing opposite Henry Fonda in *On Golden Pond*, making her the winningest actor, male or female, in Oscar history. As late as 1994, she made a cameo appearance in Warren Beatty's remake of *Love Affair*.

While one applauds her longevity in Hollywood, there is a rather radical disjunction between the Katharine Hepburn of her later years and the early, burning presence of the 1930s. As Andrew Britton cogently noted, "There was a time when, though fewer people probably cared what she did, Katharine Hepburn represented something rather different . . . One feels both that much of what was valuable about Hepburn has been lost, and that there is a connection, intimate but complex, between the monument that she now is and the offensive aberration that to so many she once was." Film critic Andrew Sarris is similarly drawn to the thirties Hepburn, whom he calls "younger, wilder, rawer, fresher, more vibrant, more vulnerable, and most of all, more menacing." Why do these often flawed vehicles still move us so? Sarris captured it well: "For a time, Katharine Hepburn's cinema was the cinema of a free woman."[67]

🦋

FOR SOMEONE WHO lived such a liberated life, Katharine Hepburn did not have much to say about women until the early 1970s. True, she did endorse the Equal Rights Amendment in 1942, long before it gained popular support, but her action was very much "in the family" since her aunt, Edith Houghton Hooker, was prominent in the National Woman's Party and her mother had been an early supporter of the ERA.

In part her silence was linked to her well-known aversion to publicity—she just wanted to do her job as an actor, and keep her opinions to herself. (One notable exception was her support for Henry Wallace in 1948 and her public stand against McCarthyism; she had also supported Franklin Roosevelt and collaborated with Eleanor Roosevelt on several occasions.)[68] More fundamentally, her silence on women's issues was part of a society-wide silence—women and feminism were just not topics of general discussion or interest until the 1960s and 1970s. But once women's liberation burst on the scene, reporters flocked to Katharine Hepburn, the epitome of the independent woman, for her views. Now that Spencer Tracy's death had removed the main reason to guard her privacy so closely, she was happy to oblige. Her new visibility in popular culture allowed her to keep herself before the public at a time when her acting career was beginning to slack off, in effect recharging her celebrity.

In the last decades of her life, Katharine Hepburn proved eminently quotable on a range of topics, with none more so than the changing roles of the sexes. "Sometimes I wonder if men and women really suit each other at all. . . . Perhaps they should live next door and visit every now and then." Many of her pithy comments, like putting on pants and living like a man, turned up repeatedly in different interviews, but articles featuring Katharine Hepburn sold magazines, especially women's magazines, so no one seemed to mind the repetition.[69]

Unlike Dorothy Thompson and Margaret Mead, Hepburn never felt she had to distance herself from feminism. "Hell, I'm a woman. I'm naturally interested in the feminist cause. I hate to see women the victims of things that are totally silly. Totally silly. For instance, jewels and dresses and stockings and shoes and a million high heels. All the desperately uncomfortable things. For what?" On another occasion, she stated forthrightly, "I'm all for women's liberation. Hell, my mother was one of the first, and I carried a banner for her more than 70 years ago, when I was 4. I wore pants when nobody else did, and I've led a life that might be considered totally emancipated." But she never saw herself as typical, or even as a role model for other women. Individualism was always her highest value. She sought to make her way as an exception to the traditional woman's role of wife and mother, a role that held no appeal for her but that she did not presume to challenge. As a commentator once observed, it was almost a case of being female without the inconvenience.[70]

At the core of Hepburn's attitudes about feminism and women's roles in the modern world was her deeply held belief that people should do what interested them most, and live with the consequences: "Being a housewife and a mother is the biggest job in the world," she told an interviewer in 1976, "but if it doesn't interest you, don't do it. It didn't interest me, so I didn't do it." She was afraid feminism had "tossed to the dogs the woman who stays at home and takes care of the children." Hepburn cited the example of her sister Peg, a farmer who brought up five children. "She goes to a lot of those functions where women are screaming and yelling about independence and she says: 'Now, wait a minute. I have done exactly what I've wanted to do, and what I've been intellectually fitted to do.' "[71]

At the same time she stood up for housewives, Hepburn was supportive of women who had other priorities. Unlike Dorothy

Thompson, who at times seemed to question careers except for all but the most exceptional women, Hepburn was all for them—if that's what you want, she'd say, go for it, but understand the tradeoffs: "I think the woman who has a career should have a career. I think a person has to make up his or her mind in life. I don't think you can have everything." Given her deeply held views about the difficulty of combining marriage and career, the biggest tradeoff concerned motherhood: "If a woman is to have a career, she should not by and large have children, because the children are the goats." "Only when a woman decides not to have children—as many do now, realizing there are already too many children—can a woman live like a man. That's what I've done." As she said repeatedly, "a woman simply can't have everything. Nor can a man."[72]

A film historian once observed that Katharine Hepburn "offers an intriguing demonstration of an acceptance of sexual difference combined with a refusal of sexist equalities."[73] She lived her whole life on the basis of complete equality with men, but she also believed that the sexes were fundamentally different: "Women simply are not men, and if we think we are, we're making a big mistake . . . . When two career people marry, something's got to give. In my day, it was always the woman. Now that's changed, and I'm all for that. But I still don't think the human animal changes." More than most, she realized what women were up against: "Naturally, I think their general situation should be equal, but anybody who's a woman, a full blooded woman, has brains enough to know that it isn't equal at all. Because the sexes are not the same—men and women are totally different."[74]

Why was Katharine Hepburn unable to imagine a world where gender roles were not so polarized that she could only think of herself as a woman living like a man? Like Dorothy Thompson and Margaret Mead, Hepburn inherited an incomplete feminist agenda from her mother's generation when she came of age in the 1920s. Told they were the equals of any man, young women were encouraged to forge their own ways in the

Birth control was the mother's cause, and so too did it become the daughter's. Here Hepburn accepts an award from Planned Parenthood for her ongoing support of reproductive rights. She is still gorgeous and elegant (and, although not visible in this shot, dressed in pants) in her eighties. (AP/Wide World Photos)

world at large, which they did with perseverance and great style. But as long as women retained primary responsibility for domestic and child-rearing duties, they would be disadvantaged as they tried to compete in the male realm. The need for a more systematic restructuring of gender roles in the private sphere to accompany the movement toward equality in the public was something that turn-of-the-century feminists like Katharine Houghton Hepburn and Emily Fogg Mead failed to anticipate. The supposed equality of the 1920s they bequeathed to their daughters, especially the sense that women could do whatever they set out to do, was far from complete.

With all her stark statements about learning "early on you can't be both," Katharine Hepburn saw this trap more clearly than most. "It's ridiculous to compete in a man's world on a man's terms," she noted at the height of the women's movement in the 1970s. Instead, she made personal choices that served as her own idiosyncratic and highly individualistic alternative to traditional gender roles. When she says that she put on pants and declared a middle road, she is talking both literally and symbolically. Her refrain begs the question, however, must women live like men to be free? She probably was smiling wryly when she replied, "That's what we're going to find out, isn't it?"[75]

𝕹

"A WOMAN MY age is not a particularly interesting object in our society, and that's a fact," a seventy-two-year-old Hepburn told columnist Rex Reed in 1979, and then proceeded to demonstrate just the opposite. Hepburn's stature as a legend increased as she aged. Unlike other actresses, she continued to snag prestigious parts well into her eighties and for the most part avoided the demeaning late roles that hurt the reputations of actresses like Bette Davis and Joan Crawford: "I was never degraded by the parts I played." Only the worsening of her Parkinson's disease, which caused a noticeable tremor in her film work as far back as the 1970s, kept her from appearing in public more.[76]

She spent as much time fanning her legend as she did acting in her later years. "It's rather the style to romanticize certain of the older actors," she noted, and then made sure she got her share of the attention. Like Martha Graham, who stopped dancing in public only in her seventies but made grand entrances and appearances into her nineties, Katharine Hepburn occupied a similar public space.[77]

Formerly reclusive and hostile to the press, Hepburn now tolerated, sometimes even relished such contact. Journalists long denied access seemed even more eager (and awed) to interview her than they were to make the trek to Margaret Mead's hidden-away turret at the museum. In 1973 Hepburn made her first ever television appearance on the *Dick Cavett Show*, reducing the usually sophisticated host to a gushing fan.[78] People really did seem to grow fonder of her as she grew older: "I'm like some weather-beaten old monument: people are beginning to realize that they'll miss me when I'm gone."[79]

As the climate for reproductive rights worsened in the 1980s, Hepburn publicly linked her name with the cause that her mother, who died in 1951, had supported alongside Margaret Sanger in the 1930s. In 1988, Planned Parenthood announced the establishment of the Katharine Houghton Hepburn Fund, which was dedicated to keeping abortion safe and legal, preventing teen pregnancy, and increasing access to family planning for low-income men and women. As a fund-raising gesture, Hepburn made a rare public speech at a Planned Parenthood banquet, keeping the audience enthralled for half an hour with her impromptu remarks about her family's long involvement in the birth control cause. In this respect Katharine Hepburn remained very much her mother's daughter.

Even though she had always maintained that she would never write about herself, the wall began to crumble when she published a slim but rather charming book in 1987 entitled *The Making of* The African Queen, *or How I Went to Africa with Bogart, Bacall, and Huston and Almost Lost My Mind*. The reception that book received emboldened her to write an autobiography, the aptly titled *Me: Stories of My Life*, published in 1991. "I'm trying to sell the book, so I'm adorable," she told a *New York Times* reporter with her new-found appreciation for favorable publicity. The book quickly shot onto the best-seller lists.[80]

Katharine Hepburn the author was no match for Hepburn the actress. The book was a superficial, self-centered, and utterly idiosyncratic look at her life, which made it sound like she had never read a book, had a serious conversation, or learned anything about the craft of film making from her years in Hollywood. It was all on the surface, which of course is what many people think Hollywood is all about. Some readers expected more from a favorite icon than such a self-centered recitation, and the legend dimmed just a bit. But many fans and admirers just accepted it as yet another bravura Hepburn performance.

Of course Hepburn couldn't care less about any of this, since she always claimed she did exactly what she wanted and never understood the mystique surrounding her in the first place. That is both true and disingenuous. True, in that there really is a dif-ference between the person and the persona, something too often forgotten when the two are collapsed: "I'm very different from the one everyone seems to know. She's a legend, that is, a creation of, by and for the public. But I really don't know her. I'm sort of like the man who cleans the furnace. I just keep her going." Disingenuous, because after decades in the limelight, Hepburn needed and craved what celebrity could bring, and was unwilling to give it up: "The only thing I *have* to do is to see to it that I maintain myself as a star because I couldn't function in any other way."[81] Surrounded in her old age by a loyal staff, a small circle of devoted friends, and her companion Phyllis Wilbourn, who was as selfless as Hepburn was selfish, she continues to live her life entirely on her own terms.

It is hard to imagine Katharine Hepburn dying with any regrets about how she lived her life. "Me, I'm like the Flatiron Building. All I can say is I could never be anyone else. I don't *want* to be anyone else, and I've never regretted what I've done in my life even though I've had my nose broken a few times doing it."[82] When the Tess Harding character in *Woman of the Year* is asked how she feels about being herself, she cocks her head and replies, "I feel good about it. Always have." Hepburn admitted there was a touch of her in every role she played, and that line rings especially true.

(*Reprinted with permission from Barricade Books Inc. From* How to Talk Golf. *Illustration by Taylor Jones.*)

F I V E

FROM TOMBOY TO LADY: BABE DIDRIKSON ZAHARIAS

HAT IS YOUR favorite sport, reporters would ask Babe Didrikson. "The one I am playing." Who's the greatest athlete? "Who's the competition?" What sport are you best at? "I'm best at everything." In exasperation, is there anything you don't play? "Yeah, dolls."[1]

They called her "The Texas Tornado," an "Amazing Amazon," and the "World-Beating Girl Viking of Texas." Mainly they just called her Babe, the first female athlete to be known by a singular name. She took the sports world by storm when she single-handedly won the team championship at the 1932 A.A.U. national championships, what United Press reporter George Kinsley called "the most amazing series of performances ever accomplished by any individual, male or female, in track and field history." Having earned a berth on the U.S. Olympic team to compete in Los Angeles several weeks later, she went on to win two golds and a silver. She defiantly told her competition that she was going to "whup" them, and then proceeded to do just that. Thirty years before Muhammed Ali, here was an athlete who was proud to say, "I am the greatest."[2]

Americans in the 1920s and 1930s were obsessed with sports. "If St. Paul were living today," a Methodist minister intoned, "he would know Babe Ruth's batting average and what yardage Red Grange made." Sports sold newspapers, and sportswriters like Grantland Rice, Damon Runyon, Ring Lardner, and Paul Gallico were household names. But the sports pages did not limit themselves to reporting the latest scores: "all dealt in the purplest hyperbole and glorification of athletes." While most of the heroes trumpeted were male, charismatic athletes like swimmer Gertrude Ederle, tennis player Helen Wills, and figure skater Sonja Henie became national idols as well. With her amazing triumphs at the 1932 Olympics, Babe Didrikson too seemed on the verge of national celebrity.[3]

But her boyish athletic body, her disdain for all things feminine, and her outspokenness made her as much a freak as a heroine in 1930s America. There was something too crude, too brash, too unpredictable about this working-class, Texas "muscle moll"—this was no well-bred Katharine Hepburn thumbing her nose at Hollywood. Growing up poor, Babe Didrikson realized she wanted to spend her life in sports, "but I had to make money too, and that isn't easy for a woman athlete." Golf eventually provided the answer, along with a transformation in her persona from brash tomboy to more conventional woman, complete with lipstick, a permanent wave, and a husband/promoter named George Zaharias. Soon she was making $100,000 a year, an enormous sum at the time. Then, just as her domination of women's golf was at its peak, she was diagnosed with cancer. She staged an amazing comeback in 1954, but succumbed to the disease in 1956 at the age of forty-five.[4]

In 1950 the Associated Press voted Babe Didrikson Zaharias the outstanding female athlete of the last fifty years. This recognition came as much from her versatility as it did from her domination of a single sport. (Jim Thorpe, chosen outstanding male athlete, shared this trait.) As sportswriter Paul Gallico, no friend of women in sports, was forced to admit, "She was probably the most talented athlete, male or female, ever developed in our country. In all my years at the sports desk I never encountered any man who could play as many different games as well as Babe." Grantland Rice, who was so closely associated with boosting the athlete that she was called "Grant's Girl," concurred: "There is only one Babe Didrikson and there never has been another in her class—even close to her class."[5]

Despite her undisputed talent, Babe Didrikson remained a somewhat imperfect role model at a time when many Americans considered the categories "woman" and "athlete" mutually exclusive. She was too individualistic to ever link up with organized feminism or participate in politics or reform. She displayed zero trace of gender solidarity, dismissing other women on more than one occasion as "sissies." Among athletes she knew she was in a category all her own. "Hi girls," she'd say to the locker room before a tournament in her Texas drawl. "Ya gonna stick around and see who'll finish second this week?" As fellow golfer Helen Dettweiler complained, "She thinks she's the whole show, which of course she is." Four decades after her death, the sports world still has not seen another all-around athlete as dazzling as Babe Didrikson Zaharias, whose legacy to the American century was her magnificent illustration of the possibilities of the female body.[6]

※

"I KNEW EXACTLY what I wanted to be when I grew up. My goal was to be the greatest athlete that ever lived." Note the absence of the qualifier "woman"—Babe Didrikson would never be limited by the mere fact of sex. Mildred Ella Didrikson was born on June 26, 1911, in Port Arthur, Texas, but she grew up in nearby Beaumont, where her family moved after a devastating hurricane struck the Texas coast in 1915. Her parents, Ole and Hannah Marie Didriksen (their daughter changed the spelling of her last name), were Norwegian immigrants who ended up in an

East Texas landscape far different from the land they had left behind. It is interesting how little attention was ever paid to their daughter's Norwegian background, a sharp contrast to other Norwegian-American athletes like tennis star Molla Bjurstedt Mallory, football coach Knute Rockne, and figure skater Sonja Henie. In Babe's case, Texas trumped Norway.[7]

Ole Didriksen supported himself with odd jobs as a carpenter and furniture restorer, and his wife occasionally took in washing when money was tight. They had seven children, of whom Mildred (first known as "Baby," later transformed into "Babe") was the sixth and the fourth daughter. Even though her family was quite poor, Babe remembered, "I had a wonderful childhood."[8]

Most girls who show signs of independence early in life are tagged tomboys, and Babe was no exception. "The way I look at it a girl that wants to become an athlete and do some winning should get that kind of start by being a tomboy. If she just goes in for games against girls when she is young, why she never gets used to being smashed around. Girls are nice to each other. Boys are rough with each other, and rougher with girls who crash into their game." With her ability to excel at any sport she tried and her amazing competitive instinct (which earned her the neighborhood reputation of "the worst kid on Doucette"), Babe took being a tomboy to new heights. As her sister Lillie said, "She was the best at *everything* we did."[9]

Except school. Babe never impressed anyone as terribly bright, and probably realized that brains alone would not get her out of Texas. Her body, in which she had total confidence, might. Remembered a male high school classmate: "I knew that winning in sports was the only way I'd ever be recognized. Babe and I were both from poor families. . . . Sports was a way of getting to be equal, and I think that's what carried Babe through and made her work so hard. . . . There was no other way to get ahead except sports."[10]

Babe Didrikson's Beaumont High School yearbook had her on

every girls team there was, including golf. That detail is significant, because she had a nasty habit of mythologizing her past,
saying on occasion that she first played golf after the 1932
Olympics. In another embellishment, a dress she made in home
economics class won first prize at the Texas State Fair, a far more
impressive accomplishment than its actual ribbon at a regional
event.

It was her basketball playing that caught the eye of Colonel
Melvin McCombs from the Employers Casualty Company of Dallas. During her senior year in high school, he offered her a job as
a typist, and the opportunity to play on the firm's basketball
team. It was 1930, and times were hard—the salary was a magnificent seventy-five dollars a month. Babe knew the money she
sent home would make a big difference, setting a pattern of helping her family financially that she proudly continued throughout
her career. Without waiting to graduate, she took the overnight
sleeper from Beaumont to Dallas, a distance of 275 miles. Babe
had never left East Texas before: "To me, that was like going to
Europe."[11]

The Employers Casualty Golden Cyclones were basically a
semi-professional basketball team. The women all worked in various capacities at the company, but they were really there to play
ball. The 1920s and 1930s were the heyday of company-spon-
sored sports programs and athletic teams, and Dallas was a
"hotbed" of industrial sports. These games drew an enthusiastic
following, and brought good publicity to their sponsors. For
women, especially the majority who could not afford college, it
was one of the few ways to play competitive sports after high
school and even get paid for it. During Babe's years there, the
Golden Cyclones went to two finals and a national championship;
she was named an All-American three times.[12]

From the beginning Babe Didrikson was out for herself. As
soon as she arrived in Dallas, she announced to her startled teammates that she now expected to be the star. While no one doubted her skill, her teammates resented her attitude, a pattern that

continued throughout her sports career. As one remembered, "She was masculine and she was an individual—she was out for Babe, honey, just Babe. We played as a team, we played as one. But I don't know how her mind run. She was not a team player, definitely not. Babe she was out for fame. There were lots of players on the Cyclones more popular than Babe was. But she got to be famous. And that's what she wanted."[13]

Since basketball only occupied one season, Colonel McCombs introduced Didrikson to track and field as a way of keeping her occupied. Soon she excelled there as well, easily picking up hurdles (which she compared to jumping over hedges in her old neighborhood), javelin throw, broad jump, high jump, and shot put. Based on her quick success, McCombs asked her to represent Employers Casualty at the 1932 Amateur Athletic Union track-and-field championships to be held at Northwestern's Dyche Stadium in Evanston, Illinois. This meet also served as the qualifier for the upcoming Los Angeles Olympics. At the beginning of the meet, the announcer introduced each team, and all its members trotted out onto the field for applause. When Employers Casualty was announced, out ran Babe, and only Babe.[14]

When the day was over, Didrikson had won five of the eight events she entered, tied one, and finished fourth in another, scoring thirty points to win the team title all by herself. Her nearest competition, the highly respected Illinois Women's Athletic Club, only managed twenty-two points despite its twenty-two-member team. Even she knew that this was something special: "It was one of those days in an athlete's life when you know you're just right. You feel you could fly. You're like a feather floating in air." As she later wrote, "This is when that stuff about me being a 'super athlete' and a 'wonder girl' started up."[15]

She quickly earned the enmity of other contestants, however, who resented the logistical nightmare that resulted when meet officials rearranged the schedules of qualifying heats and finals to accommodate Babe's participation. They also hated her brashness and cockiness, like her penchant for asking a competitor what her best time was, then claiming that she routinely beat that in practice, which, of course, she probably did.

The bragging continued on the train taking the thirty-seven-woman team out to Los Angeles. Teammates were appalled when she got off at a stop in New Mexico and yelled at the top of her lungs, "Did you ever hear of Babe Didrikson? If you haven't you will!" Noted high jumper Jean Shiley many years later, "She ran around with her medals from Evanston, saying, 'I'm the greatest, no one's better than me, Babe Didrikson.' Today I don't think her behavior would seem so outrageous. People are used to flamboyant athletes. In those days, athletes were supposed to be full of humility and modesty." Especially women athletes. Brashly taunting her opponents was in part a sign of Babe's immaturity, ill at ease in the new circles in which she was traveling. But she honestly felt that she was the best, and that she had no competition: "I'm only running against girls," she'd remind reporters dismissively.[16]

The next stop was the 1932 Olympics. Had the Olympic games been held in some distant European country, or even another part of the United States, they probably would not have attracted as much attention as they did being staged in Los Angeles. Southern California was the home of Hollywood, of celebrities, of a certain hedonism and brashness unusual in American life at the time. Babe fit right in, and the reporters lapped up her boasts and predictions. "I came out to beat anybody in sight and that's just what I'm going to do. Sure I can do anything." Her philosophy of sports never wavered: "All my life I've been competing—and competing to win."[17]

Mythologizing dogged her career even then. First, there was the matter of her age. Babe was now giving her birth date as 1914, rather than 1911, correctly surmising that her feats would seem even more spectacular when accomplished by an eighteen-year-old rather than someone who had just turned twenty-one. Later she even refashioned her body, claiming in her autobiography that she had been a mere five feet tall and 105 pounds. But newsreels and press coverage show a bigger girl, closer to five-

Babe Didrikson warms up for the javelin throw at the 1932 Olympics. Not afraid to show off her muscles and her distinctly unfeminine appearance (the unflattering skullcap covers her cropped hair), she was the epitome of the Muscle Moll. In 1930s America, this was not a compliment. (AP/Wide World Photos)

foot-five (almost her adult height) and around 120 pounds. Because of her short hair and strong body, she was often described as boyish, but she was not especially masculine-looking. "I know I'm not pretty, but I do try to be graceful," was her standard reply to reporters obsessed with her unfeminine looks.[18]

Olympic rules only allowed her to compete in three events, which was all she had qualified for anyway, and each of her competitions had some anomaly or controversy. In the javelin, she failed to warm up properly and released her first throw prematurely, which meant it stayed closer to the ground rather than arching. Yet it was a world record, and good enough for the gold. She suffered a slight muscle tear in her shoulder, however, which prevented her from duplicating the throw in later attempts, to the disappointment (and scattered boos) of the crowd. That did not keep her from giving what one sports historian has called the "first post-event radio appearance of an Olympic medal winner" on local station KHJ.[19]

In the eighty-meter hurdles, she finished in a dead heat with Evelyne Hall, but after thirty minutes of deliberation the judges gave the victory to Didrikson, despite Hall's contention that she had a welt on her neck from breaking the tape. Years later Hall still bitterly recalled that race, especially how Babe had told her on the train to Los Angeles how easy it was to influence the judges by throwing your arms up in the air and claiming victory. Hall, in contrast, had looked dejected when she finished, which she later thought influenced the judges adversely. Said Hall in 1975, "Babe had had so *much* publicity, it was impossible to rule against her."[20]

Things finally went against Babe in the high jump. She and co-competitor Jean Shiley each cleared a world record height of 5 feet 5 1/4 inches. But the judges ruled that Didrikson had dived over the bar, her head going over before the rest of her body in a then illegal "Western Roll," so they awarded the gold to Shiley. The winner's comment—"The other girls on the team were delighted, like children at Christmas, because I had beaten Babe"—says volumes about how unpopular the prima donna was among her teammates. In this case, Didrikson did have cause to cry foul, since she had used this technique before and never been called on it. The judges seemed of two minds as well, allowing the women to hold the world record jointly. And they authorized a special medal that was half silver and half gold for her second place finish, the only time this has ever been done.[21]

Ironically Didrikson's three medals at the 1932 Olympics did not translate into increased popularity for women's track and field, in fact just the opposite. In the decade after the 1932 Olympics, interest in track and field for women plummeted steadily, helped along no doubt by comments like this from United States Olympic Chairman Avery Brundage: "I am fed up to the ears with women as track and field competitors. Their charms sink to less than zero." More than other women's sports, track and field called for women to develop—and display—musculature and body physiques that seemed threateningly masculine for the times. Track and field's loss of appeal contrasted to other popular sports for women like swimming, tennis, bowling, and golf, as well as team sports like softball and basketball, all of which flourished during the Depression. This abandonment of track and field created a vacuum that African-American women moved in to fill in the 1940s and 1950s, beginning a dominance that continues to this day.[22]

What was next for Babe Didrikson? Most other Olympians simply returned home and resumed their old lives, which could be pretty grim in this the worst year of the Depression.[23] But Babe had gotten a taste of fame and fortune in Los Angeles and she wanted more. Capitalizing on her athletic skill, however, would run afoul of A.A.U. rules about professionalism. In fact, right after the Olympics she was briefly suspended by the organization for allegedly accepting money for appearing in an advertisement for a Chrysler automobile. When she explained that the ad had run without her knowledge and that she had not been paid by Chrysler, the A.A.U. relented and withdrew the ban. In December 1932, Didrikson turned professional anyway, provoking this skeptical comment from sportswriter Arthur Daley: "Miss Didrikson is probably the most naive athlete ever to turn professional. Just what form of professionalism she will engage in is somewhat vague."[24]

"These years I'm talking about were a mixed-up time for me," the athlete later recalled. "My name had meant a lot right after the Olympic Games, but it had sort of been going down since then. I hadn't been smart enough to get into anything that would really keep me up there." It wasn't just a case of being smart—there really weren't any professional opportunities for women. Or, rather, any respectable opportunities. "Once I got so hard up I almost agreed to a stunt where they'd have me running a race against a horse. But I didn't do it. I knew that wasn't really the right kind of performance for a girl to be putting on."[25]

Over the next three and a half years, Babe Didrikson did manage to earn a lot of money, perhaps as much as $40,000, most of which she sent home to her family. This was the height of the Depression, and she was able to lift her family permanently out of poverty. But her reputation was now tainted by her blatant commercialism. And she was in danger of being forever known as a freakish Muscle Moll, almost a non-woman on the fringes of respectable society. Years later she rarely talked about this period of her life.

"Sometimes, in those early barnstorming days I wasn't sure if people were laughing with or at me." The first thing she tried was vaudeville, opening at the Palace Theater in Chicago in 1933. Billed on the marquee as "Babe Didrikson—In Person—World's Greatest Woman Athlete," she had an eighteen-minute act, four or five times a day. Dressed in street clothes, she sang a parody of "I'm Fit as a Fiddle and Ready to Love," with the last words changed to "ready to go." She then stripped to a satin track suit and jumped on a treadmill where she "raced" to beat both a large clock and another woman running on a parallel treadmill. She also shared with the audience her skill at hurdles, golf, and harmonica playing. Despite advance bookings in New York for approximately $2,500 a month, she quit after one week in Chicago. "I don't want the money if I have to make it this way," she told her sister.[26]

For a while she returned to a job at Employees Casualty at the excellent salary of $300 a month, but financial pressures at home, notably medical expenses incurred by her father, sent her on the road again. She agreed to tour with a mixed basketball team called Babe Didrikson's All Americans, which was mainly men but included at least one other woman. From the fall of 1933 to March of 1934, they played almost a hundred games all the way from Muscatine, Iowa, to Thief River Falls, Minnesota, to Fort Plain, New York. Paired against local men's teams, they drew good crowds by providing cheap entertainment to Depression-era America.

When the basketball season ended, she signed on with an itinerant baseball team at a salary of between $1,000 and $1,500 a month. All the regular players had beards, so they called themselves the House of David. Enduring yet another grueling schedule, she would usually pitch an inning or two and then drive alone to the next destination, since it would have been considered improper for her to travel unchaperoned with the male team. This concern with propriety makes all the more amusing a widely-circulated crack about her time with the team. Because she did not wear a beard, she was once asked by a female spectator, "Where are your whiskers?" "I'm sitting on 'em, sister, just like you are."[27]

After her Olympic triumphs of 1932, Didrikson dropped out of the national headlines for the rest of the decade. The *Chicago Sun Times* noted, "Few sporting figures ever thudded with the ravishing rapidity that La Didrikson did." Unlike widely publicized figures like Eleanor Roosevelt, Margaret Mead, or Dorothy Thompson, who turned up regularly in mainstream magazines as well as on the radio and the lecture circuit throughout the 1930s, Babe Didrikson only rated an occasional mention in *Time* or *Literary Digest*. Since her barnstorming exploits were not conventionally athletic, she dropped off the sports pages as well. In 1943 she was the subject of a feature in the *Saturday Evening Post* called "Whatever became of . . . " At that point, however, she was just about to explode back onto the national scene with her postwar domination of women's golf, a prominence and visibility she maintained until her premature death.[28]

In the 1930s Didrikson's celebrity was more localized. She got reams of publicity, but it was mainly in the small towns of America where there were crowds and interest in her quasi-athletic exploits, mainly because of the lack of competition from other commercialized forms of leisure and recreation. Everybody had a car, however, and locals would drive for miles to see a touring basketball or baseball team, especially if the price was pegged low enough for a family to afford. These events were big news to the local press. While much of the country increasingly participated in a shared national consumer culture by the 1930s, regional and local patterns persisted. That was where Didrikson's fans and coverage were in the 1930s, not in the national magazines or press.

As long as the public was willing to turn out for her stunts, sideshows, and exhibitions, Babe Didrikson could have continued this kind of career. But it really didn't have much to do with serious athletics, and, more fundamentally, it was compromising her reputation by making her seem like a vaudeville huckster, which in many ways she was. She still yearned for the celebrity and stardom that she had first glimpsed after her Olympic triumph. In 1930s America, there were only two sports where women could become stars: tennis and golf. She chose golf. In fact, so much did she want to put this earlier part of her life behind her that she later said repeatedly, "My sports career began with golf."[29]

Babe Didrikson had set her sights on becoming a golf champion as far back as the 1932 Olympics, perhaps earlier. Soon she was working long and hard to master the difficult game. California golf pro Stan Kertes gave her free lessons, recognizing her talent and her uncertain finances (at this time, she was also supporting her large family). She played her first tournament in November 1934 but lost in the first round. Most tournaments then were match play, that is, playing elimination matches against individual opponents and moving on to the next round, rather than competing for the lowest overall score. In April 1935 she garnered her first tournament victory, the Texas Women's Amateur Championship, which was played that year at the fancy River Oaks Country Club in Houston.

Even though she had toned down her act from her barnstorming days, Didrikson's working-class, East Texas style rubbed the country-club set the wrong way. Said one snob, "We really don't need any truck drivers' daughters in our tournament." Her plans for more tournament play were squashed by the United States Golf Association, which branded her a professional for her previous commercial undertakings. Didrikson rarely confronted the powers-that-be publicly, but privately she thought she knew the reason she had been banned: "because they didn't want me to beat the rich dames."[30]

So it was back to barnstorming, although of a higher class now that she was easing her way into the country-club world of golf. She toured the country with golfer Gene Sarazen, giving exhibitions for which she earned about $150 a day. She also developed a business relationship with Wilson Sporting Goods, receiving a retainer to promote their golf products. This was what being a professional woman golfer meant in the 1930s—endorsements, commercial tie-ins, and exhibitions, but no competition or tournament play because none existed. As Babe said in 1936, "It's a sort of lonely business, being a woman pro. There's no Women's Open or Pro Championships to play in." At least she was playing the game that she loved, and making a good living from it. She would not be the first or the last female golfer to look around at the lives of secretaries, saleswomen, and teachers to say, I'd rather be golfing.[31]

In an aptly titled (and ghostwritten) 1936 article called "I Blow My Own Horn," Babe Didrikson sought to reinforce an image of herself as just a nice, normal girl. "People are always asking me, 'Are you going to get married, Babe?' and it gets my goat. They seem to think I'm a strange, unnatural being summed up in the words Muscle Moll, and the idea seems to be that Muscle Molls are not people. I look forward to having a home and children just like anybody else, maybe more than some." She then continued disingenuously, "Only I can't get married for a while yet. My contract won't let me, and I've got a three-year contract."

There was no such clause in any contract, but her next sentence was closer to the mark: "I wanted to be independent first before I got married."[32]

In early 1938 Didrikson qualified for a men's golf tournament in Los Angeles, where she was paired with George Zaharias, the professional wrestler who would become her husband and promoter later that year. "I always said I could fall in love with a man strong enough to outdrive me," she joked. She and George hit it off instantly. Like her, he had worked his way out of working-class poverty to a highly successful career as a wrestler and then as a promoter. Known as "The Crying Greek from Cripple Creek," he was at that point a handsome, if large-necked and cauliflower-eared twenty-nine-year-old wrestler nearing the end of his career in the ring. He was wealthy, had a good sense of humor, and liked her family. They were married on December 23, 1938. Didrikson was twenty-seven years old.[33]

Babe once startled an editor who asked her for the most thrilling experience of her life by replying, "The first night I slept with George." These two were a perfect match, as biographer Susan Cayleff captured: "Together they made a team of self-promoters that P. T. Barnum would have admired." George's nickname, for example, came from his tendency to break into crowd-pleasing tears in the ring when he was about to lose, a ploy that confirmed that professional wrestling was as much about showmanship as brute strength. By the time Babe met George, she had already trademarked her wisecracking style with the galleries, and she knew how to cultivate the press. He in turn easily adapted the skills he had developed on the pro wrestling tour to promoting his wife, even to the point of booking a strenuous series of golf exhibitions on what was supposed to be their delayed honeymoon to Australia in 1939.[34]

Although George Zaharias's income (reputed to be as high as $100,000 in the late 1930s and early 1940s) took the financial pressure off Didrikson, she was frustrated by the lack of competition, which was what had always driven her game to higher and

higher levels. And if she wanted competition, that meant amateur golf, since there was no women's professional circuit then.
Perhaps the biggest boost George Zaharias gave to her career was
his willingness to pay her expenses for three years while she sat
out professional golf in order to win back her amateur status.
From 1940 to 1943 she played in what tournaments there were,
but she had to refuse the cash prizes. And she could no longer
accept money for golf exhibitions or golf-related endorsements.

During her enforced hiatus from commercial athletics, Didrikson continued to work on her golf game, took up bowling (she
soon averaged a highly respectable 170), and developed a mean
tennis game. She had tried tennis once before but the residual
damage to her shoulder from her errant javelin toss at the 1932
Olympics prevented her from developing a powerful serve. That
injury finally healed, she tried tennis again, the one other sport
besides golf that promised the combination of celebrity,
respectability, and income that she craved.

Like all sports, she took up tennis with a vengeance, practicing for hours and pushing herself to master the game. "When I
go into a sport, I don't do it halfway," recalled Didrikson. "I went
all out on my tennis, just the way I had in the past on basketball
and track and field." Her coach was Alice Tennant of the Bever-
ly Hills Tennis Club, who also coached Alice Marble, Maureen
Connolly, and numerous Hollywood stars. Soon Babe was beating
her teacher, and holding her own against leading women players
like Mary Arnold and Louise Brough. But when she tried to enter
an amateur tennis tournament in 1941, her application was
denied on the grounds of once a professional, always a professional, even if she had never accepted money for tennis. "Once I
knew I could never compete in tournaments, that took the fun
out of tennis for me. It's not enough for me just to play a game.
I have to be able to try for championships." The result? She quit
tennis cold, never picking up a racket again.[35]

Wartime turned out to be not a bad time to be regaining one's
amateur status, since many major tournaments and competitions

were either scaled back or cancelled "for the duration." By 1945 Didrikson was tearing up the fairways so much that she was named Woman Athlete of the Year by the Associated Press, thirteen years after first winning the award in 1932. Few awards or honors provided sweeter vindication of her long struggle to get her athletic career back in high gear.

🏃

THERE WAS MORE involved in Didrikson's success than learning to drive, chip, and putt. She also had to create a "marketable self" suitable for public consumption, which involved leaving behind some of her rougher, brasher, and less feminine ways and bringing herself more in line with dominant notions of femininity and womanhood. Babe herself always downplayed this supposed transformation that began after the Olympics and was well on its way to completion by the time she married George Zaharias in 1938: "Some writers have said that around this time a big change took place in me. Their idea is that I used to be all tomboy, with none of the usual girls' interests, and then all of a sudden I switched over to being more feminine. Well, with almost any woman athlete, you seem to get that tomboy talk. It happens especially with girls who play things that generally aren't considered women's sports, like basketball and baseball, the way I did. . . . But I don't believe my personality has changed. I think anyone who knew me when I was a kid will tell you that I'm still the same Babe. It's just that as you get older, you're not as rambunctious as you used to be. You mellow down a bit."[36]

That statement from her 1955 autobiography is not necessarily false, but it hardly tells the whole story. Just as Dorothy Thompson, Margaret Mead, and Katharine Hepburn consciously created personae to advance careers, so did Babe Didrikson, far more aggressively. In order to leave behind her ethnic, working-class origins and the somewhat tawdry commercialism of her barnstorming days, she had to change sports to the more acceptable (and upper-class) game of golf. The world of golf had no

Contrast the track-and-field Babe to her later incarnation, where she projects a far more traditionally female demeanor. Here she smiles over plans for a line of women's sports clothing she helped design, one of the many commercial endorsements that made her one of the wealthiest athletes, male or female, of her time. (Mary and John Gray Library, Special Collections, Lamar University, Beaumont, Texas)

room for a Muscle Moll, so she had to become more feminine, too. "She studied both golf and femininity rigorously," noted biographer Cayleff. "Success in either depended on the other."[37]

In a nonsexist world, no one would care whether women athletes were pretty, butch, tomboys, or sylphs, as long as they played the game well and enjoyed it. But in the sports world of the 1920s and 1930s that Didrikson grew up in, and still in many ways today, society had a hard time reconciling the gender of women athletes with their athleticism. So much of the mythology of sports was male—competition, strength, muscular masculinity—that women were often viewed as interlopers or unwelcome participants in an athletic battle of the sexes. (Sportswriter Grantland Rice put it in couplet form, "If they keep on getting better / who will be the weaker sex?") Women athletes also walked a fine line between popular approval of their physical accomplishments and the feared loss of femininity through adoption of male competitive traits, or even worse, the development of a masculine physical appearance. No wonder women athletes had a harder time winning legitimacy and respect than their male counterparts.[38]

At the same time there was also a growing recognition that some level of athleticism and physical activity was desirable, indeed almost obligatory, for the modern woman. As the *New York Times* remarked in 1931, "Any description of the ideal modern girl invariably specifies that she must be good at outdoor sports. A long stride, a strong arm, sunburned hair, a tanned complexion have come to be regarded as part of the picture of a modern beauty. . . . Today a group picture of women swimmers, golfers, tennis players or fliers generally shows more than its average quota of good looks. And women who abhor physical effort have a reputation for being fat rather than fair." All the sports that were highlighted, including aviation, which was often classed as a sport in the 1920s and 1930s, were individual ones considered acceptable for women, where they could participate and even compete without unduly compromising their femininity. Noticeably absent were team sports with tougher, more working-class associations, like softball and basketball, and especially track and field.[39]

It was these other sports, and women's entry into them, that often proved so troubling to sportswriters and caused problems for the women who were drawn to them. Much of it came down to derogatory terms like Muscle Moll, and the supposed mannishness of the bodies of these well-trained, muscular, and fit athletes. Babe Didrikson, the nation's number one Muscle Moll in 1932, slowly learned that she needed to overcome the masculine associations of her own success.

While some early coverage simply reported her athletic accomplishments straight, most sportswriters could not resist making references to her androgynous appearance and tenuous link to conventional womanliness, often as the main lead of their story. Sportswriter Paul Gallico referred to a breed of "women who make possible deliciously frank and biological discussions in the columns of newspapers as to whether this or that famous woman athlete should be addressed as 'Miss,' 'Mrs.,' 'Mr.,' or 'It.' "[40] Only retrospectively did these men (there were no nationally prominent women sportswriters at the time) acknowledge the pain that some of their insensitive comments might have caused athletes. As Gallico later admitted, "there were no restrictions beyond good taste and libel, and I'm afraid that we often wrote as though the subjects were blind, or could not read, or would never see our articles, or had no sensibilities."[41]

Presumably Gallico considered his own dubious prose on "the Texas Babe" from 1932 to be in good taste, but it is typical of the intrusive physical interrogation of their gender credentials to which women athletes were subjected, attention that male athletes never had to endure:

> The Babe stands five feet seven inches in height. She weighs 126 pounds. She has greenish-blue eyes, an aquiline nose, a mop of brownish hair, close-cropped in back like a boy's, but worn floppy, and a little longer in front. Her mouth is large and thin-lipped. One of the girls on the swimming team said she had a mouth like a lizard's. The comparison is apt. There is light fuzz on her upper lip, her face, her neck. She has an enormous Adam's Apple. Her legs are powerful and hirsute, with large, strong ankles. Her body is slim, compact, and hard. She has the biceps of a village blacksmith. She is magnificently graceful. She looks like a boy.

If one must be a Muscle Moll, Gallico concludes, "then I suppose the next thing is to be the best one in the world, the Muscle Moll to end all Muscles Molls, as it were. When a lady athlete can perform the feats that La Didrikson can, she begins to exercise a peculiar and mysterious fascination all her own." Gallico didn't claim to have the answer to that fascination, "but it may be the same thing that keeps me lingering in front of the bearded lady and Airy Fairy Lillian, the Albino girl, or Mirzah, the snake charmer, in the ante-room of the *Freres* Ringling's entertainment, on its annual visit to Madison Square Garden."[42] In other words, he considered her a freak.

These overwrought descriptions had an effect on readers, although perhaps not always the intended one. Gallico's descriptions of Babe Didrikson as "hirsute" sent an eleven-year-old future golfer named Betty Hicks scurrying to a dictionary. From the definition in *Webster's* she constructed an image of Babe as "a totally furry creature." When she met her idol seven years later, she realized that Babe was no more hirsute than any other woman athlete, and never had been.[43]

Not all the unflattering publicity that Didrikson received was the result of sexist sportswriters. In those early years she truly did not care about female adornments like lipstick, fashion, and makeup; her hair looked like it had been butchered by a barber back home. An unsuspecting reporter once tried to pin her down on her shopping habits. "Well, Miss Didrikson, do you select your other apparel with any special care? I mean do you—er—find that binding garments—er—what I mean is . . . ." "Are you trying to ask me if I wear girdles, brassieres and the rest of that junk?" "Y-y-yes," sputtered the reporter in obvious relief. "The answer is no. What do you think I am, a sissy?" That, of course, is a revealing comment about her attitudes toward other women, and also because the word "sissy" had connotations of effeminate men. She would have nothing to do with either.[44]

Some of the transformation that Babe Didrikson went through in her twenties and thirties was in fact physical. She was not a stringbean when she competed in the 1932 Olympics, but she had hardly filled out. Photographs of a more mature Mrs. Zaharias show a striking contrast: bigger hips, a full bosom ("God*damn* these things! They sure do get in the way," she once supposedly quipped while bowling), her large frame now carrying upwards of 150 to 160 pounds, thirty pounds more than her Olympic weight. This weight gain and its redistribution were probably attributable not just to age, but to a better (and more plentiful) diet and perhaps a somewhat higher level of body fat due to a change in her training habits. (A tendency to belt down beer later in life no doubt also added a few pounds.) That she remained a superb athlete despite these dramatic changes in her physique belies the current preoccupation that there is only one kind of body for a female athlete: thin and muscular. Back in the 1930s, women athletes did not necessarily look anorexic.[45]

The transformation also included much more attention to feminine charm than Didrikson had previously manifested, the prize-winning dress at the Texas state fair notwithstanding. She let her hair grow, and had it styled and waved. Upgrading her wardrobe proved an even more dependable way of showing off her new respectability. On the golf course she dressed in skirts, and rarely wore slacks. Even after many women golfers switched to Bermuda shorts, she stuck with skirts. One exception was her win at the 1947 British Women's Amateur, where it was so cold that she resorted to a pair of borrowed slacks to keep warm.

This metamorphosis even extended to the infamous women's undergarments that just years earlier she had labeled as "sissy." Once more Paul Gallico was on the scene to record the shift: "She was older, less hoydenish, and her hair had a wave in it. We sat on a bench together to talk, and shyly, with infinite femininity she confessed, 'I got 'em,' and lifted the edge of her tweed golf skirt to disclose the silk-and-lace undergarment beneath. Then she opened her handbag and let me peer in at the usual female equipment of lipstick and compact, eye shadow and lace handkerchief. She had gone all the way and was delighted with it." A revealing choice of words: now Babe Didrikson was a woman in every sense of the word.[46]

Babe did not manage this feminization all by herself, a task fellow golfer Betty Hicks described not terribly kindly as "comparable to carving a new face on Mt. Rushmore." Her transformation was as much about class as gender: for the first time she had to learn the ways of middle-class America. She had help from a well-off Fort Worth couple named R. L. and Bertha Bowen, who had taken her under their wing when she was trying to break into golf in her home state. The childless Bowens accepted the twenty-four-year-old Babe as almost a surrogate daughter. Bertha Bowen helped her to shed her working-class mannerisms and learn how to present herself as a lady. One thing she could not get Babe to do, however, was wear a girdle, as the Texas Women's Golf Association leadership had pointedly suggested. Recalled Bertha, "We finally decided maybe Babe *should* try a girdle so she put one on and went out to play golf one day. I recall her return to our house. The car came screeching to a stop in the driveway. Babe came tearing into the house and she was shouting, 'Goddamn, I'm *chokin'* to death!' She took it off, and she never wore a girdle again, so far as I know."[47]

How complicit was Babe Didrikson in this makeover? She always had her eye on the prize, and seems to have realized that certain changes would be necessary if she were to become the national sports figure she aspired to be. Perhaps she really was ready to outgrow her tomboyish ways and the brashness of youth, but it must have been a painful process to change her persona so dramatically and suppress key elements of her style and personality—in effect becoming someone else in order to succeed. (None of the other characters in this book had to remake themselves anywhere nearly as drastically. It helped that they were already middle-class and not trying to make it in a field like sports, which was so skittish about women's athletic prowess.) On the other hand, elements of the old Babe, such as her Texas brashness and unbridled competitiveness, never disappeared—they were just repackaged.

The final element of her transformation was her 1938 marriage. Without at all suggesting that she married George Zaharias for anything other than love, he came along at a fortuitous time. As Susan Cayleff noted, his "exaggerated manliness" was a perfect contrast to her "attempted womanliness." Unlike most professional women, she was glad to take his name: "I've always competed as Mrs. Zaharias, not Babe Didrikson. George and I are a team."[48] Perhaps changing her name was yet another way of distancing herself from a past that was hampering her career. After all, the name Babe Didrikson carried a lot of baggage. Now she could start anew.

Yet even at the height of her golf career in the late 1940s and early 1950s, she found herself subjected to the same kind of attention to her appearance and personal life that had characterized press coverage of her in the 1930s. The main difference was the new emphasis on how far she had come. Mentioning her former tomboy appearance, George Farmer typically reassured *Life* readers in 1947 that all that had changed now: "Today Mildred Zaharias likes to perch a silly hat on her head, dress up in nylon stockings she once scorned, patronize the hairdresser and wear satins."[49]

By so deliberately and vigorously promoting her new public persona, Babe Didrikson Zaharias in certain ways invited this attention to her womanly attributes. But like an actress, this was the role she played in public, for her public. The real Babe Didrikson, who had in fact not changed so much from her early days and lived anything but a conventional heterosexual life, was carefully hidden from public scrutiny. So successful was she in creating this new image that when she died, almost every obituary referred to her transformation from tomboy to lady, at times even presenting that as the most important accomplishment of her life. A lost moment indeed for the history of women in sports when a superb athlete is memorialized for her femininity rather than her amazing demonstration of what the female body is capable of.[50]

🦌

SPORTSWRITER HERB GRASSIS offered this assessment of Babe Didrikson Zaharias's impact on the development of women's golf:

"Before Babe it was a game for girls . . . after Babe it was a business." "I was the first woman to play the game the way men play it," she noted with her usual lack of modesty, "I mean to hit the ball instead of swinging at it." Bob Hope, with whom she was often paired during celebrity golf exhibitions, captured it best with this quip, "There's only one thing wrong about Babe and myself. I hit the ball like a girl and she hits it like a man."[51]

Having regained her amateur status, Babe Didrikson Zaharias ran up an amazing string of fourteen straight tournament victories in 1946 and 1947, a record never matched by any other golfer. (In her myth-making she claimed it was seventeen straight, conveniently erasing from the record a minor tournament where she lost in an early round.) By far the most important was her 1947 victory at the British Women's Amateur Tournament, the first American woman to win the title. Her husband had pushed her to enter, realizing that male golfers like Bobby Jones, Sam Snead, Gene Sarazen, and Ben Hogan had dramatically enhanced their reputations by beating opponents on both sides of the Atlantic. Now she would do the same as a woman.

The effects of the recent war were very much in evidence when Babe Didrikson Zaharias arrived in England in the summer of 1947, traveling alone since George could not get away. Food rationing was still in effect, and the trains were woefully overcrowded—she had to stand most of the way to Scotland, where the tournament was being held at Gullane, outside Edinburgh. Once she arrived, she realized she had not packed enough warm clothes for the rigors of a Scottish "summer" on a seaside course. Clothes were still rationed, so she could not easily buy replacements. She mentioned her predicament to the press, and soon offers of clothing (which she dubbed "Bundles for Babe," a take-off on the "Bundles for Britain" Americans had contributed during the war) began arriving. Especially welcome was a pair of warm slacks, which she wore almost every day, despite her usual inclination to appear in public only in skirts or dresses. These "lucky pants" became part of the tournament mythology.

The British galleries, used to golfers who seriously, and humorlessly, went about their business, had never seen anything like the wisecracking, free-spirited American. She saw no reason to change the behavior that worked so well back home, and took it as something of a challenge to warm up the stodgy British crowds. She did, and then some, mainly by her powerful game of golf. When she won the tournament, she was photographed doing a Highland fling. Her victory was such big news back in the States that when she returned on the *Queen Elizabeth* she was greeted in New York harbor by a flotilla of seventy-one journalists, photographers, and newsreel reporters, plus George, all three hundred plus pounds of him, waving to her happily from the tender.

Zaharias received so much publicity from this victory, and so many offers for endorsements and exhibitions, that she gave up her amateur status to turn professional once and for all. George could have continued to pay her expenses on the tour, "but sometimes offers get so big you feel you just have to take them." One such offer, which later fell through, was a $300,000 movie deal to do a series of short golf features. There were plenty of others to make it worth her while: a contract with Wilson Sporting Goods that guaranteed her $8,000 a year, a clothing line and her own brand of golf shoes and equipment, a contract for a book on championship golf, and numerous exhibitions at $600 a shot. Her income in 1947-1948 was more than $100,000, the same as baseball star Ted Williams.[52]

The money was good, but once again Babe missed the competition. Not only would tournaments provide that, but they also would generate more publicity, which would lead to more endorsements and business opportunities. In 1948 Babe Didrikson Zaharias joined Patty Berg, Helen Dettweiler, Betty Jameson, Betty Hicks, and Bea Gottlieb to organize the Ladies Professional Golf Association (LPGA), with sports promoter Fred Corcoran as tour director. Noted Corcoran drily, "The announcement that we had formed the Ladies PGA touched off a national storm of indifference." They would have preferred to call it the Women's Professional Golf Association, but an earlier attempt to set up a pro tour had incorporated under that name in 1944 and promptly gone nowhere. (One founding member despised having the word "ladies" in the name: "It sounds like the stuff that comes out of the insides of the lobster.") The Wilson Sporting Goods Company put up $15,000 in prize money. Babe was consistently the top money winner on the tour, but the purses were so small (she made only $3,400 in a representative year like 1948) that it was impossible for any woman golfer to live off prize winnings alone. No wonder she and George were always hustling endorsements, exhibitions, and other schemes to bring in cash.[53]

There was never any doubt that the main draw for the tour was Babe herself. "How am I doin'?" she would ask the crowd, knowing they would immediately roar back their approval. Noted one sports columnist, "She will outdraw the big majority of our male heroes and pull a gallery of twenty-five hundred any old time. . . . Babe is the first woman golfer to pay attention to showmanship. She will josh her rivals and kid with the gallery—and how spectators love that sort of thing." Fred Corcoran, who represented Ted Williams, Stan Musial, Sam Snead, and other male athletes, noted, "when it came to getting headlines, Babe had them all beat. She had a fantastic feel for publicity." Far more comfortable now in public with her new persona than in the 1930s, she in turn called the press and photographers "about the best friends I've got." After all, they were just doing their job, which was to cover her.[54]

At the heart of her appeal was her bond with her fans. As she told a *Time* interviewer in 1951, "The only time the gallery will ever bother me is when it doesn't show up."[55] Babe had a stock of one-liners, which judging from their reappearances in stories and books about her life, she must have used fairly regularly. By far the most famous was variations on, "When I wanta really bust one, I just loosen my girdle and let 'er fly." (Of course, per Bertha

Bowen, there never was a girdle to loosen in the first place.)
When she was subjected to an overly long introduction, she
would mug and say, "Can we play now?" After a bad shot, "Man!
All that work and the baby's dead!" Or if a string of shots were
hooked or sliced, "Well, there must be a bottle of Scotch over
there in those bushes."[56]

Zaharias matched her quips with a powerful golf game that
had never been seen before on the women's tour. She was such a
natural athlete, and so powerful, that for most of her career she
could dominate the field with 250-yard or longer tee shots
despite her imperfect form. Gene Sarazen, who toured with her in
the 1930s and 1940s, noted, "She was too much show business to
ever develop a really sweet swing. She wanted to wallop the ball
because that pleased the public." Golfer Betsy Rawls made a similar point:

> She was the most physically talented woman I have ever seen and
> if she had started golf at an earlier age she would have been sen-
> sational. But she never developed to her full potential. . . . She
> was so strong that she didn't have to develop her swing and there
> were flaws in it. She had moments of greatness when she put it
> all together, but she had trouble being consistent because of her
> faulty swing. She was often in trouble but she was a great scram-
> bler.

Hers was the kind of golf game that was hard to teach or imitate,
as Peggy Kirk Bell pointed out: "She played the game by feel and
strength. She was a natural and she couldn't pass that on."[57]

Was Babe Didrikson Zaharias good enough to beat the top
male golfers? Probably not. She accepted that most women did
not have the strength or the stamina to beat men, except rarely.
On the other hand, she enjoyed playing in an occasional men's
tournament, as the 1938 pairing with George Zaharias at the Los
Angeles Open suggests. (She played from the men's tees in those
tournaments.) In 1947 she told a *Saturday Evening Post* reporter
that she wasn't scared of any man player, including the legendary

On the set of Pat and Mike *(1952), it's Babe who is dressed in a skirt and sweater set, while Hepburn plays in pants. There are many parallels between the Didrikson-Zaharias marriage and the relationship portrayed in the film between sports star Hepburn and her manager/promoter, Spencer Tracy. (UPI/Corbis-Bettman)*

Ben Hogan. "I'd probably get beat, but a lot of halves would drop into my lap and maybe I'd win a couple of holes. I wouldn't disgrace myself." Note the qualifier—"probably" get beat.[58]

Babe's powerful swing as well as her knack for repartee with the galleries are on display in the 1952 Katharine Hepburn movie *Pat and Mike*, where she and other golfers and tennis players played themselves. One suspects that Zaharias didn't have much trouble with that. The plot of an all-around female sports star and her male promoter, who becomes her romantic interest, has intriguing parallels to the Didrikson-Zaharias marriage. In one scene from the movie, Spencer Tracy asks Hepburn what sports she can play in addition to golf. Tennis, she replies, and shooting (skeet, range, and archery), ice hockey, basketball, and a little baseball. What about boxing, he asks facetiously. Only sixteen-ounce gloves, she replies, before he cuts her off with "That's all, honey, say no more." Babe Didrikson played all of those sports, too, including boxing, to which she could add football, swimming, diving, pool, billiards, track and field, and more. Babe's performances in twelve sports were captured on film in 1932 by Grantland Rice's Sportlight film company.[59]

The original *Pat and Mike* script called for the Hepburn character to beat Zaharias on the eighteenth hole, but the golfer vetoed that as the price of her appearing: even on screen, Babe could not bear to lose. In the film, the golfer, identified as Mrs. Zaharias or simply Babe (as in, "The Babe is on the green") mugs for her large gallery, including dropping to her knees and kissing the ball when she sinks a shot. When she wins, she is swarmed by fans and reporters alike and swept off the course. Even though Zaharias was reputed to admire Hepburn, working with her on the set caused her to remark, "Kate's double-parked with herself." When *African Queen* co-star Humphrey Bogart dropped by while they were shooting, Hepburn shouted, "Look who's here. Bogie! Bogie!" Deadpanned Didrikson, not in the least impressed, "Lady, never say that word on a golf course." Hepburn in turn said of Babe, as overheard by fellow golfer Betty Hicks: "She's rawther outspoken, isn't she?" Many golfers shared that assessment.[60]

With her attitude of "Where I go, the galleries will go, let the rest starve," Babe was not exactly a popular figure in the clubhouse. As fellow golfer Betty Dodd recalled, "I wouldn't say that Babe had a lot of friends. She was not a terribly popular person with her peers." She once lectured her fellow golfers with stunning insensitivity:

> Let me tell you girls something: you know when there's a star, like in show business, the star has her name in lights on the marquee? Right? And the star gets the money because the people come to see the star, right? Well, *I'm* the star and all of you are in the chorus. *I* get the money and if it weren't for me, half of our tournaments wouldn't even be.

The other golfers resented that attitude, especially the appearance money she could command and they could not. Perhaps surprisingly for someone with the biggest income on the tour, she was also a notorious freeloader, always hustling free meals, free accommodations, even on one occasion a Rolex watch. Betsy Rawls noted acidly, "She was rather a crude person. She added a lot of color to the tour at a time when it was needed, but she did not add any dignity to the game."[61]

Yet most of the women golfers realized the tradeoff: without Babe, there might not even *be* a women's professional tour. "You girls want to play golf," she would taunt them, "or you want to go home and work as a secretary?" Patty Berg pinpointed what she meant to the women's game: "Babe changed the game of golf for women—not only bringing along the LPGA, but by her kind of golf. She came along with that great power game and it led to lower scores and more excitement. . . . Our sport grew because of Babe, because she had so much flair and color. Her tremendous enthusiasm for golf and life was contagious—even the galleries felt good when Babe was around."[62]

The media dubbed Babe Didrikson Zaharias "Mrs. Golf," and her now giant husband often followed along on her rounds, entertaining the crowd by blowing smoke rings from his cigar to test the wind direction, or giving her a big hug if she made a tough shot. But it was pretty clear to everyone on the tour that by the late 1940s this marriage was mainly for publicity purposes. At that time divorce (except for Hollywood stars and certain anthropologists) was still taboo for a public figure, and she and George knew how to play their roles in public. What happened in private, however, was another matter.

Didrikson and Zaharias had always been a peripatetic couple, constantly on the move because of their separate careers. They had fundamentally different temperaments: she wanted to spend as much time at home as her career allowed, while he always had to be on the go. "Babe traveled because of her profession, George went because of a compulsion," noted two sportswriters. In a quote that rings true even if it sounds manufactured to fit her new domestic image, Didrikson noted that "housework has always been a treat to me": "I've spent so much of my life away on the road that when I get home I'm just aching to put my hands in the dishwasher and make up the beds, and vacuum the carpets." During their married life, they rented or owned homes in several cities, including Denver, Chicago, and Los Angeles. Not until 1955 did she and George finally realize her dream (not his) to build a home of their own on the grounds of a Tampa golf course.[63]

In her autobiography Babe paid credit to her husband's role in her career: "George has done so much to boost my career along. He's been a good judge of what things would help to build up my reputation and what things wouldn't. I lean a lot on his advice." But too often he pushed her to do too much, giving in to the temptation to schedule one more exhibition or yet another appearance at a pro shop. During one month in the 1947–1948 season she spent seventeen nights on an airplane, and this grueling schedule took its toll on her game and eventually on their marriage.[64]

Betty Hicks once described George as "a grunting grizzly bear of a man, with a deep vein of tenderness permitted to surface only if it did not interfere with a business objective." When George gave up his wrestling career to manage Babe's, he missed the limelight and the recognition. After Fred Corcoran took over much of the management of Babe's career with the establishment of the LPGA, George had even less to do. Meanwhile the once attractive wrestler ballooned up to almost four hundred pounds: in Babe's memorable quip, "When I married him, he was a Greek god, now he's nothing but a goddam Greek." Increasingly in his wife's shadow, the man who had been "once her greatest backer had become her greatest liability."[65]

Perhaps their marriage might have held together if they had children: after all, she was in her twenties when they married and was still only thirty-six in 1947 when she won the British Women's Amateur Tournament. It is hard to know whether Babe Didrikson wanted children or not. When she was asked by reporters back in 1932 about having children, she replied, "Every normal woman looks forward to having children, and I don't think I am much different from most women. At least I know I like children, and expect to have some of my own." After her marriage she had at least one miscarriage: in her lingo, all her babies had been "swimmers." Golfer Peggy Kirk Bell remembers her saying, "I'd give up every trophy I ever won if I could have a baby," but Betty Dodd, who knew her much better, recalled, "She never did say she wished she had a child. . . . It didn't sound to me like she was very upset about it. Ever." While some women on the pro tour had children, women golfers found it even more difficult to combine marriage and career than other professional women because of the extent of travel involved. More than one golfer was known to sigh that what she really needed on the tour was a wife.[66]

Probably the biggest indication that there was something wrong with the Didrikson-Zaharias marriage was the appearance of Betty Dodd on the scene in 1950. Dodd was a nineteen-year-old amateur golfer from Texas when Didrikson took her under her wing. Right away this friendship stood out, because Babe was never known for being friendly toward other women golfers. Soon Dodd was traveling with Didrikson on the tour, and she lived with her and George the rest of the time. "She's like a daughter to me" was how Babe explained Betty in her 1955 autobiography, "my pal and protege, I guess, the best friend I've got." George and Betty did not like each other, but they maintained an uneasy truce.[67]

The closeness of their bond, and its obviousness to other women on the tour, inevitably raised rumors of lesbianism. This topic was not something spoken of publicly in the 1950s, and certainly not in an image-conscious sport like golf. (For years women's professional golf has had a large following among lesbians, and a fair number of closeted players, but only in 1996 did a minor LPGA player finally come out.) When biographer Susan Cayleff interviewed Betty Dodd in 1987, Dodd was forthcoming about her deep love for the woman who had been her mentor, coach, and closest friend, but she declined to publicly frame the relationship in terms of lesbianism. In the 1950s love between women was suspect, something to be denied or left unnamed. Despite the silence of both partners, it is clear that at the end of her life, Babe Didrikson Zaharias's primary emotional commitment was to Dodd, not her husband.[68]

Babe was forty when she met Betty Dodd, and still very much at the top of her game. But her game changed as she got older, as she realized "that the time was coming for me to change over from a bashing type of game to a smoother type of game. When you begin to lose some of your power, then you have to develop more finesse. You have to change your style a little." She also faced much more competition from her peers, who were learning to hit the long ball that had been her distinctive trademark. In 1947 she told sportswriter Pete Martin, "I used to outdrive the other girls from twenty to forty yards, but I'm not far ahead of them any more. I know at least fifty or sixty girls who can outdrive eighty per cent of the men."[69]

Perhaps because her athletic career had been remarkably injury-free, Didrikson seemed to think her body was invincible, a trait fairly common among athletes. She was so reluctant to seek medical attention that she played throughout most of the 1952 season with pain from what was diagnosed as a strangulated femoral hernia. Her doctor told her, "If I'd let it go another week I might have been a goner." She returned to the tour, but still found herself dragging. Finally when she was scheduled to play in a tournament in her hometown of Beaumont in April of 1953, she consulted her personal physician, who confirmed her worst fears: She had cancer of the colon and rectum, and would need to have a colostomy. She could have had the surgery anywhere in the country, but showing how important her Texas roots were, she chose the local Beaumont hospital. Betty Dodd was constantly at her side, for long stretches sleeping on a cot in her hospital room; George basically fell apart. What Betty and George knew, and what Babe did not, was that the surgery had not been totally successful and that the cancer would likely return. Cruel as this seems, not informing the patient was fairly common medical practice in the 1950s.[70]

While Didrikson insisted that cancer was a game that needed to be won like any other, many reporters, and a few of her sponsors, believed that her career was over. Her surgery, which involved the rearrangement of her intestinal track to evacuate waste into a pouch outside her body wall, was a difficult adjustment for any cancer survivor, but especially so for an athlete in a sport where a powerful swing, superb physical condition, and timing were central to the game. Amazingly, she returned to golf just fourteen weeks after major surgery, although she was too weak and off her game to be a contender at that point.

The cancer diagnosis cemented the already strong bond between Betty Dodd and Babe Didrikson. Dodd was constantly at her side, helping her with the painful task of irrigating the colostomy and other intimate details of her recovery. When Babe began to play in tournaments again, she asked to be paired with Dodd in case anything went wrong during the round. A talented golfer herself, Dodd voluntarily subsumed her career to Babe's: "I had such admiration for this fabulous person. I never wanted to be away from her even when she was dying of cancer. I loved her. I would have done anything for her." [71]

A very uneasy trio: Betty Dodd, George Zaharias, and a cancer-striken Babe Didrikson Zaharias in a Galveston hospital in 1956. Dodd was with her almost until the end but, at Babe's request, did not attend the funeral. (Mary and John Gray Library, Special Collections, Lamar University, Beaumont, Texas)

But it wasn't all grim—they had lots of good times together. A fellow golfer once described Babe as "a great big overgrown kid who loved living" and Betty Dodd played up to this side of her: "She wanted someone to talk with her all the time, she wanted somebody to travel with her, she wanted somebody to go here, to go there, she wanted a playmate and a friend." In a telling comment about how George no longer occupied the emotional center of her life, Dodd added, "We always had a lot more fun when he wasn't around."[72]

Babe Didrikson had been pulling out her harmonica as far back as the 1932 Olympics, and Betty Dodd now joined her on guitar to make quite a musical team. Their impromptu locker room performances were among the few times that Babe interacted with her fellow players on the tour. At one point Babe borrowed some recording equipment, and she and Betty cut a demo record for Mercury. They even made a joint musical appearance on the *Ed Sullivan Show* in 1953 to benefit the American Cancer Society. The music was sort of a sidelight, because the act was mainly designed to show the public that Babe was doing fine.

Still the hustler at heart, she wangled a $1,500 appearance fee for herself and $350 for Dodd.

Everything clicked in 1954, when Zaharias won five tournaments. Probably the most emotional was the Serbin Women's Open in February 1954, the first tournament she won after her cancer operation. Just as impressive was her twelve-stroke victory in the National Women's Open in July. She was now playing not just as (in her estimation) the world's greatest female athlete but also as a cancer survivor, which is why she did not retire: "Every time I get out and play well in a golf tournament, it seems to buck up people with the same cancer trouble I had." She often visited cancer wards in cities where she was playing tournaments, offering her own special brand of heroism and courage. She even visited the White House in 1954 to raise cancer awareness. President Dwight Eisenhower was an avid golfer, and a fan of hers. Unfortunately they never got a chance to play golf together.[73]

The combination of her battle against cancer and her remarkable golf comeback made Babe Didrikson front-page news once again. The *New York Times*, which had given her very little coverage since the 1932 Olympics, now extensively covered her tournaments and charitable activities; later they would chronicle her final illness and the national response in similar detail. Coverage in the *New York Times* and magazines like *Time* and *Newsweek* brought Babe Didrikson Zaharias to a whole new national audience, an audience that had long forgotten the 1932 Olympics and did not necessarily follow golf, but that responded to this inspiring story of an athlete fighting for her life and her playing career. George Zaharias was still prominently featured, even though by now their marriage was pretty much a sham; Betty Dodd was rarely mentioned, or if so, referred to as a buddy or close friend.

During the spring of 1955 Babe worked with sports journalist Harry Paxton to write an autobiography, which appeared in five installments in the *Saturday Evening Post* and was published later that year under the title of *This Life I've Led*. As is true with many celebrity autobiographies, this one mainly retold old stories and presented as fact many of the embellishments that had crept into her record over the years. As is especially true with sports biographies, it included highly detailed (and tedious) descriptions of one round of golf after another, complete with scores, best shots, and opponents' gaffes. Evidence of Babe's uncouth behavior, disdain toward other golfers, and facets of her personality judged out of tune with her public persona were carefully excised. Although hardly a best-seller, the strategy worked. The *New York Times* review commented, "Probably many thought of her as a body without substance, a muscle moll whose personality was measured by her sinews. From her autobiography, however, Babe Didrikson Zaharias emerges as a warm, vibrant and delightful woman. . . . Thus does the real Babe shine through."[74]

Just as she and Paxton were finishing the text, she learned that her cancer had recurred, which she described in the frank discussion of her battle with the disease that informs the book. She still felt she could lick it, and defiantly ended the book with "My autobiography isn't finished yet."[75] But this time there would be no comebacks, no triumphant twelve-stroke wins. Perhaps because of her determination not to give in to the disease and her superb physical condition, she had a long, terrible, slow death, finally succumbing on September 27, 1956, at a Galveston, Texas, hospital.

The next day a somber President Eisenhower opened his press conference by saying, "Ladies and gentlemen, I should like to take one moment to pay a tribute to Mrs. Zaharias, Babe Didrikson. She was a woman who in her athletic career certainly won the admiration of every person in the United States, all sports people over the world. I think that every one of us feels sad that finally she had to lose this last one of all her battles." Eisenhower's tribute was a fitting national valedictory for an athlete who, as the *Times* editorialized, "finally lost the big one."[76]

ॐ

BABE DIDRIKSON ZAHARIAS was only forty-five years old when she died, although many obituaries erroneously accepted 1914 as her birth date and reported her as forty-two. It was still too young. Didrikson's early death robbed us of several more decades of what was bound to be an interesting life. Who knows how long she would have continued to play on the women's tour? Perhaps this was the cancer speaking, but in her autobiography she admitted to being a bit tired of it all: "And I've been putting my golf shoes on and taking them off for a long time. You can get a little tired of that. At times I feel I'd rather just ride around a course in my electric cart, or sit on the clubhouse porch, and let the rest of the girls fight it out." On the other hand, it is hard to imagine this highly competitive athlete idly sitting by in the clubhouse while (to her mind) inferior competitors battled it out without her. She had always been the star, not the chorus, and she would certainly have missed the attention.[77]

If she had been serious about retiring, she probably would have become a club professional and supplemented her income (and more importantly, her ego) by continuing to give exhibitions. Whether she would have stayed married to George Zaharias once she was out of the national limelight is debatable, since she had discussed the possibility of divorce with friends on several occasions before she became ill.

But it is equally unlikely that she would have come out as a lesbian, becoming a role model for gay women in sports thirty years before Martina Navratilova took on that mantle. Didrikson's early death, and the fact that she never talked openly about her sexual orientation, makes it difficult to determine whether she was lesbian or bisexual. In addition, like most golfers then and now, she and Betty Dodd did not see themselves as crusaders for a cause. So successful was her presentation of herself as a conventional heterosexual woman that Babe Didrikson Zaharias is remembered as George's wife, and Betty Dodd practically disappears (or is erased) from the story. When Susan Clark and Alex

Karras played Babe and George in a 1975 television movie, the plot revolved around a conventional heterosexual sports/love story. Betty Dodd, who lived until 1993, was not mentioned.[78]

If Babe Didrikson did not miss the crowds and the galleries too much, she could have sunk into the domesticity that she claimed she loved so well, puttering around the house and at last staying in one place for more than a few days at a time. The golfer actually seems a more likely candidate for the 1950s "feminine mystique" than a convert to feminism when it reemerged in the 1960s or 1970s. She had never had anything to say one way or the other about feminism or women's rights—women's issues, indeed women, did not really concern her, just herself. Sexism in sports, however, could have engaged her attention. In 1970 Billie Jean King was successfully waging battles for better treatment and more opportunities for women in sports. Were she alive (and she would have been only fifty-nine in 1970), Babe Didrikson certainly would have applauded such efforts.

Babe Didrikson Zaharias was a model and forerunner for much of what women are trying to accomplish today in sports: the right to compete; the opportunity to make a living comparable to that available to professional male athletes; the desire to be taken seriously as athletes, and not be judged by stereotypes of gender or sexual orientation; the satisfaction of a powerful, disciplined athletic body; the belief that women playing women's sports are exciting and entertaining to watch for both sexes. Babe Didrikson may have been only out for herself, but as one of the century's most gifted athletes she functioned as an undisputed role model for young girls, and no doubt more than a few young boys. Now long grown up, her former fans still remember the magic of Babe Didrikson Zaharias's heroic and inspiring life.

In a 1934 *Literary Digest* article titled, "Shall the Ladies Join Us?" writer Fred Wittner talked with mock (or perhaps not so mock) alarm about the rise of women in sports: "Go ahead," men have grudgingly condescended, "smoke our cigarettes, share our suffrage, work our jobs, but show us any of you who can play golf like Bobby Jones, or smack a tennis ball like Bill Tilden, or swim as fast as Johnny Weissmuller. That'll hold you for a while." But, he realized with a sinking feeling, the ladies wouldn't be held— they were proving themselves in the athletic realm, and by extension challenging men, just as they were in politics, work, and social life.[79]

Babe Didrikson Zaharias rarely competed head to head with men, but she was such a superb athlete that she made theories about women's physical inferiority seem outdated, if not downright silly. If anyone could overtake the men, it would be her. Women all across America took pride in her accomplishments, whose implications stretched far beyond the confines of sports. Babe Didrikson's example conveyed to them and the world at large "a dream of prowess and success, of being able to beat the men at their own games."[80]

S I X

FRONT AND CENTER:
MARTHA GRAHAM

*T*HE ALL-ENCOMPASSING phrase, "I am a dancer," sums up Martha Graham's attitude toward life. "People have asked me why I chose to be a dancer. I did not choose to be a dancer. I was chosen to be a dancer, and with that you live all your life." Graham's artistic career spanned seven decades, from the 1920s to the 1990s; so prodigious was her output (she choreographed 180 dances in all, most of them for herself) and so great was her impact on the emergence of modern dance that a critic once exclaimed, "Graham is to modern dance what Queen Victoria was to the royalty of Europe: Everybody's Grandma." Never caring much about money or worldly goods, she was intensely passionate about her work. And she knew exactly where she wanted to be: "A long time ago, I decided that my place was front and center. That's where I chose to be, and that is where I remain," a remarkable and yet entirely accurate statement from a woman then in her ninety-fifth year.[1]

Graham once described her dances as "a kind of fever chart, a graph of the heart." Pioneer dance critic John Martin, who did so much to put modern dance—and Martha Graham—on the artistic map, noted as early as 1929, "She does the unthinkable thing for a dancer to do—she makes you think." A voracious reader and consumer of all aspects of modernist culture, she brought that twentieth-century mentality to her work: "Life today is nervous, sharp, and zigzag. It often stops in mid-air. That is what I aim for in my dances." Baseball commissioner Branch Rickey had a different take: "Martha, the thing I like best in your dancing is that every time you put your arm up, the ball seems to go straight into your hand." Like all-around athlete Babe Didrikson, Martha Graham's favorite role was "the one I am dancing now."[2]

One of the most distinctive aspects of modern dance was the large, indeed central role that women played in its emergence, with Martha Graham head and shoulders (or pelvis and torso, given her technique) above the rest. No other field of art has been so affected by women and their sensibilities. Not coincidentally, the development of modern dance occurred alongside the emergence of modern feminism. A key part of this new freedom was physical: women dancers, braless, corsetless, and with bare feet instead of toe shoes, glorified in the physicality of their unbound bodies. Like women's sports, modern dance celebrated the possibilities of the female body.

Martha Graham choreographed from a woman's point of view, and even if she did not consciously identify with women's rights, her heroines embodied the same ideals of self-reliance, individualism, equality, and strength that are the essence of modern feminism. Graham's characters were never helpless—when a Graham heroine fell, there was no man to catch her. "Modern dance isn't anything except one thing in my mind," she stated forthrightly: "the freedom of women in America—whether it is Isadora Duncan or Ruth St. Denis or Clara Barton. It comes in as a moment of emancipation. . . . Modern dance is the moment when an emergence took place from behind the bustle."[3]

Martha Graham was a performer, onstage and off. People from all walks of life called her the most extraordinary woman they had ever met. So charismatic was her effect that she almost seemed to be the leader of a cult—"I thought I *was* Martha Graham," recalled dancer Paul Taylor, speaking for many others. Of course, any visionary iconoclast, and a woman at that, will have critics, and Martha Graham had more than her share. It was disquieting to have a woman running her own company, upsetting to many in the same way votes or careers for women jarred conventional norms. After Eleanor Roosevelt, Graham was one of the most caricatured public figures of the 1930s. In drama critic Stark Young's famous quip, "If Martha Graham ever gave birth, it would be to a cube." Early audiences, especially those outside New York, often failed to understand her intensely emotional and abstract dances. Others complained that they lacked beauty: "ugly girl makes ugly movements onstage while ugly mother tells ugly brother to make ugly sounds on drum," said ballet choreographer Michel Fokine, no friend to the modern dance sensibility. This bothered Graham not one whit. She aimed to shock and provoke—the only reaction she could not abide was indifference.[4]

Over the years of her remarkably long and productive career, Martha Graham developed into an American institution on a par with Eleanor Roosevelt, Margaret Mead, and Katharine Hepburn. Said a novice critic in the 1960s, "Reviewing Martha Graham is rather like being called upon to review the Grand Canyon." Her dramatic personal presentation—jet black hair pulled back from her face, exaggerated makeup, strikingly unique jewelry and clothes—was instantly recognizable, almost a trademark. She pushed her body to perform well into her seventies, too long, said many critics, but she simply could not let go. She had created those dances for her body to perform, and the hardest act of her life was admitting, if never accepting, that her dancing days were over. Three angry words summed up her struggle: "I hate age!"[5]

❦

"MY CHILDHOOD YEARS were a balance of light and dark,"
Martha Graham wrote with characteristic flair. She was contrasting her early years in Allegheny, Pennsylvania, where she was
born on May 11, 1894, with Santa Barbara, California, where her
family moved in 1908. While she would call New York her home
from the 1920s on, relocating to California was key to her development as an artist and a dancer: "My people were strict reli-
gionists who felt that dancing was a sin. They frowned on all
worldly pleasures. . . . My upbringing led me to fear it myself."
But once her family moved to Santa Barbara, all that changed:
"No child can develop as a real Puritan in a semitropical climate.
California swung me in the direction of paganism, though years
were to pass before I was fully emancipated." Climatological
determinism aside, California was enormously important to the
history of dance in America. Soon Martha Graham's name would
be added to those of Isadora Duncan, Ruth St. Denis, Ted Shawn,
and others whose artistic development was nurtured by the fresh
California spirit of optimism and experimentation.[6]

Family was always central to Martha Graham's sense of identity. When she wrote her autobiography at the end of her life, she
chose the title *Blood Memory* to underscore her conviction that
history was conveyed through successive generations: "Each of us
from our mother and father has received their blood and through
their parents and their parents' and backward in time. We carry
thousands of years of that blood and its memory." In her case, her
ancestors stretched to the beginnings of the English settlement of
North America, most notably to Miles Standish. Critics would
often intuit glimmerings of this ancestral Puritanism in her
work, especially in her austere early pieces.[7]

Allegheny was a suburb of Pittsburgh, the thriving coal, steel,
and shipping center that also produced Mary Cassatt and
Gertrude Stein. Martha's father, George Greenfield Graham, was
a doctor who specialized in nervous diseases, a staff physician at

the Western Pennsylvania Hospital Insane Department until he entered private practice in 1893. That year the thirty-seven-year-old doctor married Jane Beers, who was fifteen years his junior. Together they had four children: Martha was the eldest, followed by Mary in 1896, Georgia in 1900, and William, in 1906.

Since both parents were from the Pittsburgh area, Martha's childhood was full of relatives, including a great-grandmother who became the model for the character of the Ancestress in Graham's *Letter to the World* (1940). Equally important to her upbringing was a young Irish girl named Lizzie Prendergast, who was so grateful to Dr. Graham for medical treatment he once rendered that she promised to come work for him if he ever married. She became practically a member of the family, and stayed with them in California until she died. She was both servant and honorary older sister to the eldest child Martha, who was especially intrigued by Lizzie's lush Catholic upbringing, a stark contrast to the sparse Presbyterianism that reigned in the Graham household. Her family was Martha's first audience: "I always loved an audience from the time I was born."[8]

When author Howard Gardner included Martha Graham in a larger study on creativity (the only woman and the only American so honored), he made an observation that applies to many of the characters in this book: "As befalls highly accomplished figures, and especially ones fated to live in the media-drenched twentieth century, the young Graham has come to be surrounded with a set of virtually mandatory anecdotes." Hence the oft-repeated story of the toddler Martha dancing down the aisle of church one Sunday service, an outburst that no doubt had more to do with rebellion against a boring sermon than any foreshadowing of her later artistic bent. Dancing, with the possible exception of formal ballroom dancing, was just not part of middle-class households like the Grahams' in the 1890s and 1900s.[9]

The death of the baby William at eighteen months from scarlet fever and sister Mary's worsening asthma were the precipitating causes for the family to relocate to Southern California in 1908, when Martha was fourteen years old. Dr. Graham chose the town of Santa Barbara, but did not officially give up his practice in Pennsylvania until 1912, instead visiting his family on regular extended visits over the next several years. Martha enrolled in the local high school, where she excelled in academics, especially literature, and basketball. Her father was a strong believer in higher education for women and hoped that his eldest daughter would attend Vassar College.

A concert Martha attended in 1911 changed all that. Santa Barbara was hardly a bastion of high culture, so Dr. Graham took his seventeen-year-old daughter several hours by train south to Los Angeles to attend a performance by Ruth St. Denis, a dancer who was drawn to the themes and mythic female figures of Orientalism and the Far East. One glimpse of St. Denis performing her interpretive dances and Martha reached what she later recalled as the turning point in her life: "Miss Ruth opened a door and I saw into a life."[10]

There were two obstacles. One was her age—seventeen was quite old for initial exposure to dance training. The second was her family—proper daughters from middle-class families just did not become dancers. Even though Ruth St. Denis presented her dance as an art form, dance troupes still had connotations of vaudeville and other forms of lower-class entertainment. The fact that dancers performed in public in costumes often scanty by the day's standards reinforced its risqué reputation.

Her dream temporarily on hold, Martha finished high school in Santa Barbara in June 1913, and instead of going east to Vassar, entered the Cumnock School in Los Angeles, a junior college that emphasized self-expression through the study of literature and the arts. In 1914 Dr. Graham died suddenly, leaving Mrs. Graham with three daughters to raise. Although Martha Graham later downplayed her father's resistance to her career choice, his death removed an obstacle in her following her muse. After com-

Martha Graham as a Denishawn dancer, here dancing the lead role in Xochitl *in June 1920. The costume is not especially revealing, but it does show her sturdy legs and very strong feet. (White Studios. Courtesy New York Public Library.)*

pleting three years at Cumnock, she enrolled for the summer dance course at Denishawn, the institute that Ruth St. Denis had opened the year before in Los Angeles with her fellow dancer and new husband, Ted Shawn.

Denishawn's style of dancing presented a stark contrast to the rigidity and formalism of ballet and the frivolity and superficiality of vaudeville. Danced barefoot, it emphasized freedom of movement and physical self-consciousness of the body. Its interpretive and expressive dances relied heavily on costuming, pageants, and tableaus to suggest lush eroticism and mystery. Alongside pioneer dance interpreters Loie Fuller and Isadora Duncan, Ruth St. Denis and Ted Shawn paved the way for modern dance performance to emerge as a serious art form separate from the theater.

When Martha enrolled for the summer course, she was already twenty-two years old, ancient for a dancer to begin serious training. Soon she was a full-time student and instructor. Other than her passionate conviction that she was fated to be a dancer, it is hard to imagine what kind of professional career she envisioned for herself. Ruth St. Denis was not overly impressed with her audition or her appearance (she was far from a traditional beauty, and at that point was inclined to be overweight), and consigned her to Shawn's tutelage. He, on the other hand, saw something, as did Denishawn's rehearsal pianist, Louis Horst. Horst would be Graham's biggest supporter, eventually joining her when she launched her solo career in New York in the 1920s. He also became her lover and lifelong friend, probably the only person other than her father who could bend her will to his own. Horst, however, steadfastly refused to divorce his wife, another Denishawn dancer, which made questions of marriage between the two moot.

Ruth St. Denis kept very tight reins over the whole Denishawn enterprise, and it became clear to Martha that she could stay on as a teacher, as a group performer, and as an occasional soloist on tour (like in *Xochitl*, which Ted Shawn created for her in 1920), but that her chances to develop a professional career as a lead dancer and choreographer were distinctly limited. Graham bided her time, but in 1923, after seven years at Denishawn, she left. "I'm going to the top. Nothing is going to stop me. And I shall do it alone."[11]

Graham later said of her years at Denishawn, "I soon realized that I had to find something to dance about. I could not just go around and be an attractive young girl on a stage in a sari. I did not set out to be a rebel—I liked comfort too much—but in a funny way you don't choose these things, they choose you, and then your life is increasingly not your own." Since she was not independently wealthy, she had to find a way to support herself and to help her widowed mother and sisters. Broadway, specifically a role in a show called the *Greenwich Village Follies*, offered her the chance to earn an excellent salary and strike off on her own. It also gave her the chance to relocate to New York, the center of all serious theater and arts in the United States. Louis Horst (still married, but living apart from his wife) soon followed.[12]

Although Graham rhapsodized about the freedoms of a semitropical climate, New York's edgy, urban atmosphere suited her mood even better. As dance historian Elizabeth Kendall observed, "it was tough, it was staccato, it was unashamedly intellectual . . . it was, in short, everything she had been educated for. Martha Graham felt the change like a primal shift in the weather." Unfortunately her roles in the Follies were not all that different from the Denishawn productions, and she quickly became frustrated. She wanted to be an artist, not just a performer. When in the fall of 1925 she was asked to join the faculty at the Eastman School of Music in Rochester to develop a dance department, she left Broadway for good. Traveling back and forth between Rochester and New York City, she began to choreograph dances for herself and a few of her more talented students. In 1926 she had enough new material to offer a recital, with Horst as her accompanist. Soon thereafter she made New York her permanent home.[13]

Like struggling artists before and since, Graham did not have enough money up front to book a hall, do publicity, and print programs before ticket sales brought in cash, that is, if tickets *did* sell. The first of many financial angels, Gotham Book Mart owner Frances Steloff, came to her rescue. Steloff's influential bookstore was a gathering place for 1920s writers and intellectuals, and Graham was a frequent browser when she was in the Follies. Even though Steloff had never seen Graham dance, the bookstore owner signed a loan for $1,000 to cover the costs of the recital. Luckily people came, and the concert paid for itself.

At the time of her New York debut, Martha Graham seemed like a fresh face on the artistic scene. In fact, she was already thirty-two years old. How long do you expect to keep this up, asked a somewhat dubious friend. "As long as I've got an audience."[14]

Graham started her own company because she saw no other way to implement the vision she was developing of what modern dance (not yet so named) could be. Ditto choreography: "The only reason I became a choreographer was so that I could have the parts I wanted." Her original company was all-female for a similar reason—she knew how to choreograph for women's bodies. Another consideration was that few men would have been available anyway, given the stigma of effeminacy (or worse, homosexuality) that often attached to male dancers in this predominantly female field.[15]

Between public recitals, Graham took major steps forward in technique and content. Her debut concert still had trappings of Denishawn exoticism (Graham later dismissed these early dances as "childish things, dreadful"), but these affectations were quickly replaced by the austere and stark pieces that she called her "period of long woolens." The lack of ornamentation on stage and the simple costumes she and her dancers wore were in part a reflection of her extremely precarious financial situation in those days. All costumes were sewn by her and her dancers from material rummaged from bargain lots from nearby Fourteenth Street and Union Square; the budget was one dollar a dress.[16]

Her costumes were austere out of thrift, but also because stretch fabrics worn over a leotard-like undergarment maximized attention to the body. Unlike ballet, which works mightily to conceal physical effort, Graham wanted to show the physicality and athleticism of modern dance movement, which in turn was a vehicle to reveal nothing less than the inner core of human existence. The purpose of the body, she pontificated, was "to objectify in physical forms my beliefs." Noted *New York Times* dance critic John Martin, "Her compositions are intensely personal, a projection into spectator consciousness of her inner processes. . . . Every work, therefore, is essentially a solo, even though there are twenty people on stage."[17]

Ballet choreographer George Balanchine once said, "If I were feeling suicidal I would never try to express this in a ballet. I would make as beautiful a variation as I could for a ballerina, and then—well, then I'd go and kill myself." Graham would, and did, put those feelings into her dance. For example, in *Lamentation* (1930), a solo set to the music of Zoltan Kodaly, Graham danced sitting down in a tube-like costume of purple stretch material that only showed her feet, face, and hands. "Martha Graham does not depict grief," one reviewer noted, "she *is* grief." A woman watching Graham perform this dance who had recently lost her son in an accident finally found herself able to grieve in response to its power.[18]

Graham's all-female company, and Graham herself, did little to play up female attractiveness when they performed; in her original studio there were no mirrors. "It's not my job to look beautiful. It's my job to look interesting. We are not here to please the audience." Recalled Jane Dudley, who danced with the company in those early years, "There were no 'pretty' bodies. We looked like a collection of modern sculpture." Unlike ballet, whose dancers all seem to be cut from the same cloth, "we were all so completely and totally different," recalled Ethel Butler. "There was a tremendous sense of the individual. Not only were we different physically, as far as the structure of the body was concerned, but as people." Detractors quickly labeled them "Graham Crackers."[19]

Many of the early Graham dancers were married, and it is hard to imagine a more long-suffering group than their husbands. The men once jokingly formed a club called "The Husbands of Martha Graham's Group" to draw attention to the missed meals, ruined plans, and otherwise generally upended lives that occurred because their wives were practically at the beck and call of Graham whenever she wanted to rehearse a new piece. One husband compared his wife to a fire fighter: "You know, the fire alarm rings and down you go." There was no democracy in this operation—what Martha wanted, Martha got, on her own terms. Said her friend (and rival) Agnes de Mille, "I think Martha was *the* most selfish person I ever knew."[20]

Ruthless too, as in, "One must be ruthless to teach." As Graham worked with her dancers, either in rehearsal or in classes, she could be a stern taskmaster. "Stop sweating!" she admonished a perspiring student. "It's pure indulgence." (This story is often told, but without the final detail: was the dancer in fact able to stop sweating?) Actor Richard Boone, who later found fame on *Have Gun Will Travel* and who credited the Graham technique with helping him simulate falling off a horse, recalled her impatience at those who could not keep up: "With Martha you get it right away or jump out the window." Dancer Sophie Maslow, recalling Graham's overpowering presence in the studio, took it one step further: "If she had said 'jump out the window' in the middle of a class, I would have done it."[21]

Graham did not merely intimidate her dancers, she inspired them. She held them spellbound with casual yet stunning aphorisms that seemed to escape spontaneously from her lips: "There

is only one law of posture I have been able to discover—the per-
pendicular line connecting heaven and earth." "My dancers fall
so they may rise." Or the often repeated, "movement never lies."
Bette Davis, who like Boone had taken classes at the Neighborhood Playhouse as part of her acting training, described Graham's impact in almost religious terms: "I worshipped her. She
was all tension—lightning. Her burning dedication gave her
spare body the power of ten men. . . . Miss Graham was the modern."[22]

One characteristic of Graham's early pieces was how her body
seemed almost "riveted to the floor yet straining against it."
Whereas much of ballet is airborne, it is hard to imagine Graham
leaping or being thrown through the air—jumping perhaps, but
not leaping. This embrace of the ground was one of her main
breakthroughs in technique. Another was her emphasis on the
principle of contraction and release. In its simplest form, breath-
ing is a form of contraction and release, but Graham's conception
was far more dramatic: not just a breath, but a gasp or sob, whose
sharp intake of air by the diaphragm was literally intended to be
seen by the audience in the last row of the theater. The release was
equally strong, violent, and visible.[23]

In these early pieces Graham specifically disavowed any political undercurrents: "I do not make social or political comments
in my dances. If I had something of great social importance to
say, I would say it from a lecture platform." And yet they were
intensely political as well as personal. *Revolt* (1927) was a statement against human injustice; *Heretic* (1929) explored questions
of deviance and the group; *Deep Song* (1937) was a response to the
Spanish Civil War. Other notable compositions from this period
include *Primitive Mysteries* (1931), which reflected the influence
of a trip Graham and Horst made to the Southwest, and *Frontier*
(1935), a six-and-a-half-minute solo that many consider her
finest piece. *Frontier* was also the first of her many collaborations
with the sculptor Isamu Noguchi, whose set evoked the openness

of the frontier by angling two ropes outward from a bench. *Time* magazine called the performance "high priestess Martha Graham and her surrealist fence act."[24]

As early as the 1920s, audiences and critics were responding not just to the dances, but to Martha Graham as a performer. Her superiority as a dancer was immediately apparent to audiences, as Roy Hargrave noted about a performance of *Primitive Mysteries*: "The difference lies simply in the fact that each member of the group seems to take the first step because it is timed to a beat, whereas Graham seems to step because the beat itself has forced her to move." A former dancer from her company described the incredible stage presence that she kept well into her seventies: "When she danced, she was no longer Martha Graham; she was the character. Whenever she was onstage, she was two hundred percent onstage." So intense was Graham's preparation that she once stated emphatically, "I cannot recreate any ancient character if I don't know what she had for breakfast."[25]

This totality of commitment earned her the nickname "the high priestess of modern dance," but she always tried to distance herself from any Graham cult:

> This I hate. This is something I don't understand. I've never been a priestess and I've never thought of myself as a priestess. I've thought of myself as a skilled woman, as a woman who has been loved. My pupils used to feel that they must never be married. They felt that if they were dancers they must lead a nunlike existence. They *must* be dedicated, but if students think they can become another Martha Graham by not marrying and by not having children, that's what worries me. I don't want a cult.

Instead, she wanted to draw people to her by the intensity of her beliefs. "A dancer must have two things," she asserted: "a highly developed body technique and the ability to draw people to you. The first can be taught, the second cannot."[26]

Still popular reaction varied, from critics and the general public alike. John Martin, who was the first newspaper critic in the country hired exclusively to cover dance, helped educate audiences to this new art form, but others like Lincoln Kirstein, the wealthy Filene's department store heir who founded the American Ballet with choreographer George Balanchine in 1934, took longer to come around. (In the 1930s ballet and modern dance comprised two warring camps, each professing superiority to the other. There was also a gendered dimension to the split: ballet was mainly choreographed and produced by men, but modern dance was dominated by women.) Although Kirstein eventually acknowledged and even appreciated Graham's contributions to dance, in the 1930s he wrote about her in terms like these: "This solitary dancer, not even a girl, with her spartan band of girls seeming to press themselves into the steel woman she was, appeared either naive or pretentious, which I could never fully decide." But even he had to admit, "the force of her personality magnetized me continually."[27]

Less is known about the general reactions of the audiences who came, although the early dance recitals probably attracted more women than men. With America in the grip of the Great Depression, audiences were often a little on the scruffy side, as witnessed by one early fan letter sent to Graham: "I enjoyed your program immensely, in spite of the soggy, loose, spiritually discolored people around me, which nearly drove me from the place." Comments overheard from audiences in the 1940s were probably just as true earlier: "I didn't understand it but it was wonderful"; "I think she is terrific even if I don't know what it is all about." The reaction that Graham would probably have liked the best was this one overheard by dance critic Walter Terry: "I didn't understand it, but I felt it."[28]

Presenting yearly recitals built loyalty—people talked about a Graham cult as far back as the 1930s—but it did not pay the bills. In fact, sometimes the recitals did not even pay for themselves. Graham managed to eke out an exceedingly modest existence through teaching at various private schools and at the Neighborhood Playhouse, where she began offering dance classes as early as 1927. Even though she was living in the midst of Greenwich Village in the exciting decades of the twenties and thirties, she was not really part of the intelligentsia scene—she was too focused on her art to hang out in coffeehouses, salons, or speakeasies. And she was too poor—she did not even have a telephone until the 1940s. Her devoted student Bessie Schoenberg recalled those Depression-era days in New York: "Those were very heady times; everyone was very poor, but we really didn't care—nothing mattered except that we worked every day, that we were at the studio every day, and that there was Martha."[29]

The year 1934 was an important one for the modern dance movement. Louis Horst founded the influential journal *Dance Observer*, which over the next decades under various titles served as the major sounding board for modern dance. Just as important was the beginning of the summer festival of modern dance at Bennington. Instigated by dance educator Martha Hill (another important Martha, but when people said "Martha" everyone knew they meant Graham), the summer program was originally conceived to make year-round use of the campus of Bennington College, an experimental women's college that had opened in 1932.

Soon the name Bennington became practically synonymous with modern dance, as each summer the "Big Four"—Graham, Doris Humphrey, Hanya Holm, and Charles Weidman—relocated from the city to the green mountains of Vermont to work with students and to prepare their own dances. Neither Louis or Martha had a driver's license, so a company dancer like the practical Bonnie Bird was usually delegated to round up an old car and chauffeur the entourage north. Once they were settled in Bennington, Martha felt no restraint about occasionally taking the wheel, even though she was a terrible driver (shades of Dorothy Thompson). "Pray!" Martha Hill used to say. "With Martha's driving, that could be the end of the history of modern dance."[30]

Even though artistic rivalries were intense, summers at Bennington provided occasions for collegiality and friendship, plus much needed rehearsal and performance space. It was here that Graham premiered early versions of *American Document* (1938), *El Penitente* (1940), and *Letter to the World* (1940), often then reworking the pieces before presenting them to New York audiences.

Bennington had a special meaning for Martha Graham, for it was there that she first met Erick Hawkins, the first man to join her company and her only husband. Hawkins was born in 1909 in Colorado near the New Mexico border and raised in Missouri; with the strong encouragement of a high school teacher, he sought and won a scholarship to Harvard. While there he studied the classics and immersed himself in the worlds of art and dance. After graduation he headed to New York. Hawkins came to Bennington in 1936 with the Ballet Caravan, a small touring company of the American Ballet. Given the bad blood between ballet and modern dance, the caravan cannot have expected a very warm reception. But backstage after the concert Martha Graham surprised everyone by singling out Hawkins for his performance.

Hawkins had already expressed curiosity about modern dance technique, a rare crossover for someone trained in ballet, and in June of 1938 he took a course at Graham's New York studio. Breaking precedent, Graham allowed him to watch the rehearsals of *American Document*, then a work in progress; never before had she allowed an outsider to be present at these sessions. Next she asked him to come to Bennington for the rest of the summer, and offered him the lead in this new piece, which would be her first to use a male dancer as well as the first to use a spoken text. All this happened within four weeks.[31]

Erick's rapid ascent sent the formerly all-female group into turmoil. His vaulting to leading roles ahead of veterans who had been with her for almost a decade caused hurt feelings; long-standing company members Anna Sokolow, May O'Donnell, Gertrude Shurr, and Kathleen Slagle left to strike off on their

Martha Graham and partner Erick Hawkins at Bennington in the late 1930s, as
captured by photographer Barbara Morgan. Morgan's carefully composed pho-
tographs helped to define for posterity Graham's image as a dancer and as a woman.
(© Barbara Morgan, 1938)

own. But others such as Ethel Butler, Jane Dudley, Nelle Fisher,
and Sophie Maslow stayed. One thing that soon became clear was
that Hawkins and Graham were falling in love, and that this
would be a tempestuous relationship.[32]

Whatever the circumstances of his arrival (Hawkins was soon
joined by another man, Merce Cunningham; both went on to
major dance careers on their own, separate from Graham), it was

probably inevitable that Graham would at some point have accepted men into her company. If it hadn't happened in 1938, then certainly it would have happened after World War II, when a crop of male dancers fresh out of the army entered the field. In addition Graham—or more likely her audiences—might eventually have grown dissatisfied with choreography limited to women. After all, having dancers of both sexes opened the possibilities for dealing more explicitly with issues of sexuality, power, and domination than ever before. And the fact that these two strong personalities were passionately in love opened up new emotions for Graham to choreograph. As Erick put it once, "because my being a man let Martha be a woman, and in that role her dancing changed. . . . She came into her own as a woman and she had someone like myself to take the other side of passion."[33]

At the same time men were introduced into the company, Graham was moving away from some of her earlier severity. "I'm afraid I used to hit audiences over the head with a sledgehammer because I was so determined that they see and feel what I was trying to do," she said around 1940. "Now that we moderns have left our period of long woolens behind us, we must prove to our audiences that our theater pieces can have color, warmth, and entertainment value. . . . We must convince our audiences that we belong to the American theater." At about the same time MGM was promoting the film *Ninotchka* with the headline "Garbo laughs," Martha Graham smiled for the first time in a 1939 production of *Every Soul Is a Circus*. Walter Terry was so surprised that his review for the *New York Herald-Tribune* noted in jest, "Martha Graham ought to be reprimanded. Last night she turned out to be the Beatrice Lillie of the dance, and she's been hiding it from us all these years."[34]

Since the success of her solo *Frontier* in 1935, Graham had more consciously explored American themes. Here she was in line with the general artistic trends of Depression-era America, including New Deal arts programs, which tapped American roots for artistic expression. In 1940 she premiered *Letter to the World*,

based on the life and poetry of Emily Dickinson. The culmina-
tion of that trend was one of her most popular ballets, *Appalachian Spring* (1944), a tale of marriage in a frontier town set to music
by Aaron Copland. Dancer Tim Wengerd recalled that the Hus-
bandman was his favorite role: "Nobody dies, nobody is pun-
ished, and nobody gets turned into a swan. They are simply two
people doing what we are meant to do, loving and planning to
create the next generation in health and wholeness. That was
Martha at her best."[35]

Graham's solicitation of a score from Copland (a larger orches-
tration won the Pulitzer Prize for music for 1945, and remains
one of the most popular pieces in the classical repertoire) was typical of the close and productive collaborations she formed with
musicians. After 1933 Graham rarely choreographed to a preex-
isting score, working instead with pieces composed by Louis
Horst or others. The list of musicians from whom she commis-
sioned scores reads like a who's who of twentieth-century contemporary music: Darius Milhaud, Paul Hindemith, Samuel
Barber, Gian-Carlo Menotti, Copland, William Schuman, Norman Dello Joio, Alan Hovhaness, Vincent Persichetti, and Ned
Rorem, among others. Ironically, she herself could not read music
and did not even own a phonograph.

In this productive period Graham also choreographed dances
of deep introspection, pieces that mirrored the stream-of-con-
sciousness technique prominent in modernist writing. *Deaths and
Entrances* (1943) was a meditation on the three Brontë sisters, but
also (many felt) about Martha and her two sisters. (Georgia,
known as Geordie, had followed Martha to Denishawn and then
into her company as a dancer and later administrator, always
remaining in her older sister's shadow; she was married to the
New Yorker music critic Winthrop Sergeant. Mary married a San
Francisco doctor and died prematurely of cancer.) She also began
to mine Greek mythology in such dances as *Cave of the Heart*
(1946), based on the myth of Medea; *Errand into the Maze* (1947),

about Ariadne and Theseus; and *Night Journey* (1947), based on
Jocasta and Oedipus. This Greek phase would culminate in the
four-act masterpiece *Clytemnestra* (1958).

It is too simplistic to chart Graham's productivity in these
years against a graph of her love affair with Erick Hawkins, but
their personal relationship greatly influenced themes and compositions from this period: not just the simple happiness of a married couple in *Appalachian Spring* but also the early explorations
of Greek myth and mythology. Erick, after all, had been a classics
major at Harvard. Another significant influence was close friend
Joseph Campbell, who was the husband of Graham dancer Jean
Erdman and author of such widely read books as *The Hero with a
Thousand Faces* (1949) and the four-volume *The Masks of God*
(1959–1967). Conversations with Campbell on theology, myth,
and Jungian psychology had such a tremendous impact on Graham that he was practically an unacknowledged collaborator on
many of her dances. Graham's voracious consumption of people
and ideas was her unabashed style: "I am a thief—and I am not
ashamed. I steal from the best whenever it happens to me."[36]

Besides functioning as her lead dancer, Hawkins also took on
increasing responsibility for company administrative tasks such
as fund-raising and scheduling, which Graham had never shown
any interest in. Erick brought order, but his attempts to set himself up as a co-leader of the company were doomed to failure. She
was the genius, the driving force; his gifts, while large, paled in
comparison.

From the start there was conflict in their relationship. They
were both ambitious and controlling personalities who were passionate about their art, but destined to clash over how to achieve
it. Their creative and emotional battles were often so intense they
could not even live together; both consulted psychotherapists
throughout the 1940s. Even though it was her company and she
was the superior dancer and choreographer, he made unrealistic
demands for equal billing and solos in company performances.

Further undercutting her authority, he openly flirted with younger female dancers at the studio. Age was a significant issue here: Graham was forty-four to Hawkins' thirty when they met. The tension that their often bitterly contested relationship added to the daily routine of teaching, rehearsals, and performances can only be imagined.[37]

The tangle with Hawkins was certainly a contributing factor to the rupture that occurred between Graham and Louis Horst in 1948. It came over a trivial matter at a rehearsal, but the exchange of wounding words suggested that underlying tensions had been building for quite some time. Suddenly Graham was left without the one person who had been her steady rock since Denishawn days: "Every young artist needs a wall to grow against like a vine," he had told her then. "I am that wall." So strongly had Horst believed in Graham's artistic gifts that practically he alone could get her back on track when her creative powers stalled. And he was one of the few who could stand up to Graham's terrible temper. Now he was gone.[38]

One month later, Erick and Martha were married while on a trip to the Southwest. When they had to list their ages for the wedding license, she cut off eight years to make herself forty-six; he listed his true age of thirty-nine. (In her autobiography, she remembered the spread as even larger: "I was consistent—I took off the same fifteen years that I always had.") They had been together on and off for almost ten years, a far longer period than the marriage would last. It effectively ended less than two years later when Hawkins walked out on Graham in London after she injured her knee, causing the cancellation of their much anticipated European tour. Not only did she lose her husband, she lost her leading man, a double blow. Luckily her injury was not career-ending and after a period of rest and recuperation, she was able to resume dancing.[39]

What lay ahead was the great period of the 1950s, when Graham danced such intense and demanding roles as Judith, St. Joan, and, of course, Clytemnestra. That decade also foreshadowed the struggle with aging, which perhaps haunted Martha Graham more acutely than any other performing artist. She simply would not consider giving up dancing, even as she got older and older: age fifty as the bride in *Appalachian Spring*, fifty-six as Judith, sixty-four as Clytemnestra. After all, even a Martha Graham in decline was in a league of her own compared to most performers. The years were catching up, however, long before she was willing to slow down, let alone retire from the stage. Of all the epic stories she danced from Greek mythology, perhaps none would match her own rage at what age was doing to her body, which, since she was a dancer, was her life.

🍃

UNLIKE MANY ARTISTS or creative pioneers, who toil in obscurity and pray for eventual discovery of their special gift, Martha Graham never suffered from lack of exposure. Beginning with her first recital in New York in 1926, she attracted a band of devoted followers and her career received consistent, if not always positive, coverage in the mainstream press. Noted the *New Yorker* in 1947, "By the mid-thirties, Miss Graham was well on her way to becoming a national institution." This kind of fame did not just arise spontaneously: Martha Graham worked hard at building a persona both on and off the stage, and then she manipulated and controlled that image with savvy. She also cultivated the trappings of celebrity, modestly at first and then on a grander scale in her later years. Her goal remained the same: to do whatever was necessary to keep on dancing.[40]

Martha Graham's sense of timing was superb. Just as no one since has had the wide-open opportunities that a Dorothy Thompson or a Margaret Mead had to tailor careers in journalism and anthropology, so too did Martha Graham come along at an expansive moment in dance history. By the 1920s (but no sooner) conditions were ripe for a respectable middle-class woman to forge a career out of art-dance. Like modernist painting and sculpture, Graham's style was in synch with the times and she quickly built a reputation as dance's most startling innovator. But she was also the best performer, and American audiences were ready to accept the intense theatricality that she brought to dance.

A series of markers confirm the way in which Martha Graham became practically synonymous with the image of the modern dancer. One of the first was a spoof in *Vanity Fair* in 1934 of an "Impossible Interview" between fan dancer Sally Rand and Graham. Rand, who had wowed audiences with her bare-all performance at the 1933 Chicago World's Fair, points out that they really are in the same racket: "Just a couple of little girls trying to wriggle along." When Graham notes that Rand's performance leaves nothing to the customer's imagination and suggests she should learn to bare her soul, Rand retorts, "Say, I got to keep *something* covered." Martha points out that Sally would be frowned on in ladies' clubs, to which she replies, "And you'd be a flop in a cooch concession, kid. From now on, we'd better split fifty-fifty." A humorous piece of fluff, but also testimony to how deeply imbedded in popular culture Martha Graham's image as a modern dancer had become as early as 1934.[41]

The next year Graham found herself satirized by Fanny Brice in the *Zeigfield Follies*. In a sketch called "Rewolt," a parody of the 1927 composition of the "same" name, Brice appeared onstage in the uniform of the modern dancer (leotards and a long wrap skirt) to perform a musical parody called "Modernistic Moe" written by Billy Rose and Ira Gershwin. Her vaudeville audiences howled knowingly as she made references to the stark percussive rhythms and austere costumes of that very different performance art.[42]

Fame of a different sort came Martha Graham's way in 1937 when Eleanor Roosevelt asked her to perform at the White House, the first dancer so honored. (She would dance for seven other presidents.) Scraping together train fare for the trip to Washington, she and Louis Horst had to talk their way past a well-meaning aide who feared she would be barefoot when she met the president of the United States. After the performance, Graham and Horst encountered Eleanor planning the next day's menu with her butler. Calling back to him, "Mint jelly, too," she leaped up to thank her guests for the performance, which she wrote about in "My Day."[43]

In 1947 Graham took part in a bit of fun for the radio show "Truth or Consequences." In a popular feature, listeners tried to identify a mystery personality (Mister or Miss Hush) based on a series of rhymed clues. Jack Dempsey and Clara Bow had been the first two mystery voices, and Graham agreed to become the third, reading the following encoded jingle on the air in her highly distinctive voice:

> Second for Santa Claus, first for me,
> Thirteen for wreath, seven for tree,
> Bring me an auto, a book, and a ball,
> And I'll say Merry Christmas in spring, not in fall.

Graham had originally agreed to do the spot because it benefitted the March of Dimes, but she was totally unprepared for the notoriety it brought, such as being called "Miss Hush" on the street by strangers and having callers telephone the dance studio asking for the character.[44]

What was unusual about the episode was not Graham's desire for publicity for herself and her company, but the way in which she was unable to control its outcome. For the most part, Martha Graham kept a tight rein over her image and reputation. She granted very few interviews, and for many years a 1947 *New Yorker* profile by Angelica Gibbs was about the only biographical material available about the artist. She turned down an offer from Paramount Pictures to option a story about her life, to star Syd Charisse and Tony Martin in the Graham and Horst roles, even though her studio could have desperately used the money. "I can ruin my own reputation in five minutes. I don't need help."[45]

Some of her anxiety about the press likely came from sensitivity about her age. Many women in professional life fudged their ages, but a dancer like Graham had a special incentive. To counter the relatively late start of her dance career, as early as the 1920s Graham presented herself as being born in the twentieth century, lopping six years off her birth date to place it somewhere around 1900. Most of her friends and other dancers did not know what her actual age was, or probably care; those who did, kept silent. Her amazingly honed dancer's body and chiseled features made it difficult to pinpoint her age. Keeping the press at a distance allowed her to maintain her mystique.

This attempt to control her image also extended to the realm of photography, both still and film. Graham forbade the filming of her dance performances and rehearsals on aesthetic grounds, feeling that any reproduction was a poor substitute for the actual performance; she also feared superficial copying of her technique without the rigorous training required to master it. Unlike Katharine Hepburn's early films, which preserve her most radical and transgressive roles, that period for Graham is essentially lost. Many of her early dances can only be reconstructed from the powerful still photographs taken by Barbara Morgan in the 1930s and 1940s. But these too were carefully staged. Graham strongly discouraged friends and students from taking casual pictures of the studio, dancers on their breaks, or even summers on the Bennington campus. As a result, there are few informal pictures of Graham in the public record. In their place are artfully posed collaborations with photographers, often in silhouette and always aiming for the most dramatic effect.

So successful was her creation of this dramatic public persona that people were often surprised when they met her in person. Rather than her larger than life reputation, she was quite a small woman, only five-foot-two. Even though she looked a bit starved, she was actually quite sturdy, with a very strong back and thighs. Her early dancers also shared this sturdy physical type, a far cry from the lean and long-legged, almost anorexic look favored by many dancers today, both in ballet and modern dance. It never would have occurred to Graham or her early dancers to diet, for example, although the Depression-induced poverty of a dancer's life may have made that moot. Like Babe Didrikson, Martha Graham and her company showed that there was more than one body type available to be physically active.

Among the most distinctive aspects of Graham's body were her square, clawlike feet which "gripped the floor as though they would never let go." Agnes de Mille recalled "an instep under which you could run water, a clublike square-toed foot with a heel and arch of such flexibility and strength that she seems to use it like a pogo stick." Because almost all of her dancing was done barefoot, the bottoms of her feet were tough, almost like animal pads.[46]

Martha Graham always knew how to attract attention. Recalled an aunt fifty years later about Martha as a child, "there was something about her even then that made everyone stop and look." Her overall appearance remained remarkably consistent from her Denishawn days until she was in her sixties. Even when she barely had money for food or rent, she always looked chic, thanks to her amazing skill as a seamstress. As dancer Pearl Lang recalled, "Fabric was another dancer in Martha's hands." Her requirements for clothing were the same as for costumes: they must allow freedom of movement and expression. So thin were the lines between onstage and off that for a 1953 performance of a dance called *Voyage*, Graham danced in a black Hattie Carnegie evening gown she had bought years before.[47]

Once Bethsabee de Rothschild came into Martha Graham's life as a patron and friend in the 1940s, she was finally able to indulge her love of fine clothes and furnishings. Rothschild, who was a member of the enormously wealthy banking family, took classes with Graham during the war, although no one at first had any idea who she was. From then until she moved to Israel in the late 1950s to found the Batsheva Dance Company, she was the main financial angel of the company. She also took Martha shopping. As Agnes de Mille noted, "Under Bethsabee's patronage, Martha began to look like a star." Now she could finally afford clothes from Saks Fifth Avenue and Bergdorf Goodman, hats from John-Frederick, and necklaces from Cartier, rather than have to haunt the bargain shops on Fourteenth Street. Later the fashion designer Halston took over the role of clothing the icon.[48]

Bethsabee de Rothschild's fortuitous appearance on the scene was emblematic of Martha Graham's attitude toward money: "Money? Money's nothing. If we *need* it, we'll have it." Graham was notoriously uninterested in money matters: in her perversity the time to shop was when the account was overdrawn. If money was needed to mount a recital, she assumed it would simply appear. It usually did, although never in such quantities that it could match the increasingly expensive proposition of running a school and a dance company.[49]

Martha Graham's major early patrons were all women. (Patronage meant supporting her personally as well as her dance company, since it was impossible to draw a line between the two.) Graham's first patron had been Frances Steloff, who put up the money for the 1926 recital. Graham's connections with the Neighborhood Playhouse put her in touch with wealthy benefactors like Edith Isaacs and Rita Morgenthau, who were generous in their early support of the always-struggling company. In the 1940s a grant from Elisabeth Sprague Coolidge allowed Graham to commission composer Aaron Copland's "Appalachian Spring" suite. The actress Katharine Cornell also lent her support, as did *Readers' Digest* publisher Lila Acheson Wallace, who in 1952 made it possible for Graham to acquire the building at 316 East Sixty-third that still houses her company and school. Without a tradition of federal support for the arts, it was up to individual angels to finance culture in the United States. Martha Graham's angels were women.

By the 1940s Martha Graham's reputation as the leading exponent of modern dance was firmly established. So dominant was her image that the non-dance public often had little idea of the many other dancers, predominantly female but also by then including a few men, who were pioneering new dance techniques. One of the most important was dancer and choreographer Doris Humphrey, who never achieved the star status that Graham did, in part because she never cultivated a mystique or persona the way her rival did. Bad luck also played a role: Humphrey suffered a career-ending injury in 1945 and succumbed to cancer in 1958 at the age of sixty-three.[50]

The fact that Graham is remembered and Humphrey is not (except in the dance world, where the stature of the latter is unquestioned) speaks volumes about the construction of public personae and how certain artists like a Graham gravitate toward the limelight while others, like Doris Humphrey, follow their muses in less public but just as productive venues. Few could rival Humphrey as a choreographer, as Graham herself acknowledged: "Doris knows how to put a dance together and I don't." But Graham was a far more charismatic theatrical performer, and certainly a more colorful personality, and that package resonated with its intended audience. For every superstar put forward and kept there by an adoring public, there are often others with similar profiles and comparable gifts who remain practically anonymous.[51]

🏵

"AN AMAZONIAN WORLD of vestals," plus Louis Horst, was an apt description of the Martha Graham Dance Company in the 1930s. Graham was a charismatic leader, and she drew students to her—at that point, all women—like a magnet. Recalled Dorothy Bird: "Everyone was hypnotized, absolutely magnetized by Martha. It was like a mass falling in love, but much, much more. It was more than a crush. She opened our eyes to the arts. I was on fire." Nelle Fisher, who was in the company at the same time, recalled it as "complete dedication, like a sisterhood."

Marie Marchowsky recalled how chosen they felt: "We were the crème-de-la-crème. We didn't have to think about that. We were free. We were doing things that were little understood. We were very strong about it—we were fanatical about it. Dance was the great communicator."[52]

But not everyone could survive in this atmosphere, and many of the finest Graham dancers, female and later male, found they had to leave in order to grow. This was a very difficult decision, because it meant cutting off contact with Martha. "When you were in the company," recalled one former dancer, "Martha would die for you. The moment you left, you were gone."[53]

Given the gender inequalities of modern life, men may have found it especially problematic to work under such a charismatic female leader. Paul Taylor and Merce Cunningham, who both left to start their own companies (as did Hawkins), each made strikingly Freudian statements describing the difficulties they faced. Said Taylor, "It was marvelous working with her, but I was damned if I was going to be dominated." Cunningham concurred, "Graham's great—but unless you move quickly she does tend to castrate people."[54]

Graham's male dancers may also have felt a certain privileging of female experience in terms of technique. Given differences in human anatomy, many of the Graham exercises were easier for women to master, especially some of the floor work. Graham made a cult out of the pelvis, jokingly referring to her school as the "House of Pelvic Truth." "You are simply not moving your vagina," she might erupt to a student. (Once a cab driver nearly swerved off the road when he overheard passenger Graham dismiss another dancer with, "She never would have been a great dancer. She doesn't move from her vagina.") Critics joked that the Martha Graham dance company was the one place in America where men suffered from vagina envy.[55]

Especially in the early years, but even after men joined the company, Martha Graham created a space where women could assert themselves, as individuals and as women. Dance critic Lynn

Martha Graham—dancer, mystic, seer, genius. Dancer Glenn Tetley, encountering her penetrating gaze, thought, "Oh my God, she sees everything." (Angus McBean Photograph, The Harvard Theater Collection, The Houghton Library)

Garafola noted, "Graham found her voice in a company of women; they were her chorus and her subject, and she remade them, even as she remade herself." *New York* magazine dance critic Tobi Tobias made a similar point about Graham's choreography, especially about early pieces like *Heretic* and *Celebration* (1934): "You see the force and glory Graham found, not just in specific women with names whose souls she probed—but in womanhood itself." These were strong women, never "girls"; they projected power. This was dance for, by, and about women.[56] Sophie Maslow, one of Graham's early dancers, put it well: "When I see the old dances, the power and strength with which we moved reminds me of the women's movement today."[57]

Interestingly this portrait of a female artist surrounded by her adoring female following was rarely linked with deviant female sexuality or lesbianism, even though it was commonly assumed that many leading male dancers were gay. Although there may have been lesbians in her company, this did not surface as an issue in dance the way it did, for example, for women in sports. In fact, Graham demanded that her female dancers be sexually experienced, married or not: "I won't have any virgins in my company. I don't care if you have to stand on a street corner and get a man." Once by way of demonstration, she embraced a male dancer while both were in deep contractions (a pose close to simulated intercourse) and stated with passion, "*That* is how life begins, and if you cannot face that, *leave*!"[58]

One of the things that was most distinctive about Martha Graham was that she created dances about traditional themes like the heroic quest, but from the perspective of the woman. As Graham said forcefully, "All the things I do are in every woman. Every woman is a Medea. Every woman is a Jocasta. There comes a time when a woman is mother to her husband. Clytemnestra is every woman when she kills." *New Yorker* dance critic Arlene Croce noted that heroes were always of secondary interest to Graham, that hers was "a theatre of feminine tempests": "The difference between her and the fated heroines of nineteenth-century bal-

let—a Giselle or an Odette—is that the Graham heroine possess-
es, herself, the key to her mystery. She does not entrust it to the
hero; she herself must unlock the inner door. . . . No Graham
heroine dies unillumined."[59]

This creation of heroines and female seekers allowed Graham
to refocus the traditional patriarchal world of mythology (or real
life) by telling the story from a Medea's point of view, not Euripi-
des; Clytemnestra's, not Orestes or Agamennon. Her dances were
peopled by strong female characters, not necessarily because she
was creating with a conscious feminist perspective but because
she was creating for herself, and she craved the strength and angst
of these powerful if conflicted figures.

Although Graham dealt with critical feminist themes in her
choreography, she was far less engaged with the political side of
feminism. She displayed no awareness of the first wave of feminism—there is no record of Graham marching in a suffrage
parade, signing a petition, or otherwise participating in the cause
that energized millions of women in the 1910s. And when the
second wave of feminism appeared in the 1960s and 1970s, she
was not hostile to its aims, she just felt that it was not relevant
to her life.

Sounding very much like Katharine Hepburn, Margaret Mead,
and other independent professional women who had made it on
their own between the two waves of feminism, Graham distanced
herself from the movement in her autobiography:

> Years later, women in the movement would claim me as a
> women's liberationist. But I never thought of myself in this way.
> I was never aware of it, because I have never felt competition. I
> was brought up in a very strange way. I have been surrounded by
> men all my life so the movement really didn't touch me. But I
> never had the feeling that I was inferior. So when all this began
> in the last twenty years or so I was baffled by it. I had no affilia-
> tion with it, and I always got whatever I wanted from men with-
> out asking.[60]

As she said in the mid-1980s, "But as far as fighting for women's rights, I never thought very much about that; I've only fought by being."[61]

Graham seems to have had the same ambivalent ideas about feminism shared by many women of her generation, specifically that if she liked being a woman, never felt inferior, and most of all, if she liked men, she couldn't possibly be a feminist. "I've gotten everything I wanted from men, so I don't see any reason to exclude them or demonstrate against them. I think we need men very much." Perhaps she also associated feminism with being anti-erotic or anti-sex; certainly she was not interested in lesbianism. When asked about "girlfriends" (presumably a code for lesbian relationships), she replied, "It is impossible. I have no interest in women. I like men. If I had wanted that kind of life with a woman I would have had it. I did not. I wanted a life with men and that is what I chose." Of course her stormy relationship and short marriage to Erick Hawkins, and her less tumultuous but still tense affair with Louis Horst, suggest the difficulties that many independent and creative woman had in forging lasting relations with members of the opposite sex. But unlike some of the other women in this book, she was firm in her heterosexual identity.[62]

Despite her disclaimers of feminism, Martha Graham had more in common with its struggles than she admitted. Like many other professional women she became a Lucy Stoner when she married: "I kept my own name; I was determined to use it. I didn't want to be the wife of anybody if I had to give up my own name." Of course, if you had worked so hard to make your name synonymous with modern dance, you wouldn't want to give it up either, but there is also a lurking awareness of the dangers of submerging oneself to a man in a marriage, something she could never do.[63]

Graham also faced head-on the issue of whether to have children, deciding that having a child was incompatible with her career. The following statement suggests that she must have practiced birth control, although this political movement like most others never drew her public allegiance:

> All my life I have been a devotee of sex, in the right sense of the word. Fulfillment, as opposed to procreation, or I would have had children. I chose not to have children for the simple reason that I felt I could never give a child the caring upbringing which I had had as a child. I couldn't control being a dancer. I knew I had to choose between a child and dance, and I chose dance.[64]

Sounding remarkably like Katharine Hepburn once again, Graham used her work as a rationale for not trying motherhood, and did so with few, if any, regrets.

Like so much else in her career, her chronological age certainly played a role in her decision. When she gave her first recital in New York, she was already thirty-two years old. As she struggled to establish herself over the next decade, she lacked the stable home, income, or suitable potential father for a child, even if she had wanted to have one. When she met Hawkins, she was already in her forties and well into her fifties when they finally married, surely past childbearing age. The cycle of building her career, especially its late start, stacked the deck against having children, whatever her personal inclination.

Basically Martha Graham was an individualist, an egoist, a loner following her own muse. Aloof and self-centered, she relied primarily on herself, despite the attendant pain and loneliness. "Nothing has ever been accomplished by a group," stated the artist. "Things have only been accomplished through the glory of certain individuals and, believe me, they have suffered for it." On the other hand, as a woman she claimed never to have been held back by discrimination or sexism, primarily because she was pioneering a new field and answered to no one but herself. No wonder she did not feel it necessary to identify with modern feminism, either in the interwar period or in its subsequent incarnations.[65]

But there is plenty of material for a feminist *reading* of

Martha Graham's life, not only in her personal choices but in the work she left behind: a legacy of strong women in dance, who if not necessarily happy were at least in charge of their own destinies; the attention that her artistic and aesthetic sensibility paid to the beauty and strength of women's bodies as distinct from men's; the Martha Graham Dance Company, the oldest continuing such group in the country, where she created a space for herself and other women to dance and explore and create; a model of a female public figure of enormous stature not just in the arts but in popular culture and national life; and most of all, strong testimony that geniuses do not have to be men.

🎕

THE TWO DECADES after the breakup of her marriage to Erick Hawkins were enormously productive for Martha Graham, even though aspects of her personal life were becoming increasingly destructive. Thanks to State Department sponsorship as part of a Cold War arts initiative, the Martha Graham Dance Company won international renown on several world tours to Europe and the Far East, including a grueling sixteen-week tour in 1955–1956. The 1950s were also the peak of Graham's Greek cycle. Even though Graham was in her mid-sixties, she still could hold audiences through the sheer force of her stage presence, but it was getting harder and harder.

As her physical powers waned, Graham steadfastly refused to consider retiring from performing. Instead she choreographed pieces for herself in which she was more an actor than dancer. This stratagem produced decidedly mixed feelings in her audiences, as dance chronicler Elinor Rogosin captured: "Watching her heroic effort is upsetting, and I don't know whether to admire her courage or to cry at the futile hope of reversing time." When a friend tried to suggest that she accept her mortality, she replied, "That's difficult when you see yourself as a goddess and behave like one." Increasingly she turned to alcohol as solace, a pattern

Betty Bloomer was a student of Martha Graham's at Bennington in the 1940s. Three decades later, in 1976, her husband, President Gerald R. Ford, presented Graham with the Medal of Freedom, the first time a dancer had been so honored. (Courtesy Gerald R. Ford Library.)

of serious abuse that began during the breakup of her relationship with Hawkins.

In 1970, at the age of seventy-five, Martha Graham finally announced her retirement from the stage. The news was reported in a front-page *New York Times* story on the day she was scheduled to receive the prestigious Handel Medallion from the city of New York. At the gala that night, which was also the opening night of her company's new season, she artfully "unretired" herself with lines like, "When I retire, I'll probably go to a Greek Island and you'll know nothing about it." In fact, she did not dance in public again.[67]

Between 1971 and 1973 Graham went through a period of despair and rebirth as dramatic as any of her Greek plays. Her body finally gave out after years of abuse and at times she lingered near death in the hospital. Her company was in disarray, its very survival at stake with its charismatic leader out of the picture. Graham seemed to have lost all interest in life and dance. But then for reasons unknown she suddenly turned herself around in what dance biographer Ernestine Stodelle called "one of the greatest creative acts of her life."[68]

When Agnes de Mille came to visit her in the hospital, she noticed that Graham's hair had gone white and she suggested she keep it that way. "The hell I will," thought Graham with a flame of her old spirit. Martha Graham was not prepared to be an old lady, and the next day the hair was dyed black again, the color it stayed right up until her death. Even now, it is practically impossible to conjure up a white-haired Martha Graham.[69]

An important component of her recovery was the care and support of Ron Protas, a photographer who would be at Graham's side until her death and who took on an increasingly large role in the day-to-day running of the company. (Writer Carolyn Heilbrun noticed how both Graham and Georgia O'Keeffe at the end of their artistic lives "surrendered themselves to young men who controlled both them and their art.") His style and decisions were often controversial, and his growing influence caused upheaval and ill will in the fairly close-knit dance world. While some doubted his artistic judgment, few questioned how important he was to Graham's rebirth and recovery, including her resolve never to touch another drop of alcohol.[70]

In the 1970s and 1980s Martha Graham ascended to superstar status. In order to build financial support for her perennially struggling company, and to keep herself in the public eye, Martha Graham now became more of a fixture on the celebrity circuit than ever before. She joined Rudolph Nureyev and Margot Fonteyn to pose for a Blackglama mink ad and hobnobbed with Calvin Klein, Liz Taylor, Liza Minelli, and even Madonna, who had once studied with Graham. Agnes de Mille tagged these activities "haute tacky."[71]

In an ironic twist, Watergate and its aftermath played a role in this iconization: when Gerald Ford became president after Richard Nixon's resignation in 1974, First Lady Betty Bloomer Ford, a former Martha Graham dancer, invited her former teacher to the White House and rekindled their friendship. (Sounding a bit like Katharine Hepburn, Graham once remarked, "Oh, everyone tells me they have studied with me at one time or another. Sometimes I think I have taught half the world.") In 1976 President Ford presented Graham with the country's highest civilian award, the Medal of Freedom, one of the many awards she received in the last several decades of her life.[72]

In the 1970s and 1980s Graham continued to choreograph new works for her company, as well as stage revivals of selected earlier works, with mixed critical results. Audiences still flocked to the concerts, but critics noted a definite decline in creativity in these late compositions. *Newsweek* dance critic Laura Shapiro captured this odd process of deification in a 1984 review: "To show its allegiance to Graham, her public has thought it necessary to make her a celebrity, to praise her new dances as if they were equal to the old, and to accept the disintegration of technique in the company. We have no other way, it seems, to let a genius rest, and no way to keep a great legacy with us except by ignoring its frailty."[73]

At the core of Graham's later years was her primal fear of being outside the limelight. In a revealing aside, she once told Walter Terry, "I have a feeling that everyone is terribly lonely. And aloneness is one of our reasons for fearing death. The thing I feel with an audience is that I'm not alone." Or not dead. Like Babe Didrikson Zaharias, when she had an audience, she was always "on." If she had to stop, she would die.[74]

In her later years she developed various strategies to get the fix of public adulation that she needed to survive. Knowing audiences learned to wait for the last curtain calls after a Graham company performance, when she would take a bow herself and often make the kind of impromptu but memorable remarks that built her legend even more. Her appearances at fund-raising galas became the "magic draw for which people paid the benefit prices." She knew the effect she had on people, and she was not shy about using it. Graham could still dominate any room she entered; even her most ordinary acts, like getting out of a car, somehow seemed spectacular. "Her magnetism is as great as it was when she danced," noted Joseph Mazo. "Even if she is only taking a curtain call, she gives you a show for your money."[75]

The downside to all this, of course, was the arrogance that goes with being a diva, of always expecting to get your own way and being treated like a goddess, as well as the distinct possibility of becoming a caricature. *New York Post* dance and drama critic Clive Barnes noted two years before her death how thin the line had become between celebrity and mockery: "She is like the flag, motherhood, apple pie—everyone knows her, everyone is in favor of her, yet her very acceptability has her taken for granted as something not that far removed from a cliche, or even a joke."[76]

Martha Graham died at her Manhattan apartment on April 1, 1991, after a two-month bout with pneumonia. She had recently returned from a strenuous fifty-five-day trip to the Far East with her dance company. Just before she took ill, she completed the final draft of her autobiography, *Blood Memory*, which was published posthumously the following fall, simultaneously with Agnes de Mille's entertaining but factually flawed biography of her long-time friend and rival.

The most striking aspects of *Blood Memory* were the photographs, which captured the transformation of Martha Graham, Denishawn dancer, into the powerful and compelling presence of the 1930s and beyond. The text, however, was a mishmash of interviews, recycled quotations, and name-dropping. Arlene Croce called it "ham-handedly promotional" and "her crowning contribution to the commercialization of her empire": "Full of wisdom and glamour, it seems designed to confuse a public that is already having a hard time telling Graham apart from Georgia O'Keeffe, Katharine Hepburn, and Mother Theresa." In her ninety-sixth year, Martha Graham was still hard at work building her image.[77]

Back in 1935, Martha Graham said in an interview, "I have always fought against any dramatization of my peculiarities or my personality. If you attitudinize or dramatize yourself, your sense of touch for new things is gone. You begin living in your own past." Ironically that is precisely what happened to Martha Graham in the last years of her life: she was living her legend, not her life. Perched on a rehearsal stool looking out on invisible dancers, she was still holding that pose, "a motionless figure, her long face gaunt and heavily made up, her hair pulled back so tightly it looks painted on her scalp."[78]

And, one suspects, still raging at a body that had robbed her of the chance to keep dancing. If Martha Graham could have had her way, she would literally have danced to her grave, knowing that a still adoring audience would have followed her every step.

(© Jack Sparling)

ACROSS THE COLOR LINE: MARIAN ANDERSON

*A*RTURO TOSCANINI CALLED hers "a voice such as one hears once in a hundred years."[1] Composer Jean Sibelius said after she sang for him in his home, "My roof is too low for you." Impresario Sol Hurok remembered chills "dancing" up his spine when he happened in on a recital she was giving in Paris in 1935. Beginning in a South Philadelphia church choir back in the early years of the century, contralto Marian Anderson thrilled audiences with the three-octave range of her voice. Said operatic diva Jessye Norman, whose career in many ways was made possible by doors opened by the concert singer, "If the planet Earth could sing, I think it would sound something like Marian Anderson."[2]

Because Marian Anderson was black, her career offers a mirror on race relations in the United States over the course of the twentieth century. "Wonderful voice, it's too bad she's Negro" and "You won't be able to give her away" were the refrains in the early years of her career. Like other American artists, black and white, she had to build a reputation in Europe before audiences in this country would even consider giving her a chance at the top. And even then she could not escape the racism so deeply embedded in American life. Nowhere is this clearer than the event forever linked with her name: the open-air concert on Easter Sunday 1939 at the Lincoln Memorial in Washington, D.C., after the Daughters of the American Revolution refused her permission to perform in their Constitution Hall solely because of her race.[3]

Without underestimating Marian Anderson's talent, hard work, and perseverance in the face of discrimination, her sense of timing was opportune. As *New York Times* music critic Harold Schonberg observed when she retired from the concert stage in 1965, "Miss Anderson was the right person in the right place at the right time." By the 1930s American audiences were finally prepared to embrace an African-American singer who specialized in the classical repertoire, not just blues, jazz, vaudeville, or spirituals. Influential whites ranging from Sol Hurok, who became her manager in 1935, to Eleanor Roosevelt, who became a friend and supporter practically the moment they met, stood behind her as an artist, but also inevitably as a civil rights symbol.[4]

By her own admission Marian Anderson was a reluctant crusader, against racism or any other injustice. "It would be fooling myself to think that I was meant to be a fearless fighter," she wrote in her 1956 autobiography, *My Lord, What a Morning.* "I was not, just as I was not meant to be a soprano instead of a contralto." And yet her chosen stance on race matters—never complain, never get angry, and maintain your dignity at all times—proved an effective strategy in the period when civil rights was tentatively emerging as a national issue. W. E. B. Du Bois had predicted in 1900, "The problem of the twentieth century is the problem of the color line." Leading by example, Marian Anderson not only crossed that color line, she helped to speed its demise.[5]

A symbol of her race, but what of Marian Anderson as a woman? Here the meanings and lessons of her life are more subtle but just as telling. Supremely dedicated to her artistry, career took priority throughout most of her life; she did not marry until she was in her forties and never had children. While she rarely talked publicly (or privately) about issues of feminism or women's rights, her celebrated artistic career was a powerful demonstration of what women could contribute to American culture, indeed national life. Long-time NAACP general secretary Walter White never forgot the image of a young black girl mesmerized by the Lincoln Memorial concert: "If Marian Anderson could do it, the girl's eyes seemed to say, then I can, too."[6]

Like the other women in this book, Marian Anderson adopted a public persona that allowed her to fulfill her artistic goals and find success, indeed celebrity, in twentieth-century America. Anderson's assumption of the mantle of dignified black womanhood had special meaning for the African-American community, especially its women. The artist's personification of the tradition of racial uplift and striving for respectability placed black women at the center of the larger struggle for social change.

Long before her death in 1993 at the age of ninety-six, Marian Anderson helped to open doors for a whole generation of African Americans, including such distinguished artists as Jessye Norman, Shirley Verrett, Grace Bumbry, and Leontyne Price. In this case, leading by example, in matters both of race and gender, worked wondrous results.

🦌

LATER IN LIFE Marian Anderson acquired the moniker "The Lady from Philadelphia," but her Philadelphia was a far different place from the city in which Margaret Mead grew up or which produced Katharine Hepburn's Main Line husband, Ludlow Ogden Smith. Racial segregation and class insured that there would be little overlap between white and black, rich and poor, despite the geographical proximity.

The city of Philadelphia occupied a special place in African-American history. Philadelphia had more black residents— 45,000 at the turn of the century—than any other city except Washington, Baltimore, and New Orleans. And it was the site of

W. E. B. Du Bois's famous 1899 study, *The Philadelphia Negro*, based on an intensive house-by-house investigation of South Philadelphia's Seventh Ward. In part because of Du Bois's book the term "Philadelphia Negro" emerged as an important signifier for the African-American community, standing for those, according to scholar Nellie McKay, "who subscribed to a politics of the future 'uplift' of their race grounded in educational achievements, the accumulation of property, adherence to Victorian moral standards, and meaningful social engagement." This common identity stressed leadership, dignity, and racial solidarity in the face of prejudice.[7]

Marian Anderson's family was representative of Philadelphia's working people, a group that Du Bois characterized as "the mass of the servant class, the porters and waiters, and the best of the laborers." They were hardworking people, whose greatest drawback was the lack of good employment opportunities because of their race. They still managed to live in well kept up houses with neat parlors and often a musical instrument or two; social lives revolved around Sunday dinners and the church. Families in the respectable working class did not share the relative comfort of the black middle class, and certainly had a more difficult time than Du Bois's "best class" or "aristocracy" of clerks, teachers, professionals, and small merchants. But they were a cut above the poor, who could not even count on earning enough to keep themselves above want, and quite removed from what Du Bois identified as the vicious and criminal classes. Regardless of class, however, all of "Philadelphia's Negroes" were bound together by their experience of a deeply-rooted racism that most white Philadelphians simply took for granted.[8]

Marian Anderson was born in South Philadelphia on February 17, 1897. For most of her life, her birth date was given as 1902,[9] and sometimes as late as 1908. For the most part Anderson politely but firmly refused to divulge her age at all. As she once explained to a reporter, if she gave a specific age, some women would say, "I'll bet she's older than that," while others might react with, "I didn't know she was that old!" Like Babe Didrik-son, Anderson found it useful to shave off a few years at the beginning of her career to make her youthful accomplishments seem more striking. And like Martha Graham, she found it to her personal and professional advantage to disguise her true age as her career matured and she continued to perform well into her sixties.[10]

Probably the two most important touchstones in Marian Anderson's life were religion and family. "Religion is an anchor," she once said. "It is a pattern on which one fashions a life." So was family. Life with her parents and her two younger sisters, Alyce and Ethel, was "a thing of great joy:" "We lived in the kind of atmosphere where the family and home happened to be our whole world." (Like so many of the women in this book, and women achievers in general, Marian was the eldest child.) Her mother, Anna, had been a schoolteacher in Lynchburg, Virginia, before moving to Philadelphia; she was small in stature and light-skinned. Her darker and much taller father, John, worked for most of his life as a laborer at the Reading Terminal market, typ-ical of the menial jobs open to Philadelphia blacks; he also sold coal and ice. The homes the Andersons rented were often in mixed neighborhoods; as a child Marian played with white kids and her local grammar school was integrated. Marian did notice that on Sundays blacks and whites attended different churches, but she did not necessarily see this as a matter of color. Since most of her working-class neighbors were Irish, she simply surmised that whites were Catholics whereas her people were Methodists and Baptists.[11]

Anderson family life was shattered when Marian was ten: her father had an accident at work and died soon after, leaving Anna Anderson to care for her three daughters. Moving in temporarily with her in-laws, Mrs. Anderson was forced into the only kind of work available to black women at the time—taking in laundry, doing day work, or working downtown as a cleaning woman in a store like Wanamaker's. Soon Mrs. Anderson was able to move her family into a place of their own, where they managed to get by with a combination of cheerfulness and resourcefulness that astounded her daughter later on: "I've found this out in life, people can manage. You cut your garment according to the cloth. I do not remember a time that we needed a piece of bread or wanted something that wasn't forthcoming from someplace or another. Somehow my mother instinctively knew how to cut corners here and there and make things last." Probably the proudest moment in the singer's life came when she was making enough money from concert performances that she could call up Wanamaker's and tell them that her mother would not be coming into work anymore.[12]

Music and the church were always a special part of Marian Anderson's childhood, even though neither of her parents was especially musical. She attended Union Baptist Church (noted W. E. B. Du Bois in *The Philadelphia Negro*, "At Union Baptist one may look for the Virginia servant girls and their young men") and very quickly graduated from the children's to the adult choir. Because of the extraordinary range of her voice, she could sing all the parts, which was handy when choir members didn't show up on a Sunday morning. By the age of ten she was already giving recitals billed as "the baby contralto."[13]

The odds were certainly stacked against a young black girl from South Philadelphia achieving the kind of success she eventually did, but Marian Anderson was blessed with a support system that enabled her to forge a career out of what she saw as a gift from God—her voice. From her mother and her family, she developed self-confidence, poise, and resilience. Within her own neighborhood, she found role models not just of strong women holding families together under duress but also of women following their artistic muses. She never forgot the time she peeked through the windows of a house (even though she knew she shouldn't), drawn to the sound of music: "I saw a woman seated at a piano, playing it ever so beautifully. Her skin was dark, like mine. I realized if she could, I could."[14]

Luckily Anderson also grew up in an atmosphere that validated singing, especially when linked to religion. Tenor Roland Hayes, who was the first black singer to break into the white musical world with his combination of the classical repertoire and Negro spirituals, provided a special inspiration. Hayes took a personal interest in Marian's musical development, often asking her to join him on stage when he sang at her church. When Anderson's family could not afford singing lessons or other expenses connected with her performing, church members would take up a collection or schedule a benefit to help. (Her church did for her what black churches did for boys headed for the ministry in the nineteenth century.) At several key points these pledges of support made the difference between moving forward with her singing career and having to give it up or put it temporarily on hold.

The role of women in Marian Anderson's early life is striking, starting with her mother. "The faith my mother taught me is my foundation. It is the only ground on which I stand. . . . Her presence runs through everything I ever wanted to be." Then there was Mary Saunders Patterson, her first voice teacher, who gave her lessons for free and once loaned her a dress to wear to a concert. (Anderson kept a piece of that dress for the rest of her life.) And there was a white woman, Dr. Lucy Wilson, principal of South Philadelphia High School for Girls who rescued Anderson from the boring commercial course of study so that she could have more musical training as part of her high school curriculum.[15]

By this point it had become clear to Anderson and her supporters that she needed more formal training. Her voice was magnificent, but she had no idea of the mechanics of singing— she just opened her mouth and the notes came out. She decided to investigate music schools in the Philadelphia area. Too bad she had not read Du Bois's 1899 study, which stated flatly, "It goes without saying that most private schools, music schools, etc. will not admit Negroes and in some cases have insulted applicants." When she turned up at an unnamed Philadelphia music school to pick up an application, she was told curtly by the receptionist, "We don't take colored." She was so stunned that she did not try to plead her case, not that that would have been her style. She left silently, but deeply wounded: "I promise you I was as sick as if she'd hit me with her fist right in the middle of my stomach, and I mean really, physically sick." Characteristically she later refused to name the school, saying that its identity was unimportant.[16]

This episode became one of the seminal moments in Marian Anderson's introduction to discrimination. Another came during high school when she and her mother were on their way to a Southern concert. Forced to switch to a dirty and inferior Jim Crow railroad car as soon as they left the nation's capital, Anderson exclaimed with indignation: "One doesn't change as a person from Philadelphia to Washington!" These incidents served "to mark my growing up," and foreshadowed the racism she would have to face and surmount throughout her professional career.[17]

From the time of her graduation from high school until she left for Europe in the late 1920s, Anderson carefully and slowly built her career. (Margaret Truman once referred to these long years of artistic preparation as "the musical minor leagues."[18]) Through the generosity of friends and patrons, as well as her own hard-earned money from recitals, she studied with voice teachers like Agnes Reifsnyder, Giuseppe Boghetti, and Frank LaForge, always watching the clock as the minutes slipped away in precious (and expensive) lessons. She continued to tour and give concerts, mainly in the Northeast but occasionally in the South; the popular Philadelphia musician Billy King became her accompanist. Her fees were going up, but so were her expenses—for travel, for King's fee, for the gowns and accessories necessary to look presentable on stage. Yet too often they were playing the same places year after year, rather than reaching out to new audiences.

In 1924 Giuseppe Boghetti felt that the time was right for Anderson to give a solo recital at New York's Town Hall. Instead of advancing her career (as did Martha Graham's first New York recital just two years later), this premature concert practically derailed it. Spooked by walking out to a near-empty auditorium when she was expecting a full house, Anderson gave a lackluster performance, which failed to impress the critics. She was so discouraged that she considered giving up singing entirely. Her mother's unfailing support and a lot of prayer ("I do a great deal of praying") got her back on track, and the next year she beat out three hundred contestants to win a chance to sing with the New York Philharmonic Orchestra at Lewisohn Stadium in the summer of 1925. This concert drew more enthusiastic reviews than the Town Hall recital, but Anderson still could not escape the feeling that her career was stalled.[19]

One basic problem was that Anderson was not fluent in the languages of the songs that she was singing, and her less than stellar pronunciation was getting in the way of her luscious voice. One of the criticisms of her Town Hall concert had been that she sang as if by rote. She knew the gist of the German leider or French chansons she was singing, but did not always understand the meanings of actual words; she once forgot the words of a song and had to cover by improvising sounds. Anyone who spoke German or French would not have been fooled by her ruse, and she was deeply embarrassed by it.

Her desire to study the foreign languages in which she sang, and a general feeling that it was necessary to gain a European reputation before she could hope to conquer America, sent Marian Anderson abroad. For almost a decade until 1935 her primary musical audiences were European, although she returned to the States periodically for concerts and much-anticipated reunions with her family. Here she was following in the footsteps of Roland Hayes, who had used his European triumphs as an opening wedge to becoming a star in his native land. (In a very different context, it was not unlike George Zaharias urging Babe

Didrikson to enter the British Amateur Golf Tournament in 1947 as a way of boosting her reputation in the United States.) In the 1920s and 1930s, the rule of thumb for performing and creative artists was that you had to show your stuff in Europe first. Only then could you be "discovered" and brought back in triumph to American audiences. Martha Graham managed to escape this trap primarily because modern dance was seen as such a quintessential American art form that it would have been foolish to expect her to earn her stripes abroad.

One of the advantages for black artists performing in Europe was that they faced far less daily, grinding prejudice than in the United States. As Anderson noted, "They accepted you as an individual in your own right, judging you for your qualities as a human being and artist and for nothing else." There were no segregated trains or obstacles to finding first-class accommodations; audiences might be curious, but rarely hostile. When a Norwegian review described Anderson as "looking very much like a chocolate bar," she had far less reason to be offended than by reviews in her own country that called her a colored Negro girl or, in the South, refused to use "Miss" before her name.[20]

Despite the relative freedom from prejudice, Anderson never considered making Europe her permanent home. She would have missed her family dearly, plus she did not want to let down the friends and neighbors who believed in her. "I had gone to Europe to achieve something, to reach for a place as a serious artist, but I never doubted that I must return. I was—and am—an American."[21]

In the 1930s Anderson had her first taste of real success when she toured Scandinavia along with her Finnish accompanist, Kosti Vehanen. "Ah, a Negro singer with a Swedish name! She is bound to be a success in Scandinavia," a promoter reasoned, and soon the papers were talking about "Marian Fever." In order to have a serious concert career, however, she had to master German so that she could sing leider. She worked diligently at both her technique and her language skills, and in 1933 made a successful debut in Berlin. For the next two years she traveled the continent, culminating her tour with engagements in Vienna and at the Mozarteum in Salzburg. Music critic Herbert F. Peyser called her "a sensation of the Vienna music season" in an extremely laudatory review that ran in the *New York Times*. This helped to lay the groundwork for her eventual return.[22]

Her most important break came practically by chance. Impresario Sol Hurok, who had built a successful concert management business in the 1920s and 1930s by presenting European talent to American audiences, was in Paris in the summer of 1935 on one of his talent-scouting trips when he saw a flier for a concert by an American contralto named Marian Anderson. He decided to drop in, and was mesmerized by what he later described as a "tall, handsome Negro girl." (She was then in her mid-thirties.) Going backstage after the concert, he introduced himself and asked Anderson and Vehanen to come by his office the next day. She was flustered, since she had tried several times in the 1920s to interest him in her career but to no avail. In her words, this opportunity was "big time." After winning a release from her current American manager, who could not compete with the terms the Hurok organization was offering, Anderson put herself in Hurok's hands. From then until her farewell tour in 1964–1965, the marquee always read "S. Hurok Presents . . . Marian Anderson."[23]

Hurok quickly made plans for his new discovery to give a Town Hall concert in New York City in late December. In the meantime she had to make an important musical and symbolic decision: should she reunite with her old African-American accompanist, Billy King, or should she stay with Kosti Vehanen, who was white. As she remembered the dilemma, "If I did not use Billy King some of my own people might be offended. And particularly in the South, where I knew I would be singing, people might take offense that a white man was serving as my accompanist." She made the decision, she said, purely on musical grounds, selecting Vehanen, but the choice had its own symbol-

ic meanings, too. Few images were as powerful a symbol of inter-
racial cooperation as the black hand of Marian Anderson joining
the white hand of her accompanist as they took their bows at the
end of each concert.[24]

The long-awaited Town Hall concert almost didn't happen.
On the boat back to the United States, Anderson fractured her
ankle and found herself in a cast up to her knee. She determined
that she could still sing, if she leaned gently against the piano; as
long as she was already on stage behind a curtain when the audience assembled, her evening gown would easily cover the cast.
Why all the deception? She was horrified that pity might get in
the way of audiences and critics reacting to this most important
concert of her career. "I was there to present myself as an artist
and to be judged by that standard only." (Not coincidentally, that
was her approach to the issue of race as well.) The ruse worked.
When the audience was informed at intermission of the reason for
the unusual stage setting, they had already been completely won
over by her voice.[25]

The reviews the next day hailed a major new American star.
Harold Taubman's for the *New York Times* began: "Let it be said
at the outset: Marian Anderson has returned to her native land
one of the great singers of our time." Hurok immediately
announced a second concert at the larger Carnegie Hall to take
advantage of the excitement surrounding her return to America.[26]

Under Hurok's management, all the years of training and
exposure in Europe finally began to pay off, and Anderson was
poised to vault into the top echelons of concert stardom. By the
1937–1938 season, she was booked for seventy concerts, and by
1938–1939, ninety. The balance also shifted between the United
States and the continent: while she still made yearly trips to
Europe, the majority of her performances were now at home. In
retrospect it is lucky that she found her American audience when
she did, because the coming of World War II would close down
Europe for most artists starting in the late 1930s, with deleteri-
ous effects on the careers of European-based performers.[27]

Marian Anderson projected a dignified, almost regal presence. Music critic Howard Taubman called her "the voice of a race." (Courtesy University of Pennsylvania, University Libraries, Department of Special Collections.)

What Marian Anderson could not have anticipated, and surely would have shuddered at with horror if she had, was what Heywood Hale Broun called "one of the most monstrous and stupid things that have happened in America in years": the refusal by the Daughters of the American Revolution to allow her to sing in their Constitution Hall because of a contract clause that restricted its use to white artists only. Anderson did not want to force a showdown over segregation; she merely wanted to appear in Constitution Hall because it was the largest and best auditorium in the nation's capital and she felt she deserved to sing there. As she soon realized, events moved beyond her control.[28]

Eleanor Roosevelt played a central role in this story. The deep and long-lasting friendship between Marian Anderson and the First Lady dated to 1936 when the singer was invited to present a private recital at the White House. As often was the case when she performed near Philadelphia, her mother accompanied her.[29] Kosti Vehanen noted the "dignified atmosphere of tradition and also of the democratic spirit" of the event, plus this scene after the concert:

> Mrs. Roosevelt, our charming hostess, took Marian's mother by the hand, and led her over and introduced her to the President. I shall never forget seeing these two ladies enter the room. Mrs. Roosevelt's manner was sure and free, as becomes a woman of the world, happy to welcome the mother of America's best-known singer. In all of Mrs. Anderson's being, there was evident the feeling that this was one of the greatest moments of her life. Her face reflected her gratitude and the pride she felt.

When it came time for Marian to meet the president, he piped up, "You look just like your photographs, don't you?" which so flustered her that she completely forgot the little speech she had prepared for the occasion.[30]

Marian Anderson called Eleanor Roosevelt "one of the most admirable human beings that I have ever met" and then added, "I suspect that she has done a great deal for people that has never been divulged publicly. I know she did that for me." In the case of the DAR controversy, Roosevelt's support for Anderson was quite public, starting with her resignation from the organization upon learning of its stance. In a February 28, 1939, "My Day" column, Roosevelt talked about her decision, sharing her reasoning that in this case it was better to protest the policy publicly than to stay in the organization and try to work for change. Although she did not mention the DAR by name, reporters soon guessed the group's identity and the link to the aborted Anderson concert.[31]

Although Eleanor Roosevelt always claimed that "My Day" had nothing to do with politics, by the late 1930s she was becoming bolder in her advocacy of causes in which she believed. The DAR controversy was one of the first times she used her popularity and political clout to mobilize public opinion through her column, in effect making what could have been just a local brouhaha into a national issue. She received more mail supporting her resignation than on any other issue in 1939, and Gallup polls showed that 67 percent supported her decision. Martha Graham, on the other hand, was unable to get her mother to follow Mrs. Roosevelt's example and resign from the DAR. "They give such nice parties," objected Mrs. Graham.[32]

While Marian Anderson continued on her already scheduled national tour and tried to avoid reporters' questions about the escalating controversy, efforts intensified to find a way for Anderson to appear in the nation's capital after all. Eleanor Roosevelt was but one of a number of concerned citizens, both in official Washington and in the black community, working to this end. For a while it looked as if Anderson would be allowed to appear at the large Central High School auditorium, but this compromise collapsed when the school board refused to bend the strict segregation of the D.C. school system—the high school in question was for whites only.

It is not clear who originally came up with the idea for Anderson to give an open-air concert at the Lincoln Memorial, but Secretary of the Interior Harold Ickes, his assistant Oscar Chapman, and Eleanor Roosevelt strongly endorsed the idea. Franklin Roosevelt's feelings were clear: "I don't care if she sings from the top of the Washington Monument as long as she sings." In the end, the event was presented by Howard University and Associated Sponsors under the auspices of the Interior Department, which controlled the Lincoln Memorial; sponsors of the event included members of the Supreme Court and Congress, members of the cabinet, as well as civil rights leaders and representatives from the world of music and entertainment, including Leopold Stokowski, Geraldine Farrar, Tallulah Bankhead, and Katharine Hepburn. Eleanor Roosevelt was also a sponsor, but she made sure she was out of town the day of the concert so as not to overshadow it.[33]

Marian Anderson found herself in the extremely uncomfortable position of being the central figure in a battle that she would not have chosen to wage herself. Reluctantly she realized that her significance as an individual was small: "I had become, whether I liked it or not, a symbol representing my people. I had to appear. . . . I could not run away from this situation." Her own feelings were ones of sadness rather than pride or excitement: "I was sorry for the people who had precipitated the affair. I felt that their behavior stemmed from a lack of understanding." As she later said, "I had no bitterness, and I have no bitterness. If you are all right on the inside, you don't have to worry about things like that. They will eventually take care of themselves."[34] They did.

On Easter Sunday, April 9, 1939, before an integrated crowd of 75,000 and a national radio audience, Anderson delivered when the stakes were as high as any performance in her career. Secretary Ickes introduced the singer by declaring that "genius draws no color line" and linking the event to the legacy of Lincoln, who indeed seemed to look down benignly on the proceedings from inside the memorial. Then Anderson stepped forward, dressed in a fur coat and hat against the late afternoon chill and sang "America the Beautiful." Accompanied by Kosti Vehanen, she followed with arias by Donizetti and Schubert, and the spirituals "Gospel Train," "Trampin'," and "My Soul Is Anchored in the Lord." After the thunderous response, she also briefly addressed the crowd, although she had to read what she had said in the papers the next day because, so overcome by emotion, she had no memory of what words came out of her mouth.[35]

Anderson's dignified and powerful performance at the Lincoln Memorial cemented her place as one of the leading American concert artists and a prominent symbol of her race. She had already been chosen as the 1938 recipient of the Spingarn Medal given annually by the National Association for the Advancement of Colored People for "the highest and noblest achievement by an American Negro"; Eleanor Roosevelt presented her with the medal in a July 1939 ceremony with these words, "Your achievement far transcends any race or creed." In 1940, Anderson won the equally prestigious Bok award presented to the Philadelphian who had contributed the most to the city in the past year. She in turn used the $10,000 prize money to establish a scholarship for aspiring artists regardless of race.[36]

The Lincoln Memorial concert had a monumental impact on Anderson's career. When the whole DAR story broke, conservative columnist Westbrook Pegler publicly speculated that it was a publicity stunt on behalf of a "hitherto obscure Negro singer." Pegler's charge was ridiculous, yet it is hard to imagine impresario Sol Hurok being able to orchestrate anything with publicity value equal to what actually happened. Instead of being just the fifty-ninth stop on the concert tour of a well-known singer, the Washington performance became a national event. The DAR had created another personality for her, noted one writer, "that of the noble and persecuted Negro woman."[37] Her fees doubled, and she found herself booked two years in advance; Eleanor Roosevelt invited her back to the White House to perform for the King and Queen of England. She had finally reached the pinnacle of her profession, and would stay there until her retirement in 1965.

Coming just months after the Lincoln Memorial concert, the awarding of the NAACP Spingarn medal for "the highest and noblest achievement by an American Negro" to Marian Anderson received even more attention than usual. And who was more appropriate to present the medal than Eleanor Roosevelt. (UPI/Corbis-Bettman)

JUST AS SPORTS provided Babe Didrikson's ticket out of the Texas poverty she grew up in, music opened up whole new worlds for Marian Anderson, giving her the chance to travel around the world and meet many interesting people over the five decades of her performing career. The downside was that she was always on the move, her life scheduled and booked months, indeed years in advance. Once she showed up for a photo shoot with Carl Van Vechten in the midst of a raging blizzard. "Why didn't you wait for an easier time?" he asked. She replied matter of factly, "In my life there are no easy times, I am always busy. One hour or one day is like the next."[38]

Marian Anderson could never have handled the demands of her career without the help of her manager, Sol Hurok. "I owe more than I can say to this fabulous man. There must be other performers who were better equipped for a great career and who were simply not lucky enough to have Mr. Hurok at the helm." (Martha Graham was under Hurok's management for two seasons in the 1940s, but her company's national tours lost so much money that Hurok could not afford to present her.) Hurok's personal interest in Marian Anderson's career ripened into a warm and long-lived friendship; one of the most vibrant chapters in his autobiography, *Impresario*, covered his association with the artist, and she would deliver the eulogy at his Carnegie Hall funeral in 1974.[39]

Hurok once pointed out that audiences only saw the polished performance, not all that went into getting the performer on the stage:

> They do not stop to think—nor should they—of the many months in a concert artist's life during which her only home is the drawing room of a train, her most intimate horizon the impersonal plains and mountains of America speeding past the window, her human relationships the fleeting handclasp of a welcoming committee, the ministrations of a hostess in the few hours between train and concert, between concert and train.

In the hectic years of the late 1930s, Anderson might perform close to a hundred concerts a year. At the time it seemed wonderful to be in such demand, but she later had second thoughts:

"When I look back on that kind of schedule I realize how silly it was. How could I be at my best every night?"[40]

Marian Anderson only sang music she believed in: "There are things in the heart that must enrich the songs I sing." Her favorite composer was Schubert, followed by Brahms, Schumann, Hugo Wolf, and Richard Strauss. She displayed no affinity for modern music, but did like to feature lesser-known American and European composers. And following the precedent of Roland Hayes, every concert included a set of spirituals. "They are my own music, but it is not for that reason that I love to sing them," Anderson explained. "I love the spirituals because they are truly spiritual in quality; they give forth an aura of faith, simplicity, humility, and hope." Her favorite was "He Has the Whole World in His Hands," but audiences were most moved by her haunting rendition of the "mumblin' words" of "The Crucifixion." Besides displaying the richness of the contralto's voice, singing spirituals drew attention to the struggles of the African-American people and thus served as a powerful statement against racism.[41]

Even before the DAR controversy, Marian Anderson had established herself as one of the few artists who could regularly guarantee a sell-out box office. In 1938, music critic Marcia Davenport attributed this appeal to the sort of musical attraction that people meant when they spoke of "the good old days": "Like the 'old-time religion,' the old time concert is waning; today there is nothing in it, as a rule, vital enough to compel the loyalty of millions." Like the lecture tours that brought Eleanor Roosevelt, Margaret Mead, and Dorothy Thompson to communities across the country, Marian Anderson's recitals provided a viable way for her to reach her public and build a following, especially under Hurok's skilled management. Opera, however, remained out of the question for any black artist at that time, no matter how talented or popular.[42]

One of the demands that Anderson made early on, and which

Hurok fully supported, was a refusal to sing in segregated halls, in which whites were given the better orchestra seats and blacks relegated to the upper balconies. If an open seating plan was not feasible, Anderson insisted on vertical segregation of the races, that is, blacks would have access to the most expensive seats and the cheapest in the same proportion as whites. In concerts, especially in Southern cities, she would often bow extra long to the section of the concert hall where "her people" were seated. Once the recital was over, however, there was no segregation backstage, and "my own people always streamed backstage almost triumphantly": "They were so delighted at the recognition I was getting that they felt the auditorium was theirs for an evening."[43]

Ironically, given the many times that race intruded on her career, the fact that Anderson was a black performer also enhanced her stature and appeal. Music critic Robert T. Jones noted that in 1935 "black singers singing music by Italian and German and French composers had a novelty value that was highly commercial—at least in certain areas." In Anderson's case, it set her apart from the constellation of other touring artists, many of them European—how many in the general public could distinguish between Lotte Lehman, Jarmila Novotny, and Elisabeth Rethberg? On the other hand, everyone had heard of "the sensational Negro contralto," a phrase that Hurok used in his promotional material for the 1936–1937 season.[44]

With Anderson's growing box-office appeal went other trappings of stardom, such as radio broadcasts and recording contracts. She recorded exclusively for RCA Victor Red Seal from 1936 on, but she missed the electricity of a live concert in her studio work. "I cannot stress too strongly how significant a role the audience plays in any concert. Although I sing with my eyes closed, I have a picture of the audience out front." Unlike Martha Graham, who refused to authorize filming of her performances, Anderson left a legacy of recorded performances and studio recordings; new audiences today can discover for themselves the majesty of Anderson's voice in its prime, thanks to digital remastering. These recordings represented a significant source of income. Her rendition of "Ave Maria" alone had sold 750,000 copies by the mid-1950s.[45]

The star received an enormous volume of mail, including requests for concerts, benefits, sponsorships, and other demands on her time. Sometimes fan mail was sent to the artist at Carnegie Hall or to her farm in Connecticut; one letter got to her with an address that would surely flummox today's automated postal system: Marian Anderson, Famed Contralto, c/o Postmaster, Danbury, Connecticut. Anderson was a terrible correspondent and tried in vain to keep up with her mail, often lugging it with her on concert tours only to return home with it still unread and unanswered. When she did finally get to it, her responses (like the singer herself) were gracious and generous. To her, every letter writer was a friend, and "One is always happy to hear from friends."[46]

One of the great advantages of being managed by the Hurok organization was the support staff that it provided. In Marian Anderson's case, Isaac Jofe traveled with her to oversee the day-to-day logistics of touring. (Given that Anderson traveled with upwards of twenty pieces of luggage, including a sewing machine, sleeping bag, iron, hot plate, and record player, as well as formal gowns and street wear, this was probably especially helpful.) Also traveling with her was her accompanist Franz Rupp, who had replaced Kosti Vehanen when he returned to Europe after war broke out. For eight or nine months on the road, she spent most of her time with these two white men, a highly unusual situation at the time. No matter how many eyebrows this trio raised, they made quite a companionable group, all being indefatigable sightseers.

The calmness so evident in Anderson's stage demeanor came in handy when facing the inevitable slights and insults that came her way traveling in the still-segregated America of the

1930s, 1940s, and 1950s. "Sometimes it's like a hair across your cheek," she remembered. "You can't see it, you can't find it with your fingers, but you keep brushing at it because the feel of it is irritating." Hurok and Jofe tried to shield her from these incidents, but they were not always successful. At times the Hurok organization had to resort to blackmail, such as threatening to withdraw all Hurok bookings from a hotel or concert hall, to make sure that Anderson was welcome. Even then she could often tell when an exception had been made in her case, an experience she described as a "cool breeze that blew from the persons who were waiting on me." She often ate in her room, which she claimed was more restful, but it also removed the possibility of being denied service in the dining room. Rather than cause a scene over these small indignities, she focused all her energy on her performances. "It is better not to know for sure," she once said of these situations. "It is more comfortable not to think about it if I can avoid it."[47]

She wore these selective blinders as a form of protection: even though she stood for the race publicly, she tried to orchestrate or control exposure to racism in her personal life. Take the matter of travel and accommodations—here was one of the top artists in the entire country, earning perhaps $100,000 a year in the late 1930s, the same as Dorothy Thompson or Eleanor Roosevelt. Why shouldn't she be able to have a decent sleeper berth on a train rather than being forced to sit up all night because of prejudice against a black passenger sharing the washroom with a white in the morning? As she once said, she didn't see this as a social opportunity; she merely expected comfortable accommodations. Why should a famous singer have to stay in private homes when she could afford the best suite at any hotel in town? (Anderson stayed at the home of former Pennsylvania governor Gifford Pinchot and his wife Cornelia before the Lincoln Memorial concert because all of Washington's hotels were closed to blacks.) Why would a taxi driver, when he picked up Anderson in midtown Manhattan to take her uptown to her apartment, assume that she was coming from a day's work as a domestic rather than a meeting with Sol Hurok? She excused these slights with this simple yet empowering philosophy: "As long as you keep a person down, some part of you has to be down there to hold him down."[48]

As in all other aspects of her life, Anderson chose a dignified and measured response to racial matters. "If I were inclined to be combative, I suppose I might insist on making issues of these things. But that is not my nature, and I always bear in mind that my mission is to leave behind me the kind of impression that will make it easier for those who follow." For example, she was extremely meticulous about tipping those who gave her good service when she traveled, from porters to bellhops to maids to waiters. She also tipped stagehands and others who helped backstage at concerts. These tips were not extravagant (and she carefully kept track of them, in part because she was reimbursed by the Hurok organization for her expenses), but one suspects that she was walking a fine line: not to give too much and appear to be flaunting her wealth, and not to be so stingy as to reflect poorly on a member of her race who had made good. She was determined to show America what a Negro of wealth and character looked like.[49]

Anderson also learned to be gracious when a white hostess took her back into the kitchen to meet the cook or other domestic help, who were invariably black. Anderson did not object to this (probably because she understood the way in which she was revered by her own people), but she did wonder if the same woman would have taken a white artist back to meet the help. If the hostess did not specifically introduce the visiting artist to blacks who were serving at the event, Anderson would try to find some way to acknowledge their presence. And yet Anderson would never initiate conversations with white help—"I'm afraid they'll think I'm getting above myself," she told a frankly astonished white friend.[50]

Soloists depend on their accompanists; Marian Anderson and Franz Rupp formed an especially close relationship. When they appeared together on stage at the end of a performance, black hand clasped in white, it paid tribute to their musical collaboration. The gesture was also a profound if subtle statement of racial harmony. (Courtesy University of Pennsylvania, University Libraries, Department of Special Collections.)

This sense that Anderson was not just performing as an individual but as a representative of her entire race reinforced the special attention she paid to her wardrobe and appearance. "I began to realize, particularly when I appeared in the South, how important one's appearance was. I think that my people felt a sense of pride in seeing me dressed well." Like most performing artists, she hired a dressmaker to make her clothes rather than buying them off the rack; dress fittings were as much a part of the routine of preparing for a season of concerts as choosing music with her accompanist. She called evening gowns her "working uniform," but was reluctant to wear clothes she considered showy or flamboyant—once while touring in Scandinavia she cut off the train to a dress because she thought it too extravagant. "No one needs to tell me that I am not a glamour girl, and I do not try to dress like one," she said. "I do not go in for things that dazzle, for I am not a dazzler." Dazzler or not, she learned to present an elegant presence on stage, one which audiences rarely failed to notice. And she took more pleasure in her wardrobe over the years, keeping favorite gowns long after she could no longer fit into them.[51]

Her clothes style when she wasn't performing was simple, elegant, and classic—suits and dresses, hats and simple purses, and what seems to have been a penchant for expensive shoes.[52] Sometimes when she was sightseeing, she wore tailored pants, which looked fine on her figure. She wore her hair chin length and with a slight wave; the fact that her hair color stayed the same very dark black for her entire performing career suggests that at some point she began dying it. Anderson was tall—almost five-foot-nine—and statuesque. She was not especially concerned with her weight, but sometimes she was heavier than at others, although never to a point where she could be called seriously overweight. Like so much else about her demeanor, she carried it well.[53]

As part of her carefully crafted persona as a representative of her race, Anderson could never afford to be sloppy or inappropriately dressed. As her mother had so often said, "Remember, wherever you are and whatever you do, someone always sees you." When members of her church choir were interviewed for a PBS documentary, the strongest memory of one elderly black woman was of Anderson just back from Europe. "A colored lady in a black persian lamb coat," now that was something! What do most people remember about Anderson standing up before the Lincoln Memorial on that Easter Sunday in 1939? The fur coat that she was wearing. (Her nephew, conductor James DePriest, has since donated the coat to the Smithsonian Institute.) These items of expensive clothing were confirmation that success could happen. More to the point, the simple and understated way that Anderson wore these clothes underscored that black wealth and affluence could be tasteful, not garish, a rejoinder to the popular vaudeville and film stereotypes of suddenly rich blacks flaunting their diamonds, loud clothes, and other symbols of conspicuous consumption.[54]

Marian Anderson was proud of her successes but she also heeded another of her mother's dicta that "grace must always come before greatness." Perhaps Fanny Hurst had that in mind when she said at a Hurok-sponsored gala on the tenth anniversary of Anderson's Town Hall debut, "She has not grown simply great, she has grown great simply." She refused to act like a celebrity and hated to be the center of attention, which made her seem smaller and less imposing off stage than on. She learned to cooperate with reporters, but disliked publicity. In fact, she could barely force herself to talk about herself in the first person, invariably resorting to "we" when describing the accomplishments of her career.[55]

In a tribute to the artist after her death, the *New Yorker* noted, "Marian Anderson represented an old style of American gentility. She did not cherish disturbances." She never threw temper tantrums, never had an argument with her accompanist, never walked off the stage during rehearsals; her personal life was free from scandal or impropriety. The musical world of the 1930s and 1940s would not have been ready for a tempestuous black diva, but acting that part would have been entirely foreign to Anderson's upbringing and style. She chose a different route. Every aspect of her life, from her family to her career to larger political questions, she approached with a philosophy that preached "One could be black and succeed in a white world with dignity."[56]

At the core of Marian Anderson's being was a certain alone-ness, an emotional self-sufficiency that Kosti Vehanen once described in this way: "Marian's heart is like a little golden cas-ket that is extremely difficult to open; perhaps no one will ever do that. . . . She guards it carefully in order, one feels, that no liv-ing being can come near enough to disturb the great calmness of her soul." This inner calm and serenity stood her in good stead throughout her career, but one has to wonder at the psychologi-cal cost of keeping her emotions so tightly bottled up inside in what Nellie McKay called "her life inside her silken cocoon." Like so many other aspects of her private life, Anderson chose not to share her scars or disappointments with the world at large.[57]

Marian Anderson's choices and personal demeanor make more sense when placed in the larger social and political context of black women's history. Many black women exhibited a strong collective sense of community, including a commitment to racial self-help and uplift to counter the indifference or outright hostil-ity of white America. Religion was often central to their hopes for their race and their identity as women. Marian Anderson's life can be seen as a musical variation on this pattern of black women's work in the culture of uplift: through her voice, her deep spiri-tuality, and her modest yet determined behavior she embodied the highest ideals of what was then proudly called "Negro wom-anhood."[58]

Anderson was hardly the first black woman to adopt this strat-egy. Claiming respect and respectability had long been the goal of the vibrant black women's club movement, which flourished from the 1890s on. Even more than black men, black women were the subjects of a range of demeaning and damaging stereo-types, ranging from the devoted Mammy to the oversexed Jezebel to the controlling wife Sapphire who lords it over the timid black male.[59] As club women worked to improve their communities, they also worked to uplift the image of black womanhood, "lift-ing as we climb" in the memorable slogan of the National Asso-ciation of Colored Women. This strategy was especially important in the South in the bleak years after the introduction of Jim Crow, when black women stepped into the vacuum in the public sphere created by the disfranchisement of black men.[60]

This struggle for respect was also, according to historian Eve-lyn Brooks Higginbotham, the key to understanding the role of black women in the Baptist church in these years. By asserting that African Americans could be decent, moral, respectable citi-zens (what Higginbotham calls "the politics of respectability"), black church women were struggling to be allowed to define themselves at the same time they were challenging racism. They sought "reform of individual behavior and attitudes both as a goal in itself and as a strategy for reform of the entire structural system of American race relations." In this way an emphasis on morals and manners, indeed class, was an important political statement. And it was one that black women were uniquely qual-ified to make.[61]

So when an elegant, beautiful black woman like Marian Anderson became a success, and did so with dignity and class, this message undermined the basis for racism in the first place, by revealing a black woman who in every way but her skin color matched the most successful whites. This is not to imply, obvi-ously, that the only goal for blacks was to make it in a white world on white standards; Marian Anderson's aspirations were far more complex than that. Anderson refused to let race be used against her to deny her the privileges to which she was entitled by virtue of her artistry, status, and celebrity. And she demanded that black women be given the same respect that white women received in the culture at large. In the America of the 1930s,

1940s, and 1950s, just *being* Marian Anderson could be a powerful political—and potentially feminist—statement.

§

SOME OF MARIAN Anderson's friends thought "her destined to
be forever rootless, a career-woman who traveled the world's great
cities, singing before kings and presidents," a perennial "bache-
lor girl." A 1942 Associated Press biographical blurb on the
artist stated starkly, "She never married." The piece incorrectly
listed a birth date of 1908, which would have made her only thirty-four, a little early to have given up on marriage, it would seem.
Less than a year later Marian Anderson proved both the Associated Press and her friends wrong by marrying Orpheus K. Fisher,
an architect she had known since high school. He was forty-three,
she was forty-six, although the announcement in the press gave
her age as thirty-eight.[62]

The young singer first met her future husband, who was usually called King, on a concert trip to Wilmington, Delaware,
around the time of World War I. Alice Moore Dunbar, widow of
the noted black poet Paul Laurence Dunbar, introduced the two,
who saw more of each other once Fisher moved to Philadelphia to
attend art school. He was far more eager for marriage than she
was; whenever he pressed, she pulled back. "I knew he was always
there because I knew that he was an interested person and I was
interested in him to a degree, but at that time music was the
most important thing in my life. He had his own career as an
architect, and we would see each other from time to time or he
would write, but it was not often." Referring to herself in the
third person in her autobiography, she said simply, "one gets
swept up in a career, and one has time for little else." But neither
one married as the years passed, and at some point they seem to
have decided that if they ever married it would be to each other.
Rumors about an impending match circulated in the black press
in 1939, 1940, and 1942, so theirs must have been a fairly open
relationship. They finally tied the knot on July 17, 1943, in

Bethel, Connecticut, although the press did not report the wedding until November of that year.[63]

The decision to get married was linked to Anderson's decision to buy a country retreat, which she had done in 1939 in Danbury, Connecticut. Although they were not yet married, King participated in the often frustrating search for a suitable property. As soon as sellers learned that the famous contralto was interested in their property, one of two things happened: the property was withdrawn from the market entirely or the price was jacked up, either to discourage her from buying or to capitalize on her widely-reported high earnings. "In the end," Anderson reported with more acerbity than usual in a 1960 article, "we had to buy a place with twice the amount of acreage we needed so we wouldn't contaminate the neighborhood." It was worth it. She named it Marianna Farm, a combination of her name and her mother's. Every summer Anderson recuperated there from the rigors of her performing schedule, welcoming her mother, sister, and beloved nephew for extended visits.[64]

The 115-acre property came with an old farmhouse, and after their marriage Fisher began to remodel it. In the 1950s they decided to build a modern, single-story house on another part of the property; he designed the house and supervised its construction, serving as his own contractor to cut costs. The new house was completed in 1954. One of the special attractions of the setup was a separate state-of-the-art recording and practice studio for Anderson, where she could work with her accompanist Franz Rupp to prepare recitals for the following season. Having labored under a lifelong (and probably unnecessary) fear of disturbing neighbors or guests with her practicing, she could now sing without bothering a soul.

Anderson jokingly referred to herself as "just a plain dirt farmer" and she loved puttering around the place. She was an avid gardener, and grew so many vegetables that Marianna Farm sold the surplus at local markets. The farm was filled with the animals that she and King loved, including horses, cattle, German shepherds, a Kerry Blue called Falla, and a pair of pigs named Phyllis and Pontiac. She and her husband invested a lot of energy and cash in the farm, but like Dorothy Thompson's Twin Farms in Vermont, it tended to eat up money faster than it made it. Sighed Fisher, "We'd like to think the farm pays its way, but it doesn't."[65]

The farm also allowed Anderson, in the revealing words of a television documentary, "to merely be a woman." This wasn't simply one of those 1950s paeans to domesticity that Hollywood churned out, with Joan Crawford or Betty Grable in an apron gamely making toast or pushing a broom. Marian Anderson, like Babe Didrikson, genuinely enjoyed spending time as a homemaker as a respite from the months she spent on the road. "I find it a pleasure to keep house," she told readers of her autobiography in 1956; when asked what she planned to do after her retirement, she said simply, "To be a homemaker." And yet her time devoted to housewifery was distinctly limited to summers on the farm, and then only when she felt like it. Like most women of her economic status, she depended on a staff of full-time servants.[66]

Photographs of Anderson puttering around Marianna Farm, often in slacks, were prominently featured in the souvenir programs that the Hurok organization put together. Audiences were interested in seeing what the famous artist was like when she was not performing, and the curiosity factor was perhaps a little higher when the artist was black. *Ebony*, the leading magazine directed at middle-class Negroes in the 1940s and 1950s, also ran several spreads about the farm that allowed readers to sample Anderson's gracious country living. In one such feature in *Ebony* in February 1954, a photograph of Orpheus Fisher was accompanied by this caption: "Because of his ruddy complexion, Fisher is often mistaken for a white man." It was true, so true that one wonders if concertgoers seeing a photograph of her husband in a souvenir book might have assumed that the artist was married to a white man.[67]

In 1960 Anderson shared with readers of the *Ladies' Home Jour-*

In the early days of her career, Marian Anderson usually traveled by train, but in the 1950s she began to fly, especially when touring abroad. Sometimes her husband, Orpheus Fisher, came along. Photographs like this suggest how the light-skinned Fisher might have been mistaken for white. (Courtesy University of Pennsylvania, University Libraries, Department of Special Collections.)

nal the fact that for years her husband had passed as white. He did it "for the same reason a good many other Negroes who are able to, pass. Economically, it's greatly to their advantage. . . . You know yourself, no one, to look at him, would ever suppose he is a Negro. So he took advantage of that in order to get started on a career." According to Anderson, King held one job long enough to prove that he could pass, but then he grew tired of the burden of living the deception on a daily basis and quit. "If white people think Negroes enjoy passing they're very much mistaken," Anderson told the white interviewer who was also her friend. "It's a terrible decision to make."[68]

Just as Anderson was criticized for touring with a white accompanist rather than a member of her race, she may also have been criticized (privately, never in print) for marrying such a light-skinned husband, a touchy issue for many in the African-American community. On the other hand, in certain quarters she was probably admired for it, because light skin was often seen as a marker of higher status. Either way she certainly would have dismissed such judgments as an intrusion on her personal privacy.

By all accounts she and King had a very satisfactory marriage. She called him an "understanding person, and without such a man our marriage could not have worked out, for I am still away from home entirely too much." He kept an office at the farm and conducted his architectural practice from there. He did not usually accompany her on tours, so they exchanged nightly telephone calls; Anderson's long-distance phone bills back to Connecticut and to her mother in Philadelphia probably rivaled Dorothy Thompson's.[69]

Yet it cannot have been entirely easy to live as Marian Anderson's husband. (Yes, he did occasionally get mail addressed to Mr. Anderson.) She was the primary wage earner in the family, and her income made possible their affluent lifestyle. In this marriage, she wrote the checks, giving him a monthly allowance to cover farm and other expenses. While she obviously kept her name for professional purposes, their friends usually referred to her as Mrs. Fisher, as did he: "We have a good marriage because we never do anything without consulting each other. . . . Mrs. Fisher is a very remarkable woman and that's a reward in itself." Showing just the slightest touchiness on the subject, he announced to the Connecticut staff right after their marriage, "The first person who calls my wife Miss Anderson is going to be fired." No one ever was, and King was good-spirited enough to agree to an interview with *Ebony* entitled "How to Live with a Famous Wife."[70]

Perhaps not surprisingly given the ages at which they married, theirs was a marriage without children. "Having children is a great responsibility, and we sincerely believed that they would have been a great joy to both of us. We have been sorry that when we decided we wanted a family, it was a bit late." But it was not just a matter of timing—not having children was a "sacrifice" determined by the burdens of her career:

> When we were married we made plans to have a family. But I had more concert work than ever before, and we postponed other things. We both felt that we wanted to raise our own children, not to turn them over to nurses. Certainly I did not want to drag a child with me on my travels.

Anderson later wondered whether they made the right decision, especially since she believed that her husband would have been a good father and that children made a home complete. "We have animals, on whom we lavish much attention, but they do not take the place of children. I admire the women in my profession who manage to sustain singing careers and raise families. Perhaps I should have been more daring. But one has to be true to one's own nature, which left me no choice but to make this additional sacrifice, which King shares."[71]

Like Katharine Hepburn and to a lesser degree Martha Graham, Anderson also harked back to memories of her childhood and found herself not up to the standards that her own mother had set. Whenever Anderson thought about what kind of parent she would have been, "I thought of my mother. She was always there. To leave your child with someone else is never the same. Something is missing." On another occasion, she put the legacy in more positive terms: "My great desire if I could have had a family, was to devote as much time to our children as my mother did. If we had been half as successful as she was with us, we would have done a very good job."[72]

More so than any of the other women in this book, Marian Anderson seemed to use her marriage as a buffer against the public world. She and King cultivated an elegant yet understated lifestyle, befitting her celebrity. They enjoyed their private time together when Marian was not on tour, especially if they were surrounded by friends and beloved family members like Mrs. Anderson (who lived until 1964) and Marian's favorite nephew James. Husband and wife depended on each other, and yet each accepted the long separations necessitated by the demands of her career. The fact that they waited so long to marry, and married with their professional careers in place, probably added to the evenness and strength of this relationship, which lasted until Orpheus Fisher's death in 1986.

🦜

MARIAN ANDERSON'S ROUTE home from high school in the 1910s took her under a railroad trestle. She later admitted dreaming about the trains rumbling overhead, " 'Oh, if just one of these days I could be on a train with the Metropolitan Opera Company going somewhere.' And so I prayed to the evening star, and I prayed, and I prayed." In 1954 her prayers were finally answered, when she was invited by Metropolitan Opera manager Rudolph Bing to perform at the Met. When she made her operatic debut in January 1955 as Ulrica in Verdi's *Un Ballo in Maschera (The Masked Ball)*, she was the first black person ever to sing on the stage at the Metropolitan.[73]

Anderson's Metropolitan debut can be read in two not necessarily contradictory ways: outrage that racism kept her from major operatic roles until her voice was past its prime (she was then fifty-seven years old), or as a historic turning point, breaking the color bar at the Met and immediately opening its stage to rising generations of talented black singers. Anderson, as was her wont, avoided recriminations and focused on the positive meanings of the event: "The chance to be a member of the Metropolitan has been a highlight of my life. It has meant much to me and to my people. If I have been privileged to serve as a symbol, to be the first Negro to sing as a regular member of the company, I take greater pride from knowing that it has encouraged other singers of my group to realize that doors everywhere may be open increasingly to those who have prepared themselves well." To the press Anderson put it even more simply, "Now one is speechless."[74]

Even though she dreamed as a young girl of singing with the Met, realistically Anderson seemed to have known that opera was out of the question for a black performer in the United States in her youth. There was no law or ordinance; it was just a deeply rooted convention that had never been challenged. Europe was different. On a trip to the Soviet Union in the 1930s, she was offered the chance to sing Carmen, but she passed on the opportunity. "I was young, and time stretched invitingly before me. What was the hurry?" When her career took off back in the States, she focused entirely on recitals, with occasional orchestral appearances. Luckily it was still possible to build a career that way, a different situation from today when world-class singers blend opera with solo concerts, and in fact often use their operatic fame as springboards to successful solo recording and performing careers. In effect, Marian Anderson did it in reverse. "Welcome home," said a stagehand backstage at the Met.[75]

As performers (and the public) have long realized, opera and concertizing demand very different stage personae. Anderson's majestic but unflamboyant recital style, indeed her whole approach to life, was in many ways the antithesis of the kind of theatricality necessary to be a good opera performer. When she rehearsed the part of Ulrica, she had to force herself to overcome her tendency to stay rooted in one spot on the stage. She had by then been performing for more than four decades, and it could not have been easy to venture into this new musical venue, especially when she knew how many eyes would be watching.

Like her performance at the Lincoln Memorial concert sixteen years before, Anderson rose to the occasion. Her part was fairly small, and she did not appear onstage until the beginning of the second scene. Sporting a long black wig and wearing a gypsy costume of long skirt, peasant blouse, and scarves, she sang while stirring a cauldron. (Without diminishing the gravity of the occasion or her performance, in her costume she bore an uncanny ressemblance to the gypsy woman onstage in *A Night at the Opera* at whom Groucho Marx yells "boogie-boogie" from the balcony.) She was not especially pleased with the first performance, but received an overwhelming response from the audience, which included her husband, her mother, and members of the Hurok organization. With great pride she repeated the performance several weeks later on tour with the company in her home town of Philadelphia.

In the aftermath of the concert, the Met approached the Hurok organization about her availability for the next season. "You didn't think that we were doing this as a stunt, did you?" they told the somewhat surprised managers. Instead of demanding a larger part, she asked to play Ulrica again. Always the perfectionist, she wanted to do it better.[76]

Marian Anderson always remained grateful to the Met for the tasteful way in which the entire situation was handled, and she never forgot the incredible response from the public. "I may have dreamed of such things, but I had not foreseen that I would play a part in the reality." There was probably a sigh of relief in the opera world that this arbitrary yet embarrassing barrier had toppled so easily. Doors opened immediately to other African Americans to sing at the Met, starting with Robert McFerrin and Mattiwilda Dobbs that same year. So striking was the flowering of operatic talent among black singers, male and female, that it quickly became difficult to imagine a lily-white Metropolitan production.[77]

Marian Anderson's Metropolitan debut joined such other symbolic racial breakthroughs of the immediate postwar years as Jackie Robinson's signing with the Brooklyn Dodgers in 1947 and Althea Gibson's winning Wimbledon in 1957. When asked if her Metropolitan debut was comparable to Jackie Robinson's baseball breakthrough, Anderson replied, "One hopes so. It would be a matter of pride." That statement reads differently when you realize Anderson was a rabid Dodgers fan, but the sentiment is just as true.[78]

Being the "First Negro" (or the "first woman") inevitably placed enormous pressure on those who broke barriers. Althea Gibson had "always wanted to be somebody," but like Marian Anderson, she never considered herself a crusader. "I am not a racially conscious person," she wrote in 1958. "I'm a tennis player, not a Negro tennis player. I have never set myself up as a champion of the Negro race." Like Anderson, "I feel our best chance to advance is to prove ourselves as individuals." That was not the only strategy available to advance the cause of civil rights, but it was a viable one.[79]

In contrast to the attention focused on Marian Anderson as a leader of her race, far less publicity came to her as a symbol of women. One reason was that she herself never talked about women's issues or feminism. When the women's movement revived in the 1960s, reporters did not rush to her concerts to ask her about Betty Friedan's *The Feminine Mystique*, the Presidential Commission on the Status of Women, or the founding of the National Organization for Women. They did, however, ask her about Little Rock, Selma, and the March on Washington. Although she was a much-admired woman, she was not generally associated in the public's mind with women's issues per se, probably because at that time feminism was seen primarily as relevant to white women, whereas black women were thought to be more concerned with racial matters.

By the time of her Met debut, Marian Anderson had settled comfortably into the upper echelons of star status—her reputation was secure and her popularity continued to grow. She no longer had to prove herself year after year, she just had to continue to do what she had been doing, and her loyal public would follow. In 1956, she sat down to write her autobiography, timed no doubt to capitalize on the publicity surrounding her new operatic career. Its apolitical tone, in keeping with the 1950s, was probably intentional. Not at all introspective and filled with many silences, the narrative nonetheless told an inspirational story of hard work and achievement by a person who was in the best sense of the word "a Philadelphia Negro."[80]

In 1957, the State Department arranged to send Marian Anderson on a hugely successful good will trip to Asia. The highpoint was her visit to India, where she was the first foreigner ever invited to speak at Gandhi's shrine. After delivering an already eloquent eulogy, she lapsed into a moment of silence and then moved the crowd by unexpectedly beginning to sing "Lead, Kindly Light." When critics charged that Anderson's visit was merely a propaganda tool for the United States government, Dorothy Thompson used one of her last "On the Record" columns to come to Anderson's defense. (The next year Thompson seconded Anderson's nomination to New York's elite Cosmopolitan Club, calling her "not only one of the greatest artists in this country today, but one of the greatest spiritual forces in the world.") Anderson's tour was the basis for a December 1957 Edward R. Murrow "See It Now" documentary called *The Lady from Philadelphia*, which brought Anderson's story to a nationwide television audience.[81]

The symbol of a black American touring on behalf of the United States in the racially charged 1950s no doubt gave President Dwight Eisenhower the idea of appointing Anderson an alternate delegate to the United Nations in 1958–1959, what Harold Schonberg called "the other voice of Marian Anderson." While she was honored to be following in the footsteps of Eleanor Roosevelt, Anderson characteristically demurred that she was not qualified for the post, and felt awkward at having to present the views of her country rather than her own. Mainly, however, she found the job "confining," since she was used to an active concert schedule. Once the session ended, she happily returned to her first love, music.[82]

Around this time, critics began to discuss in print what many had been talking about in private for quite a while—should Marian Anderson retire? Her voice was definitely past its prime at the time of her Met debut, but she had not become an embarrassment on stage the way Martha Graham was by the late 1960s. With Anderson's blessing, the Hurok organization announced a farewell tour for 1964–1965, to culminate in an Easter Sunday concert at Carnegie Hall in New York. Audiences across the country had the chance to see their idol in person one more time, embracing her now not only for her voice (or memories of it) but with perhaps a bit of nostalgia for her nonconfrontational approach to race relations, as an increasingly polarized country grappled with the explosive issue of civil rights throughout the 1960s.

Once she retired from the concert stage, Anderson stayed retired, enjoying the opportunity to spend more time at Marianna Farm with her husband and her family. As befits a personage of her stature, her later years were marked by awards and milestones: election to the Women's Hall of Fame in 1975, a seventy-fifth birthday gala in 1977 with Leontyne Price, Clamma Dale, and Shirley Verrett, and Marian Anderson Day in Philadelphia in 1979, highlighted by a benefit concert by Luciano Pavarotti, which raised $100,000 for the University of Pennsylvania, where her papers and memorabilia were deposited. She rarely appeared in public, although the now white-haired Anderson shared spirited and moving memories for a 1991 documentary about her life. After she was widowed, Anderson remained on her Connecticut farm until 1992 when she moved to Portland, Oregon, to live with her nephew James DePriest. The next year she suffered a stroke and died. She was ninety-six years old.

Sounding a lot like Katharine Hepburn, in 1976 Marian Anderson dismissed her stature as a symbol and a role model by saying, "I've been around for a long time." As usual, she underestimated her impact on the world around her. As far back as her Town Hall debut in 1935, music critic Harold Taubman observed, "If Joe Louis deserves to be an American hero for bowling over a lot of pushovers, then Marian Anderson has the right to at least comparable standing."[83]

At the gala for Marian Anderson's eightieth birthday, at which Shirley Verrett and Grace Bumbry (both recipients of Marian Anderson scholarships) performed, Verrett observed, "She was a dream-maker, giving us the right to dream the undreamable, reach for the unreachable, and achieve the impossible." That is perhaps the artist's greatest legacy to the American century—her demonstration that leading by example could be an instrument for social change, the doors she opened for others to follow. At the same time her triumph and survival remind us of how much she had to overcome.[84]

Marian Anderson captured both of these legacies in a simple but poignant passage from her autobiography, one of the few times she allowed herself to voice anything approaching anger or bitterness at the events of her life. "Things are changing in our country, and I am hopeful. But I cannot suppress a private regret. I still wish that I could have gone to a music school."[85]

E P I L O G U E

GROWING OLD GRACEFULLY
IN PUBLIC

WHAT IF THESE seven exceptional women had had the chance to gather to reflect about their lives? And not on some public forum sponsored by a women's college or magazine, but in an informal get-together: girls' night out, the grown-up equivalent of a sleepover.

If they felt like getting away to the country, they could have met at Marian Anderson's Danbury farm, the Hepburn compound on the Connecticut shore, or further north, at Dorothy Thompson's Twin Farms in Vermont. If it was easier to meet in the city (which for each of these women, except for Babe Didrikson, would have meant New York City), they might have gathered at the Cosmopolitan Club, where four of them were members. Katharine Hepburn would likely have munched on chocolate, Dorothy Thompson might have ordered scotch, and Babe Didrikson, probably feeling a bit out of place, would have asked for a beer. And then they would have begun comparing notes.

There would be so many topics to talk about: husbands, lovers, marriages, children; whether they were comfortable with their appearances; how they were portrayed in the press; how they felt about modern feminism and their lives as women; whether they had second thoughts about personal or professional choices they had made; how important wealth and economic independence were to them; what advice they would give to rising generations about balancing public and private lives.

Although some of these women were casual acquaintances, none were close personal friends, nor were they the gossipy type, so it is hard to imagine such a gathering evoking deep secrets or confidences. On the other hand, once these women started talking about people they had known, places they had visited, and milestones they had achieved, their wide-ranging conversation would have provided a window on twentieth-century American life and culture.

At some point the conversation would certainly have turned to the nexus between celebrity and aging for women. One common denominator in their lives was the challenge, indeed the difficulty, of maintaining the acclaim to which they were accustomed as they grew older—of getting through what Katharine Hepburn had identified as the tricky middle years of a woman's career. If she survived, she became an institution, a legend, revered like an old building. If not, her stardom and celebrity, to say nothing of her livelihood, ran the risk of vanishing into thin air.

In many ways celebrity was like a drug for all seven of these remarkably talented but somewhat egocentric women: they were hooked, they needed their public to sustain them in who they were. As they aged, they had to find ways to adjust their public images in order to hold onto their audiences, whether they were dancer, actor, politician, or journalist. If their retooled images still clicked with the public, then prospects were good for spending the remainder of their careers just where they had always been: squarely in the public eye.

Older women in popular culture were caught in the bind. Men

often saw their stature and popular authority rise to reflect their years of accumulated experience, but rarely was there a corresponding benefit to women. The elder statesman was always more prevalent than the female equivalent; the leading man could have romantic interludes with younger women, but older women involved with younger men raised eyebrows. Whereas grey hair and wrinkles signified maturity and competence for men, for women they seemed only to draw attention to the passage of time. Societal pressure on women to appear younger than they were, which compelled many women to lie about their ages and try desperately to hold onto their youthful appearances, was just one manifestation of the unequal weight of aging that fell on women.

But just because popular culture preferred younger, attractive women does not mean that all women were cast aside at a certain age. The women in this book had an advantage: they all entered the public domain earlier in the century when they were not subjected to as rigorous a standard of how women in popular culture were supposed to look. (It helped that this was the pre-television era.) As these women matured, they adapted their own personal styles to their chronological age and level of professional visibility. They were less concerned with their physical appearance (it is hard to imagine Eleanor Roosevelt or Margaret Mead having a face lift, although Martha Graham and Katharine Hepburn succumbed to the temptation) than with their moral authority, political influence, or artistic integrity. The strategies they adopted to maintain a toehold in popular culture varied, but each one met this final hurdle with different degrees of success and varying amounts of style.

Babe Didrikson had already undergone one transformation from tomboy to lady, but she would have faced a much greater challenge holding on to her celebrity once her competitive athletic career was over. Didrikson's whole life had been sports, and she had prepared herself for little else; society doesn't offer too many roles for ex-jocks, especially the female variety. Her premature death kept her from confronting the full force of the transition to mid-life and beyond, but it also cemented her reputation. By dying young, and almost at the top of her form, she became the rare phenomenon: a female sports legend.

The problem Dorothy Thompson faced—how to keep the public interested in the ideas and opinions she had to offer, and how to keep those ideas fresh and appealing in the immediate postwar period—was only tangentially related to age, although its consequences were just as chilling. Because Thompson never found the postwar equivalent of her campaign against Hitler, readers had no reason to turn to her column for an insight or opinion they could get somewhere else. Plus her forte—impassioned and often quite personal political commentary—now faced stiff competition from newer forms of media, especially television. Unwilling and unable to tailor her opinions to match postwar popular taste, she plugged along as always, resigned but also a bit resentful about her diminished audience. When she died in 1961, what was left of her reputation died with her.

Martha Graham's rage against age was the most extreme manifestation of a celebrity's unwillingness or inability to let go of the limelight. She managed to prolong her performing career into her seventies, an amazing if ultimately self-defeating accomplishment, by counting on the power of her stage presence to make audiences suspend belief about her actual age. She also learned to choreograph roles for herself that were gentler in their demands on her body and ones that audiences could accept an older female dancing. Once she could no longer dance, she kept on performing as the head of the Martha Graham Dance Company, turning her now ancient body into the personification of modern dance itself. She became a legend, but her struggle in her declining years to continue to be Martha Graham was as poignant as it was inspirational.

Marian Anderson had a far less tortured experience than Martha Graham accepting the changes that growing older had on her celebrity, although she too put off the moment for as long as possible. Anderson's stately and dignified appearance had a certain timeless quality to it, which deflected attention away from the diminished range of her voice in later years. Due to careful management by the Hurok organization, she never became overexposed, and her farewell tour in 1965 was handled with customary good taste. In the remaining twenty-five years of her life, Anderson certainly could have milked her fame much more, but she rarely appeared in public, preferring the privacy of her happy personal life. (Royalties from her still popular recordings removed any financial pressure to capitalize on her legend.) After years of being on display as a representative of her race and sex, Anderson may have been the only character in this book who was glad finally to be rid of the spotlight.

Margaret Mead got better, if more exposed, as she got older, exploiting the new medium of television to cement her celebrity in the last decades of her life. In her younger incarnation, Mead was the globe-trotting anthropologist, always ready to draw parallels between the societies she studied and her own. In later years, Mead became a guru, a highly visible public figure who had opinions on every topic imaginable. She even made her dowdy appearance, the antithesis of modern media's emphasis on youth and slimness, work to her benefit, using her grandmotherly exterior as a cover for her often controversial views, which found a receptive public right until the very end of her life. Margaret Mead was so curious and eager for new experiences that she just could not slow down, even when her body gave out on her. "The last man from Raratongo might die today," she was probably saying on her deathbed, "I must hurry."

The respect for Eleanor Roosevelt increased as she aged, and she became that rare creature: a true elder stateswoman. After Franklin's death freed her from the constraints of being a politician's wife, Eleanor Roosevelt lived the last two decades of her life as a public figure with a degree of freedom she had previously lacked. Her opinions on a range of important postwar subjects, including world peace, human rights, and liberalism, were critical to national discourse. (Her stand on civil rights still remained controversial.) Until her final illness sapped her strength, she was meeting new people, taking on new causes. Her domestic and international vision seems just as compelling and farsighted today as it did when she was alive. No other female public figure has even come close to the impact that Eleanor Roosevelt had on the American century, nor is any likely to. She remains the epitome of public-spirited womanhood, a true woman of conscience.

Of these seven women, Katharine Hepburn found the best niche in popular culture as she grew older, with the result that she was probably more revered in her dotage than at any other point in her life. This renown had little to do with her acting—although she did continue to snag quality parts into her eighties—and more to do with her change of heart toward publicity. After Spencer Tracy's death freed her from her former circumspection about her private life, she entered a new phase of celebrity. Hepburn's outspokenness and quirky personal style proved appealing and marketable to fans old and new, many of whom were also rediscovering her films through the new availability of video and cable. With the revival of feminism, Hepburn's brand of personal independence and autonomy seemed a spirited affirmation of what many women were seeking to accomplish for themselves. And as the stars of the Golden Age of Hollywood died off, Hepburn came to embody that lost era. She truly was the last survivor.

These seven women may not have solved the problem of growing old gracefully in public, but they provide compelling evidence that women don't have to be young and beautiful to command the attention of twentieth-century popular culture. They were all survivors from an earlier age where public renown had to be earned, where fame actually stood for something. They gave to the twentieth century seven shining examples of what women could contribute to public life and national culture. That kind of celebrity has staying power.

Ever ready with a pithy quote for public consumption, these

women would have had no trouble summing up their philosophy of life for future generations. Here's what each, from Roosevelt to Anderson, might have chosen:

"Life was meant to be lived."

"Stick to your principles, no matter how unpopular."

"Never stop learning."

"Paddle your own canoe."

"Compete to win."

"Your body is a temple."

"Anchor your soul in the Lord."

A handy set of principles for modern women's lives, then and now.

NOTES

CHAPTER 1: FIRST LADY OF THE WORLD: ELEANOR ROOSEVELT

1. Eleanor Roosevelt, *The Autobiography of Eleanor Roosevelt* (New York: Harper and Row, 1958), p. 428. This volume is an abridged version of the three autobiographical volumes Roosevelt published over the years: *This Is My Story* (New York: Harper and Brothers, 1937), *This I Remember* (New York: Harper and Brothers, 1949), and *On My Own* (New York: Harper and Brothers, 1958). It also includes a new section called "The Search for Understanding."
   The reference to Teddy Roosevelt was perhaps more apt than she realized. According to Roosevelt's sister, "Eleanor was my brother Ted's favorite niece. She is more like him than any of his children." Quoted in Joseph P. Lash, *Love, Eleanor: Eleanor Roosevelt and Her Friends* (Garden City, N.Y.: Doubleday, 1982), p. 127.
2. Raymond Clapper, "The Ten Most Powerful People in Washington," *Look* (January 28, 1941).
3. Susan Ware, "Very Much a New Yorker," *New York Times*, August 23, 1996, p. C1; Joseph P. Lash, *"Life Was Meant to Be Lived": A Centenary Portrait of Eleanor Roosevelt* (New York: W. W. Norton, 1984), p. 55; Betty Boyd Caroli, *First Ladies* (New York: Oxford University Press, 1987), p. 195; Tugwell quoted in Joan Hoff-Wilson and Marjorie Lightman, eds., *Without Precedent: The Life and Career of Eleanor Roosevelt* (Bloomington: Indiana University Press, 1984), pp. 10–11; Joseph P. Lash, *Eleanor and Franklin* (New York: W. W. Norton, 1971), p. 594.
4. Maurine H. Beasley, *Eleanor Roosevelt and the Media: A Public Quest for Self-Fulfillment* (Urbana: University of Illinois Press, 1987), p. 186; Hoff-Wilson and Lightman, *Without Precedent*, pp. 218–19; Ruby A. Black, "Is Mrs. Roosevelt a Feminist?" *Equal Rights* (July 27, 1935), p. 164.

5. Doris Kearns Goodwin, *No Ordinary Time: Franklin and Eleanor Roosevelt: The Home Front in World War II* (New York: Simon and Schuster, 1994), p. 397; Lash, *"Life Was Meant to Be Lived,"* p. 160. Pegler's other pet names for the First Lady included "The Great Gab," "La Boca Grande," "Emperor Eleanor," and later "the Widow."

6. Quoted in Beasley, *Eleanor Roosevelt and the Media*, p. 34.

7. Caroli, *First Ladies*, p. 190; Blanche Wiesen Cook, *Eleanor Roosevelt, Volume One, 1884–1933* (New York: Viking, 1992), p. 14.

8. Eleanor Roosevelt, *Autobiography*, p. 3

9. *Ibid.*, p. 9.

10. Eleanor Roosevelt, "Wives of Great Men," *Liberty* 9 (October 1, 1932), pp. 12–16, found in Allida M. Black, ed., *What I Hope to Leave Behind: The Essential Essays of Eleanor Roosevelt* (Brooklyn, N.Y.: Carlson Publishing, 1995), p. 215.

11. Lash, *Eleanor and Franklin*, p. 198.

12. Cook, *Eleanor Roosevelt*, p. 167.

13. Eleanor Roosevelt, *Autobiography*, p. 62.

14. Lash, *"Life Was Meant to Be Lived,"* p. 30.

15. Lash, *Love, Eleanor*, p. 53; Cook, *Eleanor Roosevelt*, p. 170; Lash, *"Life Was Meant to Be Lived,"* p. 30.

16. Cook, *Eleanor Roosevelt*, p. 183.

17. Lash, *Love, Eleanor*, p. 67.

18. Eleanor Roosevelt to Joseph P. Lash, October 2, 1943, quoted in Lash, *Eleanor and Franklin*, p. 302; *ibid.*, p. 311. While many believe that after this point Eleanor and Franklin never again had sexual relations, there remains the question of whether she still loved Franklin. Her lifelong friend Esther Lape thought she did. Speaking specifically of Franklin, Lape reflected, "I don't think she ever stopped loving someone she loved." Quoted in Lash, *"Life Was Meant to Be Lived,"* p. 122.

19. Geoffrey Ward, *A First-Class Temperament: The Emergence of Franklin Roosevelt* (New York: Harper and Row, 1989), contains an excellent discussion of FDR's struggle with polio.

20. Cook, *Eleanor Roosevelt*, p. 292.

21. Eleanor Roosevelt, "Women Must Learn to Play the Game as Men Do," *Redbook* 50 (April, 1928), in Black, *What I Hope to Leave Behind*, pp. 195–200; Hoff-Wilson and Lightman, *Without Precedent*, p. 30; Cook, *Eleanor Roosevelt*, p. 16.

22. *Ibid.*, pp. 462, 452.

23. Eleanor Roosevelt, *Autobiography*, pp. 193, 279.

24. Susan Ware, *Partner and I: Molly Dewson, Feminism, and New Deal Politics* (New Haven: Yale University Press, 1987), p. 205.

25. Beasley, *Eleanor Roosevelt and the Media*, photo insert between pp. 50 and 51.

26. Lash, *Eleanor and Franklin*, p. 920, has another version. Eleanor had come into Franklin's cocktail hour armed with an agenda. Remembered daughter Anna: "Father blew his top. . . . What she wanted was o.k. but for him it was one more thing at the end of a tough day."

27. Eleanor Roosevelt, *Autobiography*, p. 280.

28. *Ibid.*, p. 123.

29. Joseph P. Lash, *A World of Love: Eleanor Roosevelt and Her Friends, 1943–1962* (Garden City, N.Y.: Doubleday, 1984), p. 551; Margaret Mead with Rhoda Metraux, *A Way of Seeing* (New York: William Morrow, 1974), p. 105.

30. Goodwin, *No Ordinary Time*, p. 453.

31. Hoff-Wilson and Lightman, *Without Precedent*, p. 21.

32. *Ibid.*, p. 49.

33. It was Elliott, in a somewhat sensationalized book he co-authored about his parents after Eleanor's death. See Goodwin, *No Ordinary Time*, p. 121.

34. Caroli, *First Ladies*, p. 201. Goodwin, *No Ordinary Time*, is the best source on Missy LeHand.

35. Joseph P. Lash, *Eleanor: The Years Alone* (New York: W. W. Norton, 1972), p. 233.

36. This pattern is still striking among the surviving associates who worked closely with Roosevelt during her life—they always refer to her as Mrs. Roosevelt when they speak of her, never as Eleanor. Margaret Mead pointed out that it was often her opponents who called her by her first name only, as in the "We Don't Want Eleanor Either" campaign buttons, as a way of stripping her of her dignity; "those who loved and trusted her called her 'Mrs. Roosevelt.'" Mead, *A Way of Seeing*, p. 105.

37. Susan Ware, *Beyond Suffrage: Women in the New Deal* (Cambridge: Harvard University Press, 1981), p. 124. See also Ware, *Partner and I*, for a discussion of the Dewson-Roosevelt friendship.

38. Cook, *Eleanor Roosevelt*, p. 434.

39. He told it to Joe Lash. See Lash, *Love, Eleanor*, p. 122.

40. Goodwin, *No Ordinary Time*, p. 222. For more on Hickok's career, see Doris Faber, *The Life of Lorena Hickok: E.R.'s Friend* (New York: William Morrow, 1980).

41. Eleanor Roosevelt to Lorena Hickok, March 7, 1933, quoted in Hoff-Wilson and Lightman, *Without Precedent*, pp. 15–16.

42. Lorena Hickok to Eleanor Roosevelt, December 5, 1933, quoted in Faber, *The Life of Lorena Hickok*, p. 152.

43. Lash, *Love, Eleanor*, p. 223. The letter dates from 1934 or 1935.

44. Lash, *Eleanor and Franklin*, p. 709. Lash uses the quote anonymously in the text, but does identify himself as its source in the footnotes.

45. Once during the governorship years, Frances Perkins, who served as FDR's Industrial Commissioner, and Eleanor Roosevelt had to share a room together because the governor's mansion was too crowded. There Roosevelt told Perkins the story of her lonely childhood, although presumably not about Lucy Mercer since the two women were not all that close. Perkins was touched by the story, and treated it in strictest confidence. The very private Perkins was therefore quite shocked to see many of the same details appear in the first volume of Roosevelt's autobiography. Quoted in George Martin, *Madam Secretary: Frances Perkins* (Boston: Houghton Mifflin, 1976), pp. 234–35.

46. Lash, *A World of Love*, p. 43; Cook, *Eleanor Roosevelt*, p. xiv.

47. A subcurrent focuses on Hickok's appearance—she weighed upwards of two hundred pounds and was not exactly a traditional beauty—with the assumption that Eleanor couldn't have wanted to go to bed with her because she was not sexually attractive. Says who, replies biographer Cook, who reminds us

that "friendship and love are rarely about straight teeth or bony clavicles." *Ibid.*, p. 460.

48. I use the term bisexual despite fears of transposing current notions of sexuality and sexual practice back onto an earlier time, and with a certain reluctance because of the shock value associated with the term. It is not meant as a moral judgment one way or the other about Eleanor Roosevelt's life, although I realize that certain readers may not feel as comfortable with the term as I am. In the end, however, I concluded that this straightforward term offered the best and most useful way to describe Eleanor Roosevelt's emotional life, that is, as someone who loved both men and women. Note that my definition does not demand or assume that there was a sexual component to this love. Nor does it rule it out.

The best popular source on bisexuality and the challenge it poses to notions of fixed sexual identity is Marjorie Garber, *Vice Versa: Bisexuality and the Eroticism of Everyday Life* (New York: Simon and Schuster, 1995). Garber notes that the term bisexual used to convey "having both sexes in the same individual" before its more modern meaning switched to a person "sexually attracted to members of both sexes." (p. 237) But as Garber notes, there is no agreement whether bisexual means the potential to have such feelings, the potential to act on them, or the actual sexual acts themselves (p. 249). That wide penumbra of meanings certainly leaves room to include Eleanor Roosevelt, and several other women in this book.

49. Cook, *Eleanor Roosevelt*, p. 318. The comment had been caused by her reading Margaret Kennedy's *The Constant Nymph* (1924).

50. Lash, *Love, Eleanor*, p. 1.

51. Eleanor Roosevelt, *It's Up to the Women* (New York: Frederick A. Stokes, 1933), p. 204; Eleanor Roosevelt, "Women in Politics," *Good Housekeeping* (January, March, and April, 1940), found in Black, *What I Hope to Leave Behind*, pp. 256, 263.

52. Eleanor Roosevelt, *It's Up to the Women*, in Black, *What I Hope to Leave Behind*, pp. 238–39; Roosevelt, "Wives of Great Men," in *ibid.*, p. 218; Roosevelt, "Women at the Peace Conference," *Readers' Digest* 44 (April 1944), in *ibid.*, p. 528.

53. Susan Ware, ed., *Modern American Women: A Documentary History* (New York: McGraw-Hill, 1997), pp. 144–45; Eleanor Roosevelt, "Women Must Learn to Play the Game as Men Do," in Black, *What I Hope to Leave Behind*, p. 195.

54. Hoff-Wilson and Lightman, *Without Precedent*, p. 246; Lash, *"Life Was Meant to Be Lived"*, p. 188.

55. Eleanor Roosevelt, *Autobiography*, pp. 60, 103.

56. Eleanor Roosevelt quoted in Black, *Equal Rights* (July 27, 1935), p. 163; "Dear Mrs. Roosevelt," *Democratic Digest* (February 1938), p. 9, quoted in Ware, *Beyond Suffrage*, p. 129.

57. Black, *Equal Rights* (July 27, 1935), p. 163.

58. Eleanor Roosevelt, "What Are the Motives for a Woman Working When She Does Not Have To, for Income?" unpublished article (August 1945), in Black, *What I Hope to Leave Behind*, p. 280.

59. For background on the history of women's entrepreneurship, see Debra Michals, "Beyond Pin Money: The Rise of Women's Small Business Owner-

ship, 1945 to the Present" (forthcoming Ph.D. dissertation, New York University).

60. Beasley, *Eleanor Roosevelt and the Media*, p. 72.

61. *Ibid.*, pp. 189, 82.

62. Lash, *Eleanor and Franklin*, pp. 928–29. Roosevelt's autobiography has slightly different wording: "Father slept away. He would expect you to carry on and finish your jobs." Eleanor Roosevelt, *Autobiography*, p. 276.

63. Allida Black, *Casting Her Own Shadow: Eleanor Roosevelt and the Shaping of Postwar Liberalism* (New York: Columbia University Press, 1996), p. 53; Beasley, *Eleanor Roosevelt and the Media*, p. 153; Lash, *"Life Was Meant to Be Lived,"* p. 126.

64. Many of these activities were done as a way of funneling money to her children. For example, in 1948 and 1949 Anna was a co-host on a fifteen-minute daytime radio talk show carried by the American Broadcasting Company network; in 1950 and 1951 Elliott was the producer of "The Eleanor Roosevelt Show," a forty-five-minute syndicated radio program broadcast five afternoons a week. In a similar gesture, Henry Morgenthau, III, son of her beloved friends Elinor and Henry Morgenthau, Jr., produced "The Prospects of Mankind," which appeared on educational television (the forerunner of PBS) in the late 1950s and early 1960s. Beasley, *Eleanor Roosevelt and the Media*, pp. 171–73, 183.

65. Her old nemesis Westbrook Pegler for a while was threatening to draw attention to how she had not mentioned that Lucy Mercer Rutherford was with the president when he died, but nothing came of this. Lash, *A World of Love*, pp. 311–12.

66. Lash, *Eleanor: The Years Alone*, p. 182.

67. Eleanor Roosevelt, *Autobiography*, p. 299.

68. Hoff-Wilson and Lightman, *Without Precedent*, p. 23; Lash, *"Life Was Meant to Be Lived,"* p. 134. The friend was Joe Lash.

69. Eleanor Roosevelt, *Autobiography*, p. 412.

70. Black, *Casting Her Own Shadow*, p. 127. Black has an excellent discussion of Eleanor Roosevelt and civil rights.

71. Kennedy approached this meeting with trepidation, and a dash of hubris. "It's the raft at Tilsit," he told a friend, referring to the meeting between Napolean and Czar Alexander I that resulted in the Treaty of Tilsit in 1807, "and I want an ally with me." See Lash, *Eleanor: The Years Alone*, p. 293, and Black, *Casting Her Own Shadow*, p. 189, for their accounts of the outcome.

72. Lash, *Eleanor: The Years Alone*, p. 298; Eleanor Roosevelt, *Autobiography*, p. 389.

73. Lois Scharf, *Eleanor Roosevelt: First Lady of American Liberalism* (Boston: Twayne, 1987), pp. 174–75.

74. The cartoon is reproduced in Lash, *"Life Was Meant to Be Lived,"* p. 196.

CHAPTER 2: "SHE RIDES IN THE SMOKING CAR": DOROTHY THOMPSON

1. See, for example, Don Wharton, "First Lady of American Journalism," *Scribner's* 101 (May 1937), pp. 9–14.

2. Dorothy Thompson, *"I Saw Hitler!"* (New York: Farrar and Rinehart, 1932), p. vi; John Gunther, "A Blue-Eyed Tornado," *New York Herald-Tribune* (January 13, 1935), p. 6.

3. Peter Kurth, *American Cassandra: The Life of Dorothy Thompson* (Boston: Little Brown, 1990), p. 219; Vincent Sheean, *Dorothy and Red* (Boston: Houghton Mifflin, 1963), p. 255.

4. Marian Sanders, *Dorothy Thompson: A Legend in Her Time* (Boston: Houghton Mifflin, 1973); Julia Edwards, *Women of the World: The Great Foreign Correspondents* (New York: Ballantine, 1988), p. 93. Boadicea was the warrior queen of ancient Britain, although one suspects this allusion was lost on many of Johnson's audience. It is not clear what specific article or column Longworth was referring to—perhaps she means the hysterectomy that Thompson had in 1939 (see below). Alice Roosevelt Longworth is of course the same person who once cattily said of Franklin Roosevelt's affair with Lucy Mercer, "He deserved it. He was married to Eleanor." Joseph P. Lash, *"Life Was Meant to Be Lived"* (New York: W. W. Norton, 1984), p. 34.

5. Jack Alexander, "The Girl from Syracuse," in John E. Drewry, *Post Biographies of Famous Journalists* (Athens: University of Georgia Press, 1942), p. 432; Kurth, *American Cassandra*, p. 303. Lippmann did not say this publicly; it was contained in a letter to his wife. The language was remarkably similar to the description of the Katharine Hepburn character, Tracy Lord, in *The Philadelphia Story*.

6. Quoted in the review of Kurth, *American Cassandra*, by Geoffrey C. Ward, "Wonder Woman," *New York Review of Books* 37 (August 16, 1990), p. 40. Kurth's well-researched biography is an excellent introduction to Thompson, and more reliable and balanced than the earlier biography by Marian Sanders.

7. At some point in her career, she began to give the date as 1894, and she stubbornly refused to give the correct date even when her brother confronted her with the evidence of her mistake. Her tombstone, however, records the correct date.

8. "Dorothy Thompson: An Autobiography" (5 pp. mimeo), released by the Bell Syndicate, September 5, 1957, found in the Dorothy Thompson papers, Department of Special Collections, Syracuse University [hereafter DT, Syracuse].

9. Dorothy Thompson Christmas radio broadcast, December 22, 1940, in DT, Syracuse.

10. According to Thompson's memoirs, Grandma Grierson had decided "against her daughter's knowledge" to induce a miscarriage through herbs and other abortifacients to spare her the burden of another pregnancy. When she began to hemorrhage, the grandmother was afraid to confess and a doctor sewed her up, which caused Margaret Thompson to die of septicemia within forty-eight hours. Local townspeople said she had died in childbirth. See Kurth, *American Cassandra*, pp. 18–19.

11. *Ibid.*, p. 27.

12. Dorothy Thompson, "Chapter One," draft of unpublished autobiography, found in DT, Syracuse.

13. Dorothy Thompson, "My First Job," *Ladies' Home Journal* (April 1957), p. 198.

14. Kurth, *American Cassandra*, p. 3; Sanders, *Dorothy Thompson*, p. 71.

15. *Ibid.*

16. *Ibid.*, p. 85. There is some confusion about whether Sigrid Schultz was the first, when she inherited the Berlin Bureau for the *Chicago Tribune* from George Seldes. Kurth, *American Cassandra*, p. 95, says Thompson was first; so does Kay Mills, *A Place in the News: From the Women's Pages to the Front Page* (New York: Dodd, Mead, 1988), p. 32. Edwards, *Women of the World*, pp. 54 and 87, gives the nod to Schultz; and Ishbel Ross, *Ladies of the Press* (New York: Harper and Brothers, 1936), p. 365, doesn't fall into the "first" trap, identifying Thompson in 1925 as one of two women in Europe to head a bureau.

17. Charles Fisher, *The Columnists* (New York: Howell, Soskin, 1944), p. 37; Kurth, *American Cassandra*, p. 50; Autobiographical mimeo, September 5, 1957, in DT, Syracuse.

18. Sanders, *Dorothy Thompson*, p. 104; Margaret Case Harriman, "The It Girl," *New Yorker* (April 20, 1940), p. 28.

19. Sanders, *Dorothy Thompson*, p. 151.

20. Dorothy Thompson to Sinclair Lewis, undated letter (c. 1930–1931), in DT, Syracuse; Sanders, *Dorothy Thompson*, p. 152.

21. Kurth, *American Cassandra*, p. 167. Around this time (1931) Thompson was approached about being the managing editor of *The Nation*. Sinclair Lewis thought it might be a good idea, but Thompson had grander visions than being tied down to a desk. "How *can* I take the *Nation*? What about Vermont? Europe? I *see* you staying home and minding the baby. *Du!*" *ibid.*, p. 158.

22. Thompson, *"I Saw Hitler!,"* pp. 3, 14.

23. Mark Schorer, *Sinclair Lewis: An American Life* (New York: McGraw Hill, 1961), p. 539; Autobiographical mimeo (September 5, 1957), in DT, Syracuse.

24. Sanders, *Dorothy Thompson*, p. 202; *New York Herald-Tribune* advertisement (1936), found in DT, Syracuse.

25. Kurth, *American Cassandra*, p. 220; Fisher, *The Columnists*, p. 16; Margaret Case Harriman, "The It Girl," *New Yorker* (April 27, 1940), p. 24.

26. *Ibid.*, p. 28; Dorothy Thompson to Eleanor Roosevelt, January 29, 1941, in DT, Syracuse; Kurth, *American Cassandra*, p. 331.

27. A prime case in point is the announcement in her column of her resignation from the DAR over its denial of Constitution Hall to Marian Anderson. See Chapter Seven.

28. Eleanor Roosevelt, "Women in Politics," *Good Housekeeping* (January, March, April, 1940), found in Allida M. Black, ed., *What I Hope to Leave Behind: The Essential Essays of Eleanor Roosevelt* (Brooklyn: Carlson Publishing, 1995), p. 255.

29. Harriman, "The It Girl," *New Yorker* (April 27, 1940), p. 28.

30. Kurth, *American Cassandra*, pp. 197, 165.

31. *Ibid.*, pp. 209, 265; Sheean, *Dorothy and Red*, p. 257. Radio was a significant source of her income, and a major place for corporate advertising. Her radio shows were sponsored at various points by Pall Mall, General Electric, Savarin Coffee, and Clipper Craft Clothes.

32. Gunther, "Blue-Eyed Tornado," p. 6; Kurth, *American Cassandra*, pp. 258,

259. For a discussion and a photograph of Sophie Tucker, see Joyce Antler, *Journey Home: Jewish Women and the American Century* (New York: The Free Press, 1997).

33. Kurth, *American Cassandra*, p. 268. She really did receive many "Woman of the Year" awards, which makes the link to the Katharine Hepburn movie even more apt.

34. Fisher, *The Columnists*, p. 29.

35. Dorothy Thompson to Sinclair Lewis, April 29, 1937, in DT, Syracuse.

36. Kurth, *American Cassandra*, p. 254; Dorothy Thompson, "A Party for Twenty," *Current History* 50 (May 1939), pp. 45–46. A contributing cause may have been Thompson's progressive loss of hearing, first noticed around 1941. Her increasing deafness reinforced her lifelong tendency to dominate conversations.

37. Kurth, *American Cassandra*, p. 166. Sinclair Lewis wickedly parodied Dorothy in his 1944 novel *Gideon Planish* as the character Winifred Homeward, as in "Winifred Homeward the Talking Woman": "She was an automatic, self-starting talker. Any throng of more than two persons constituted a lecture audience for her, and at the sight of them she mounted an imaginary platform, pushed aside an imaginary glass of water, and started a fervent address full of imaginary information about Conditions and Situations that lasted till the audience had sneaked out—or a little longer." Full quote in Kurth, p. 245.

38. Sheean, *Dorothy and Red*, p. 255; Schorer, *Sinclair Lewis*, p. 622; Kurth, *American Cassandra*, p. 243.

39. Dorothy Thompson, "Oh, Professor," *Ladies' Home Journal* (June 1958), p. 11; biographical blurb in *True Confessions* (1945), found in DT, Syracuse; Sanders, *Dorothy Thompson*, p. 242.

40. Nancy F. Cott, *The Grounding of Modern Feminism* (New Haven: Yale University Press, 1987), p. 180.

41. Dorothy Thompson to Rose Wilder Lane, September 3, 1921, in William Holtz, ed., *Dorothy Thompson and Rose Wilder Lane: Forty Years of Friendship* (Columbia: University of Missouri Press, 1991), p. 19.

42. Betty Boyd Caroli, *First Ladies* (New York: Oxford University Press, 1987), p. 307.

43. Alexander, "The Girl from Syracuse," in Drewry, *Post Biographies*, p. 474.

44. Sara Terry, "Revisionist History," *Boston Globe*, June 1, 1995. Since 1993, Twin Farms has been run as a luxurious fourteen-room country inn where rooms cost $700 to $1,500 a night. Meals and drinks are included, but not the sparkling conversation (and the lurking tension) of the old days when Dorothy Thompson and Sinclair Lewis called it home. See also *Gourmet* (September 1996), pp. 99–100.

45. Kurth, *American Cassandra*, pp. 274, 138, 270.

46. Sheean, *Dorothy and Red*, pp. 179–80.

47. Sanders, *Dorothy Thompson*, pp. 160, 242; Dorothy Thompson to Sinclair Lewis, February 2, 1931, and April 29, 1937, in DT, Syracuse.

48. Kurth, *American Cassandra*, pp. 459–60.

49. *Ibid.*, p. 295. Sinclair Lewis, who was also upset by Wells's death, found a cruel way of lashing out by calling Thompson's cancellation "a publicity stunt."

"Dorothy's just putting on an act. She wasn't his mother. It's all self-dramatization." *Ibid.*, pp. 370–71.

50. Holtz, *Thompson and Lane: Forty Years of Friendship*, p. 22. Comments Thompson shared with *Ladies' Home Journal* readers in 1937 show how torn many of her friends were over this issue: "Among my personal acquaintances I can count a dozen women who postponed having children in their youth. . . . Almost all of them have lived to regret it bitterly. Their lives after thirty have been spent seeking advice as to how they can now have children, only to find that they have missed earlier opportunities and it is now too late. Looking ahead, a decade ago, they were afraid. Looking back now, they say, 'We could have managed it, after all.' " Dorothy Thompson, "To Live and Create Life," *Ladies' Home Journal* (May 1937), p. 12.

51. Sanders, *Dorothy Thompson*, p. 61.

52. Dorothy Thompson to Sinclair Lewis, April 29, 1937, in DT, Syracuse.

53. For Thompson's fluctuating sexual identity, see Sanders, *Dorothy Thompson*, pp. 27, 108, 179–82; and Kurth, *American Cassandra*, pp. 178–83. This quote is from Kurth, p. 101.

54. *Ibid.*, p. 101.

55. Sheean, *Dorothy and Red*, pp. 215–16, 220.

56. *Ibid.*, p. 223; Dorothy Thompson to Sinclair Lewis, March 30, 1933, in DT, Syracuse.

57. See John D'Emilio and Estelle Freedman, *Intimate Matters: A History of Sexuality in America* (New York: Harper & Row, 1988), for general background. See also Estelle Freedman, *Maternal Justice: Miriam Van Waters and the Female Reform Tradition* (Chicago: University of Chicago Press, 1996), for discussion of a woman who loved other women, but did not consider herself a lesbian in early- to mid-twentieth-century America.

58. See Marjorie Garber, *Vice Versa: Bisexuality and the Eroticism of Everyday Life* (New York: Simon and Schuster, 1995), for a historical and literary discussion of this phenomenon.

59. Kurth, *American Cassandra*, p. 347; Sanders, *Dorothy Thompson*, p. 296. Less charitably, Geoffrey Ward referred to him as "the perfect wife" (Ward, "Wonder Woman," p. 40).

60. Dorothy Dunbar Bromley, "Feminist—New Style," *Harpers* (October 1927), found in Susan Ware, ed., *Modern American Women: A Documentary History* (New York: McGraw Hill, 1997), p. 146.

61. Dorothy Thompson, "Women Correspondents and Other New Ideas," *The Nation* (January 6, 1927), p. 11; Holtz, *Thompson and Lane: Forty Years of Friendship*, p. 11.

62. Dorothy Thompson, "I Write of Russian Women," *Ladies' Home Journal* (March 1956), p. 11.

63. Dorothy Thompson, "Women Correspondents," p. 11.

64. Dorothy Thompson, "The Married Woman's Right to Earn," *Equal Rights* (February 29, 1936), pp. 411–12; Dorothy Thompson speech in *Changing Standards: Proceedings of the Fourth Annual New York Herald-Tribune Women's Conference on Current Problems* (September 26–27, 1934), p. 197.

65. *Ibid.*, p. 191.

66. Dorothy Thompson, "If I Had a Daughter," *Ladies' Home Journal* (September 1939), p. 4. Here is more of the quote: "In the joys of the new opportunities open to them, thousands of them have attempted the impossible. . . It is an illusion. One woman in a thousand can do it. And she is a genius. Most women are not geniuses, even though they may be gifted. And most of those who attempt what is, by its nature, too much, break their hearts."

67. Dorothy Thompson, "The Century of Women's Progress," *Ladies' Home Journal* (August 1948), p. 12; Dorothy Thompson, "The World—And Women," *Ladies' Home Journal* (March 1938), p. 4. In a letter to her *Ladies' Home Journal* publishers, she used a telling analogy: "They often remind me of negroes, who struggling for equality with whites, give up, or themselves come to hold in contempt, qualities in which—at least from the viewpoint of their happiness—they are *superior*. (For instance the profound religious instinct and responsiveness to nature which they have.)" Dorothy Thompson to Bruce and Beatrice Gould, July 23, 1951, in DT, Syracuse.

68. "Occupation: Housewife" is reprinted in Dorothy Thompson, *Courage to Be Happy* (Boston: Houghton Mifflin, 1957), pp. 203–208. Friedan's attack is found in *The Feminine Mystique* (New York: W. W. Norton, 1963), pp. 35–36.

69. Dorothy Thompson, "It's a Woman's World," *Ladies' Home Journal* (July 1940) p. 25; Thompson, "Oh, Professor," p. 11.

70. "Cartwheel Girl," *Time* (June 12, 1939), p. 47; Fisher, *The Columnists*, p. 44.

71. Betty Rose Bartholomew to Dorothy Thompson, June 3, 1960, in DT, Syracuse.

72. Harriman, "The It Girl," *New Yorker* (April 27, 1940), p. 25.

73. Kurth, *American Cassandra*, p. 451.

74. Sanders, *Dorothy Thompson*, p. 331.

75. Eleanor Roosevelt to Dorothy Thompson, January 23, 1953, in DT, Syracuse; Kurth, *American Cassandra*, p. 398.

76. Sanders, *Dorothy Thompson*, p. 353.

77. Dorothy Thompson, "There Is a Time," *Ladies' Home Journal* (November 1952), pp. 14, 186.

78. Dorothy Thompson, "The Boy and Man from Sauk Center," *Atlantic Monthly* (November 1960), pp. 39–48.

79. Sheean, *Dorothy and Red*, p. 255.

CHAPTER 3: COMING OF AGE WITH MARGARET MEAD

1. Jane Howard, *Margaret Mead: A Life* (New York: Simon and Schuster, 1984), p. 111; Jane Howard, "Margaret Mead, 'Self-appointed Materfamilias to the World,' " *Smithsonian* 15 (September 1984), p. 118; Howard, *Margaret Mead*, pp. 374, 378.

2. *Ibid.*, p. 325.

3. *Ibid.*, p. 400; Gail Sheehy, "Why Can't a Woman Be More Like Margaret Mead?" *New York* (August 13, 1973), p. 39; Betty Friedan, *The Feminine Mystique* (New York: W. W. Norton, 1963), p. 139.

4. David Dempsey, "The Mead and Her Message," *New York Times Magazine* (April 26, 1970), p. 23; Friedan, *The Feminine Mystique*, p. 139; Howard, *Mar-*

garet Mead, p. 429. Gregory Bateson developed the insight about Mead's importance at her memorial service.

5. Margaret Mead and Rhoda Metraux, *A Way of Seeing* (New York: McCall Publishing, 1970), p. 192; Margaret Mead, *Blackberry Winter: My Earlier Years* (New York: William Morrow, 1972), p. 2.

6. Howard, *Margaret Mead*, p. 61; Dempsey, "The Mead and Her Message," p. 74.

7. Mead, *Blackberry Winter*, p. 45; Margaret Mead, *Letters from the Field, 1925–1975* (New York: Harper and Row, 1977), p. 8.

8. Rhoda Metraux, ed., *Margaret Mead: Some Personal Views* (New York: Walker and Company, 1979), pp. 170, 266.

9. Mead, *Blackberry Winter*, p. 19; Rosalind Rosenberg, *Beyond Separate Spheres: The Intellectual Roots of Modern Feminism* (New Haven: Yale University Press, 1982), p. 209.

10. Mead, *Blackberry Winter*, p. 92.

11. Metraux, *Some Personal Views*, p. 253.

12. Mead, *Blackberry Winter*, p. 108; Howard, *Margaret Mead*, p. 52.

13. *Ibid.*, pp. 35–36; Luther Cressman to *New York Times*, May 3, 1983. This letter, titled "Mead's First Husband Comes to Her Defense," was in response to the Derek Freeman controversy, which is discussed at the end of the chapter.

14. Columbia compiled an enviable record in supporting women in anthropology: between 1921 and 1940, twenty men and nineteen women received Ph.D.s; looking at a slightly longer period, which would include Ruth Benedict, between 1901 and 1940, twenty-nine men and twenty-two women got the degree. Margaret M. Caffrey, *Ruth Benedict: Stranger in This Land* (Austin: University of Texas Press, 1989), p. 270; Margaret Mead, *Ruth Benedict* (New York: Columbia University Press, 1974), p. 29.

15. Mead, *Blackberry Winter*, p. 115.

16. *Ibid.*, p. 292. For background on American anthropology and the importance of research on Native American topics, see Eliza McFeely, "Palimpsest of American Identity: Zuni, Anthropology, and American Culture at the Turn of the Century" (Ph.D. dissertation, New York University, 1996).

17. At that time, this last concern was really one about *sexual* vulnerability. Popular stereotypes portrayed "primitive" or "savage" men as unable to control their sexual impulses, which in turn was thought to put unattached white women at grave risk. By the 1920s, however, a tradition of women missionaries, explorers, and ethnographers had lessened those fears, although this racialized discourse still lurked just below the surface. See Louise M. Newman, "Coming of Age, but Not in Samoa: Reflections on Margaret Mead's Legacy for Western Liberal Feminism," *American Quarterly*, 48, #2 (June 1996), pp. 233–72.

18. 1938 manuscript draft on qualifications for field work, found in Margaret Mead papers, Library of Congress [hereafter MM, LC]. At her memorial service, a colleague remembered her quizzing a young scholar about to go off into the field about his preparation. Go spend a night riding around New York City in a police car; if you haven't seen a baby born, go to a hospital to watch a delivery; make yourself familiar with what death looks like, etc. See David

Hurst Thomas, "Remembering Margaret Mead," *New York* (February 5, 1979), p. 11.

19. Boas to Margaret Mead, July 14, 1925, MM, LC. This warm letter shows the concern that Boas took with his students, especially over issues such as guarding their health. "If you find that you cannot stand the climate do not be ashamed to come back. There are plenty of other places where you could solve the same problem on which you propose to work." Besides female adolescence, he also suggested she look out for the "excessive bashfulness of girls in primitive societies" and crushes among girls. The final word? "Don't forget your health."

20. Her father had previously offered her such a trip if she did not marry Cressman, but had not prevailed. To his credit, he coughed up the money this time.

21. Howard, *Margaret Mead*, p. 82.

22. Mead left very evocative descriptions of her time in Samoa in *Blackberry Winter* and in *Letters from the Field*.

23. Mary Catherine Bateson, *Composing a Life* (New York: Atlantic Monthly Press, 1989), p. 89.

24. Material on the Society of Women Geographers can be found in MM, LC, and the Society of Women Geographers papers, also at LC.

25. Margaret Mead, *Coming of Age in Samoa: A Study of Adolescence and Sex in Primitive Societies* (New York: William Morrow, 1928), p. 187; Mead to William Brownell, March 10, 1930, MM, LC; Arthur Cooper review of *Blackberry Winter* in *Newsweek* (November 13, 1972), p. 105: "When I was in college during the uptight, sexually repressed 1950s, everyone was reading *Coming of Age in Samoa* and dreaming of polymorphic Polynesian pleasures. That the book was 30 years old didn't matter. Margaret Mead was a guru to my generation, just as she was to the one before and would become to the one after."

26. Dempsey, "The Mead and Her Message," p. 100; Mead, *Coming of Age*, p. 19. As one critic noted, Mead "becomes the first of a long line of anthropologists to live among people eaters, but never get eaten." [Leonora Foestal and Angela Gilliam, eds., *Confronting the Margaret Mead Legacy: Scholarship, Empire, and the South Pacific* (Philadelphia: Temple University Press, 1992), p. 113.] On her next research trip to New Guinea Mead would actually visit a people that had only recently given up cannibalism (and not get eaten).

27. Margaret Mead to William Ogburn, August 9, 1928, MM, LC; Mead to William Morrow, January 25, 1928, MM, LC.

28. Advertisements and clippings found in MM, LC; William Morrow to Margaret Mead, January 11, 1929, MM, LC; Howard, *Margaret Mead*, p. 182.

29. *New York Times Book Review* (November 4, 1928), p. 18; *The Nation* 127 (October 24, 1928), p. 427; R. H. Lowie review in *American Anthropologist* 31 (July 1929), p. 532; Robert Redfield review in *American Journal of Sociology* 34 (January 1929), p. 728; and Mary Austin, *Birth Control Review* (July 1929), pp. 165–66.

30. Order blank, with quotes and description, in MM, LC.

31. Isidor Schneider review in *New Republic* 64 (November 5, 1930), p. 329; Margaret Mead to Thayer Hobson, January 30, 1941, MM, LC. In 1939 Morrow

published the three books together under the title *From the South Seas: Studies of Adolescence and Sex in Primitive Societies*.

32. Howard, *Margaret Mead*, p. 327; clipping, no date (1970s), Biography File, Schlesinger Library, Radcliffe College.

33. *Literary Digest* (November 11, 1933), p. 11. In her seventies she was disconcerted to find herself described in her medical records as an "obese white female," but according to her daughter, she then told the story on herself, "not only observing herself but observing herself being observed." Mary Catherine Bateson, *With a Daughter's Eye: A Memoir of Margaret Mead and Gregory Bateson* (New York: HarperCollins, 1984), p. 258.

34. See Margaret Mead to Henry Romeike Inc., March 13, 1930, MM, LC. The clippings are found in MM, LC.

35. Mary Alden Hopkins to Margaret Mead, December 26, 1930, MM, LC.

36. As early as 1928, her publisher warned her that her popular writing might backfire among fellow scholars whose opinions would count in her as-then still young career. [William Morrow to Margaret Mead, June 20, 1928, MM, LC.] Morrow was right, but Mead was never headed for just an academic career. She probably published more "serious" monographs in addition to her popular works than most anthropologists did in their careers, which may have added to the resentment. As Mead once told Barbara Walters, "Men who would never begrudge success to women bicycle riders, women opera singers, women jugglers begrudge it to me. Especially when they are drunk, they come to me and say, 'You have it all. It's not fair.' " Quoted in Howard, "Margaret Mead, 'Self-appointed Materfamilias to the World,' " p. 126.

37. Mead, *Blackberry Winter*, p. 201.

38. *Ibid.*, pp. 211, 217.

39. *Ibid.*, p. 240.

40. This was actually fairly typical of most anthropologists' careers. The difficulty of winning grants, the high cost of travel and research, residual health problems from earlier trips, and the tendency to acquire spouses and children as they aged, all help explain this phenomenon. While not the focus here, Mead did keep traveling, returning to New Guinea at various points throughout her life to follow up on her earlier research.

41. Howard, *Margaret Mead*, pp. 386; Howard, "Margaret Mead, 'Self-appointed Materfamilias to the World,' " p. 123.

42. Mead, *Blackberry Winter*, p. 100; Howard, *Margaret Mead*, p. 336.

43. Margaret Mead to Professor William Ogburn, April 27, 1927, MM, LC. Here is the full quote: "Do you remember my asking you once what my drive was and you said 'I don't know Margaret, You just got drive!' " She herself saw her drive as "just a need for something to think about," but clearly it was much stronger than that.

44. "Grandmother to the World," *New York Times* (November 16, 1978), clipping found in MM, LC.

45. Margaret Mead, "Bisexuality: A New Awareness," in Margaret Mead and Rhoda Metraux, *Aspects of the Present* (New York: William Morrow, 1980), pp. 269–275. The quote is from p. 271.

46. Bateson, *With a Daughter's Eye*, p. 142; Howard, *Margaret Mead*, p. 367.

47. Bateson, *With a Daughter's Eye*, p. 140; Caffrey, *Ruth Benedict*, pp. 188–200. The vast dimensions of the Mead-Benedict love affair make one reread or reinterpret so many aspects of their professional lives, like their habit of reviewing each other's books in national forums like the *New Republic* or the *New York Times*, which would clearly be seen as inappropriate now. Plus Mead wrote two books on Benedict, and in the eyes of some biographers, deliberately made it seem like Benedict was having an affair with Edward Sapir in order to deflect attention away from Benedict's essentially lesbian nature. And of course, little of her complicated personal life was mentioned in Mead's autobiography.

48. *Ibid.*, p. 201; Bateson, *With a Daughter's Eye*, p. 150.

49. Mead, *Blackberry Winter*, p. 244; Caffrey, *Ruth Benedict*, p. 84.

50. Mead, *Blackberry Winter*, p. 245.

51. *Ibid.*, p. 206.

52. Bateson, *With a Daughter's Eye*, p. 24; *Lactation Review* IV (1979), p. 6.

53. Howard, "Margaret Mead, 'Self-appointed Materfamilias to the World,' " p. 118. Eichelberger had been devoted to Mead since Barnard, and was enormously helpful behind the scenes in Mead's life. To call her a "go-fer" does a disservice to the enormous depth of their ties, but she did often take care of the practical details Mead so easily left to others, such as finding cotton dresses that traveled well to the Pacific. An unmarried social worker, Eichelberger handled Mead's finances and acted as her attorney. Mary Catherine Bateson captured the depth of this very private relationship with this exchange between her mother and Eichelberger: "You just looked at me across the room and fell in love with me." Bateson, *With a Daughter's Eye*, pp. 16–17.

54. Howard, *Margaret Mead*, pp. 258, 253; Mead, *Blackberry Winter*, p. 271.

55. Bateson, *With a Daughter's Eye*, p. 148; Howard, *Margaret Mead*, p. 73.

56. *Ibid.*, pp. 295, 320.

57. Bateson, *With a Daughter's Eye*, p. 137. This insight comes from 1955.

58. *Ibid.*, p. 153, 239.

59. Thomas, "Remembering Margaret Mead," p. 11.

60. *The Nation* 140 (May 29, 1935), p. 634.

61. Margaret Mead, *Sex and Temperament in Three Primitive Societies* (New York: William Morrow, 1935), pp. 321, 322.

62. Peggy Reeves Sanday, "Margaret Mead's View of Sex Roles in Her Own and Other Societies," *American Anthropologist* 82 (June 1980), p. 343; Margaret Mead, *Male and Female: A Study of the Sexes in a Changing World* (New York: William Morrow, 1949), p. 348.

63. Mead participated in a panel on *The Second Sex* in the *Saturday Review* 36 (February 21, 1953), pp. 30–31, and was actually fairly supportive of Beauvoir, although recognizing how much of it was linked to her personally: "The whole book is an impassioned, often overly elaborate, statement of the misery a gifted woman can feel in twentieth-century France. . . . Stripped of its personal bias and its over-decorative paraphernalia, the main argument—that society has wasted women's individual gifts by failing to institutionalize them—is a sound one."

64. Peter Kurth, *American Cassandra*, p. 435. Unlike Mead, Thompson found its overall argument unconvincing.

65. Mead, *Male and Female*, p. 51.
66. Friedan, *The Feminine Mystique*, pp. 130, 138, 127–28, 134.
67. *Ibid.*, p. 137; Howard, *Margaret Mead*, p. 426. Friedan's full quote is more revealing, and far more self-serving: "I felt that Mead, who was born twenty years before me, had gone as far as she could with feminism and that I, in reacting to her, took it a step further and was in a way her heir. I felt part of a procession."
68. *Ibid.*, pp. 362–63; "Margaret Mead," *Publishers Weekly* 202 (December 11, 1972), p. 10; forward by Margaret Mead to Helen Wortis and Clara Rabinowitz, *The Women's Movement: Social and Psychological Perspectives* (New York: AMS Press, 1972), p. xv; *Publishers Weekly* (December 11, 1972), p. 10.
69. Clipping from *Harvard Gazette* (1977), found in Biography File, Schlesinger Library; Howard, *Margaret Mead*, p. 405. Here is the full quote, which is quite revealing about a political philosophy so different from Eleanor Roosevelt's or Dorothy Thompson's: "I've never spoken against anything. If you speak out, you just mobilize hostility. I never spoke out against fascism. I never spoke out against communism. . . . I never spoke out against anything. I always speak positively. That's why I never had any trouble with the Attorney General's list." Mead was actually proud of this record.
70. *New York Times* (April 25, 1971), Biography File, Schlesinger Library; *Harvard Gazette* (1977), *ibid.*; *Publishers Weekly* (December 11, 1972), p. 10; Margaret Mead, "Women: A House Divided," *Redbook* (May 1970), p. 55.
71. Margaret Mead to Davis Thomas, Curtis Publishing Company, June 22, 1964, MM, LC.
72. Howard, "Margaret Mead, 'Self-appointed Materfamilias to the World,' " p. 126.
73. Metraux, *Some Personal Views*, pp. 43–44. The *Redbook* column is from 1974.
74. Margaret Mead to Mrs. Thomas Palmer, April 19, 1974; Mead to Maria Sweitzer, April 19, 1974; and Statement on ERA, dated September 12, 1975, all in MM, LC.
75. Quoted in letter from Pat Schroeder to Jimmy Carter, December 6, 1978, MM, LC, encouraging him to award her the Presidential Medal of Honor posthumously, which was done in 1979.
76. Mead, *Blackberry Winter*, p. 289; Howard, *Margaret Mead*, p. 228; Bateson, *With a Daughter's Eye*, p. 119. Here is another of her formulations: "Motherhood is like being a crack tennis player or ballet dancer—it lasts just so long, then it's over . . . . We've found no way of using the resources of women in the 25 years of post-menopausal zest." "Student and Teacher of Human Ways," *Life* 47 (September 14, 1959), p. 147.
77. Howard, *Margaret Mead*, p. 375.
78. *Ibid.*, p. 327.
79. *Ibid.*, pp. 385, 392.
80. *Saturday Review* (November 25, 1972), p. 66; Howard, *Margaret Mead*, p. 400.
81. "Margaret Mead, 1901–1978," *Natural History* 88 (January 1979), p. 6.
82. Jane Howard, "Angry Storm over the South Seas of Margaret Mead," *Smithsonian* 14 (April 1983), p. 67.
83. Note that no one is really asking the Samoans themselves what it was like to be analyzed by these outsiders. Anthropologist Eleanor Leacock quoted a

poignant comment from a young Samoan woman friend on what it felt like to read *Coming of Age*: she said that the behavior described rang true to her youth, but she hated the way Mead wrote about it. Foestal and Gilliam, *Confronting the Margaret Mead Legacy*, p. 11.

84. Roy A. Rappaport, "Desecrating the Holy Woman: Derek Freeman's Attack on Margaret Mead," *American Scholar* 55 (Summer 1986), pp. 317, 315.

85. Howard, "Angry Storms over the South Seas of Margaret Mead," p. 72.

86. Cheryl M. Fields, "Controversial Book Spurs Scholars' Defense of the Legacy of Margaret Mead," *Chronicle of Higher Education* (May 11, 1983), p. 28. See also Lowell D. Holmes, *Quest for the* Real *Samoa: The Mead/Freeman Controversy and Beyond* (South Hadley, Mass.: Bergin and Garvey, 1987).

CHAPTER 4: LIVING LIKE A MAN: KATHARINE HEPBURN

1. Clipping from *New York Times*, May 21, 1985, found at Film Studies Department, Museum of Modern Art, New York, New York. Hepburn used this image repeatedly to describe her life choices.

2. Homer Dickens, *The Films of Katharine Hepburn* (Secaucus, N.J.: Citadel Press, 1971), p. 29; Katharine Hepburn, *Me: Stories of My Life* (New York: Knopf, 1991), p. 225.

3. Sheridan Morley, *Katharine Hepburn* (Boston: Little, Brown, 1984), p. 44; clipping from *Los Angeles Herald-Examiner*, January 15, 1976, found in Hepburn Biography File, Academy of Motion Picture Arts and Sciences Library, Los Angeles [hereafter Academy Bio]; Morley, *Katharine Hepburn*, p. 155; Julia Shawell, "Hollywood's Strange Girl," *Pictorial Review* (April 1934), p. 75.

4. Anna Quindlen, "Life in the 30's," *New York Times*, March 2, 1988; Quindlen, "Reading Hepburn," *New York Times*, October 23, 1991.

5. Nancy Friday, *My Mother, My Self* (New York: Delacorte Press, 1977), p. 233.

6. Cleveland Amory, "The Strength of Katharine Hepburn," *Parade Magazine* (November 27, 1983), p. 5.

7. Garson Kanin, *Tracy and Hepburn: An Intimate Memoir* (New York: Viking, 1971), p. 235. Elaine May had not met Hepburn when she made the statement, and had only (like so many of us) admired her from afar.

8. MGM Press Release, 1943, Academy Bio; Christopher Anderson, *Young Kate* (New York: Henry Holt, 1988), p. 14.

9. In Hepburn's case, it is even more complicated. After her brother Tom's suicide (see below), a doubly inaccurate birthdate of November 8, 1909, entered the public record. See Barbara Leaming, *Katharine Hepburn* (New York: Crown, 1995), p. 212.

10. Anne Edwards, *A Remarkable Woman: A Biography of Katharine Hepburn* (New York: William Morrow, 1985), p. 127. For a fuller discussion of Mrs. Hepburn and her reform activism, see Susan Ware, "Katharine Hepburn, Her Mother's Daughter," *History Today* (April 1990), pp. 47–53, and Leaming, *Katharine Hepburn*.

11. Morley, *Katharine Hepburn*, p. 18. Hepburn paints a warm, and often funny, picture of Lewis's visits in *Me*, pp. 24–25.

12. Mary Cantwell, "Hepburn: 'I Had a Corner on the Rich, Arrogant Girl,'" *New York Times*, November 15, 1981.

13. John Bryson, *The Private World of Katharine Hepburn* (Boston: Little, Brown, 1990), p. 88; Hubert Saal, "Kate and Coco," *Newsweek* 74 (November 10, 1969), p. 78.

14. Ware, "Her Mother's Daughter," p. 50; Katharine Hepburn 1985 Commencement Address, and "Katharine Hepburn with the Class of 1973," both found in the Bryn Mawr College Archives, Bryn Mawr College.

15. Anderson, *The Young Kate*, p. 247; Lee Israel, "That's No Lady, That's Katharine Hepburn," *Ms.* (February 1973), p. 26; Morley, *Katharine Hepburn*, p. 165.

16. 1942 statement in support of ERA, circulated by the National Woman's Party, found at Schlesinger Library, Radcliffe College; Barbara Lovenheim, "Katharine Hepburn Takes the Movies' Measure," *New York Times*, September 27, 1987, found in Biography File, Schlesinger Library.

17. Kanin, *Tracy and Hepburn*, p. 311.

18. Leaming, *Katharine Hepburn*, p. 268; Lupton A. Williams and J. Bryan, III, "The Hepburn Story," *Saturday Evening Post* 214 (December 13, 1941), p. 24. In her films, Katharine Hepburn often found ways to display these attractive limbs to her advantage. The best example is the scene in *Woman of the Year* where Tess Harding first meets Sam Craig, leaning on the side of a desk (in a rare skirt) while adjusting her stockings.

19. Morley, *Katharine Hepburn*, p. 27; Hepburn, *Me*, p. 154. Some of the beaus that Hepburn brought home to Fenwick found it a bit odd that ex-husband Luddy was so much part of the family. Howard Hughes, who failed the Hepburn test of being interesting and was thus dismissed, was especially unnerved by Luddy's habit of taking home movies all the time. Hughes complained while playing golf with Dr. Hepburn, prompting this reply: "Howard, Luddy has been taking pictures of all of us long before you joined us and he will be taking them long after you've left. He is part of the family. Go ahead, drive. You need a seven iron." (Leaming, *Katharine Hepburn*, p. 358). In the 1970s Hepburn became close again to her ex-husband, who had since remarried. Only an older, mellower Hepburn could appreciate someone who seems to have been an absolute joy.

20. Ron Homer, "Katharine Hepburn," *Ladies' Home Journal* (March 1977), p. 54. Other times she faced her selfishness more directly: "Egocentrics should keep to themselves and not torture little children. I would have made a terrible parent. The first time my child didn't do what I wanted, I'd kill it." Curtiss Anderson, "Katharine Hepburn's Personal Scrapbook," *Good Housekeeping* 118 (January 1978), p. 106.

21. Remarks by Katharine Hepburn, March 14, 1988, "Celebrating Two Generations of Individual Courage," Planned Parenthood Federation of America, New York, New York.

22. Hepburn, *Me*, p. 417.

23. Israel, "That's No Lady, That's Katharine Hepburn," p. 26; Hepburn, *Me*, p. 131.

24. Lee Israel, "Last of the Honest-to-God Ladies," *Esquire* (November 1967), p. 114.

25. For example, Boze Hadleigh, *Hollywood Lesbians* (New York, 1994) makes no mention of Hepburn, nor does Marjorie Garber in her extensive discussion of

bisexuality in Hollywood and popular culture in *Vice Versa: Bisexuality and the Eroticism of Everyday Life* (New York: Simon and Schuster, 1995).

26. Hepburn, *Me*, p. 227; Edwards, *A Remarkable Woman*, p. 254.

27. *Los Angeles Herald-Examiner*, February 16, 1968, Academy Bio.

28. Gregory Speck, "Interview with Katharine Hepburn," *Interview Magazine* 15 (September 1985), pp. 217–21, Academy Bio.

29. Ronald Bergan, *Katharine Hepburn: An Independent Woman* (New York: Arcade Publishing, 1996), p. 101.

30. For background on women in Hollywood, see Wendy Holliday, "Hollywood's Modern Women: Screenwriting, Work Culture, and Feminism, 1910–1940" (Ph.D. dissertation, New York University, 1994); and Lizzie Francke, *Script Girls: Women Screenwriters in Hollywood* (London: BFI, 1994). Janet Thumin, " 'Miss Hepburn Is Humanized': The Star Persona of Katharine Hepburn," *Feminist Review* 24 (Autumn 1986), p. 75, gives this definition of persona: "a public image which derives from the performance and utterances of the person and is constructed over time in specific ways."

31. Ralph G. Martin, "Katharine Hepburn: My Life and Loves," *Ladies' Home Journal* 92 (August 1975), p. 109.

32. Morley, *Katharine Hepburn*, p. 61.

33. Andrew Britton, *Katharine Hepburn: Star as Feminist* (New York: Continuum, 1984, 1995), p. 13.

34. Bergan, *An Independent Woman*, p. 84.

35. *Los Angeles Herald-Examiner*, April 14, 1968, Academy Bio.

36. There are several variations of this scene. This is from Edwards, *A Remarkable Woman*, p. 195, which notes that Spencer Tracy often claimed the line, but most attributed it to Mankiewicz. Another variation is found in Leaming, *Katharine Hepburn*, p. 391.

37. Hepburn, *Me*, pp. 246, 400.

38. *Ibid.*, p. 407.

39. Leaming, *Katharine Hepburn*, p. 465.

40. Hepburn, *Me*, pp. 275, 396.

41. Leaming, *Katharine Hepburn*, pp. 400–1.

42. Barbara Leaming, for example, noted, "To watch them together was to wonder why this fierce, independent woman had so totally subordinated herself to Tracy's will" while he seemed to take her for granted. [Leaming, *Katharine Hepburn*, pp. 400–1.] Leaming's book sparked impassioned letters from John Ford's grandson and Spencer Tracy's authorized biographer, denying this view of Tracy. See *New York Times Book Review*, May 14, 1995, p. 30. Perhaps as a rebuttal to Leaming, Christopher Anderson paints the relationship in a generally positive light in *An Affair to Remember: The Remarkable Love Story of Katharine Hepburn and Spencer Tracy* (New York: William Morrow, 1997).

43. Morley, *Katharine Hepburn*, p. 9. Later (p. 109) Morley notes that Hepburn and Tracy were generally regarded as untouchable, but more basically as "unenthralling" by the gossip press, adding: "it was as if Mrs. Roosevelt had settled down quietly in her middle-to-late years with Harry S. Truman. Somehow they still wouldn't have been the Kennedys." While Eleanor Roosevelt and Harry Truman sounds pretty juicy to me, Morley is probably correct that theirs really wasn't the juice that tabloid stories were made of, even now.

Forty-something actress who has never been a sex symbol involved with an older, respected leading man with a drinking problem—as scandals go, that one was pretty tame.

44. Edwards, *A Remarkable Woman*, p. 366.
45. Morley, *Katharine Hepburn*, p. 174.
46. Bryson, *The Private World of Katharine Hepburn*, p. 162; Mary Cantwell, "Hepburn: 'I Had a Corner on the Rich, Arrogant Girl.' " See also Carrie Donovan, "Hepburn Style," *New York Times Magazine* (January 19, 1986), pp. 42, 44.
47. Morley, *Katharine Hepburn*, p. 155.
48. Edwards, *A Remarkable Woman*, p. 15.
49. For Joan Crawford and her shoes, see the introduction by Shari Benstock and Suzanne Ferriss to *On Fashion* (New Brunswick, N.J.: Rutgers University Press, 1994), pp. 1–3.
50. *Los Angeles Herald-Examiner*, January 3, 1963, Academy Bio; Edwards, *A Remarkable Woman*, p. 269; Donovan, "Hepburn Style," p. 44.
51. *New York Post*, March 12, 1986, Academy Bio.
52. Morley, *Katharine Hepburn*, p. 59; Israel, "That's No Lady, That's Katharine Hepburn," p. 26; Lupton A. Wilkinson and J. Bryan, III, "The Hepburn Story," *Saturday Evening Post* 214 (November 29, 1941), p. 9; Caryn James, "Katharine Hepburn: The Movie," *New York Times*, September 1, 1991; Morley, *Katharine Hepburn*, p. 159.
53. Bergan, *An Independent Woman*, p. 32; Leaming, *Katharine Hepburn*, p. 279.
54. *Los Angeles Times*, January 24, 1975, Academy Bio.
55. Britton, *Star as Feminist*, p. 211. In 1938 Howard Hughes had wanted Hepburn to star in *The Amelia Earhart Story* about the aviator's last flight, but the film was never made.
56. *Ibid.*, p. 76.
57. *Los Angeles Times*, August 4, 1935, Academy Bio; Edwards, *A Remarkable Woman*, p. 145; Speck, *Interview*, Academy Bio.
58. Jeanine Basinger's *A Woman's View: How Hollywood Spoke to Women, 1930–1960* (New York: Knopf, 1993), p. 32, alerted me to *Dragon Seed*. Here is her description of seeing the movie as a child: "A woman poisons the Japanese army! Perhaps I should learn to cook, after all. Because she flirts and because a woman belongs in the kitchen, Katharine Hepburn helps to win World War II."
59. Other guests included Clare Boothe Luce, Alice Roosevelt Longworth, Noel Coward, Henry Mencken, and Sir Willmott Lewis of the London *Times*. She added tellingly, "Sinclair Lewis, Dorothy Thompson's husband, can come to all my parties, and not because it is his right. Nobody living talks better, if he likes the party. Nobody can kill a party sooner, if he does not. But he'd like this party." Condensed from "On the Record" and published in *Current History* 50 (May 1939), pp. 45–46.
60. Marian K. Sanders, *Dorothy Thompson: A Legend in Her Time* (Boston: Houghton Mifflin, 1973), p. 290.
61. *Independent Woman* 21: 65 (March 1942), p. 65. The editorial was on the whole quite praiseworthy of the film as an entertaining comedy.
62. Thumin, " 'Miss Hepburn Is Humanized,' " p. 96; Britton, *Star as Feminist*, p. 183.

63. Bergan, *An Independent Woman*. p. 96.

64. Molly Haskell, "The Hand of Kate," *Village Voice* (April 1, 1986).

65. Leaming, *Katharine Hepburn*, p. 450; Hepburn, *Me*, p. 250. Barbara Leaming (p. 449) suggests that Hepburn may also have modeled her performance on her mother and members of the suffragist generation. Of Eleanor Roosevelt, Hepburn said, "I admired her strength of character," but she thought her mother had a more original mind. Speck, *Interview*, Academy Bio.

66. Basinger, *A Woman's View*, p. 170; Britton, *Star as Feminist*, p. 218.

67. *Ibid.*, pp. 232–33; Andrew Sarris, "The Premature Feminism of Katharine Hepburn," *Village Voice* (August 26, 1981), p. 39.

68. Hepburn had visited both the big house at Hyde Park and Val-Kill; she also supplied the narration and Eleanor Roosevelt the commentary for a wartime film called *Women in Defense* produced by the Office of War Information. See Edwards, *A Remarkable Woman*, p. 251; Martin, "Katharine Hepburn: My Life and Loves," p. 109; Bergan, *An Independent Woman*, p. 93.

69. Morley, *Katharine Hepburn*, p. 109.

70. Israel, "That's No Lady, That's Katharine Hepburn," p. 26; Cantwell, "Hepburn: 'I Had a Corner on the Rich, Arrogant Girl.' "

71. *People* (October 11, 1976), p. 66; December 1984 clipping, Biography File, Schlesinger Library; *Los Angeles Times*, October 10, 1976, Academy Bio.

72. *Screen Stories* (1969), Academy Bio; Colin Dangaard, "Back on TV, Hepburn Still Puts 'Career before Everything,' " *Us* (February 6, 1979), Academy Bio; Homer, "Katharine Hepburn," p. 54. Here is the full quote: "Of course, I'm not one to champion the traditional woman's role. And in a sense I'm competitive with men. But I haven't been handicapped by children. Nor have I handicapped children by bringing them into the world and going ahead with my career. I have lived like a man to the extent of taking care of myself with no one protecting me. I've taken my chances. But a woman simply can't have everything. Nor can a man."

73. Thumin, " 'Miss Hepburn Is Humanized,' " p. 101.

74. Cleveland Amory, "The Strength of Katharine Hepburn," *Parade Magazine* (November 27, 1983), p. 6; "Katharine Hepburn with the Class of 1973," Bryn Mawr College Archives.

75. Homer, "Katharine Hepburn," p. 54; T. Mathews, "Kate," *Newsweek* 110 (August 31, 1987), Katharine Hepburn Biography File, Lincoln Center Archives, New York Public Library.

76. Britton, *Star as Feminist*, p. 232; David Lewin, "Katharine Hepburn at 75," *New York Post*, April 13, 1985, Biography File, Lincoln Center. Some might disagree with Hepburn's assessment, based on some of the vanity vehicles she did for television in the late 1980s and early 1990s. I am a lifelong fan of Hepburn, but at that point I chose not to watch any more. Like Anna Quindlen crossing the street to avoid meeting the star, I wanted to keep my memories untarnished.

77. Hepburn, *Me*, p. 225.

78. Transcript, October 3, 1973, found at Academy of Motion Picture Arts and Sciences Library. Hepburn had remained a doubtful guest until the very end, and then just showed up to check out the set. Once there, she said they might

as well do the interview right then, which might explain why Cavett was somewhat flustered. But he was clearly in awe of her.

79. Morley, *Katharine Hepburn*, p. 158.
80. James, "Katharine Hepburn: The Movie," *New York Times*, September 1, 1991.
81. Speck, *Interview*, and *Screen Stories* (1969), both found in Academy Bio.
82. Britton, *Star as Feminist*, p. 238.

CHAPTER 5: FROM TOMBOY TO LADY: BABE DIDRIKSON ZAHARIAS

1. Susan E. Cayleff, *Babe: The Life and Legend of Babe Didrikson Zaharias* (Urbana: University of Illinois Press, 1995), p. 23; " 'Best at Everything': Babe Garners Another Trophy," *Newsweek* 5 (May 4, 1935), p. 19. Cayleff's groundbreaking book, the first feminist scholarly biography of the sports figure, greatly shaped my understanding of Babe Didrikson Zaharias.
2. Sue Macy, *Winning Ways: A Photohistory of American Women in Sports* (New York: Henry Holt, 1996), p. 80.
3. William Oscar Johnson and Nancy P. Williamson, *"Whatta-Gal": The Babe Didrikson Story* (Boston: Little, Brown, 1975), pp. 91, 92.
4. Babe Didrikson Zaharias as told to Harry Paxton, *This Life I've Led: My Autobiography* (New York: A. S. Barnes, 1955), p. 5.
5. Cayleff, *Babe*, p. 257; Grantland Rice, *The Tumult and the Shouting: My Life in Sport* (New York: A. S. Barnes, 1954), p. 240; Johnson and Williamson, *"Whatta-Gal,"* p. 111.
6. Cayleff, *Babe*, p. 164; Betty Hicks, "Next to Marriage We'll Take Golf," *Saturday Evening Post* (January 23, 1954), p. 37.
7. BDZ, *This Life I've Led*, p. 27; Cayleff, *Babe*, p. 73.
8. BDZ, *This Life I've Led*, p. 7.
9. Cayleff, *Babe*, p. 33; Johnson and Williamson, *"Whatta-Gal,"* p. 51; Cayleff, *Babe*, p. 36.
10. Johnson and Williamson, *"Whatta-Gal,"* p. 54.
11. BDZ, *This Life I've Led*, p. 3.
12. Susan K. Cahn, *Coming On Strong: Gender and Sexuality in Twentieth-Century Women's Sports* (New York: Free Press, 1994), p. 43.
13. Johnson and Williamson, *"Whatta-Gal,"* p. 75.
14. McCombs certainly knew the publicity value of this stunt, but by sending only Babe Didrikson he in effect robbed other Employers Casualty team members of the chance to qualify for the 1932 Olympics. See Doris H. Pieroth, *Their Day in the Sun: Women of the 1932 Olympics* (Seattle: University of Washington Press, 1996), p. 44.
15. BDZ, *This Life I've Led*, p. 48; Cayleff, *Babe*, p. 65.
16. *Ibid.*, p. 67; Johnson and Williamson, *"Whatta-Gal,"* p. 85; Cayleff, *Babe*, p. 90.
17. Johnson and Williamson, *"Whatta-Gal,"* pp. 101, 99; BDZ, *This Life I've Led*, p. 5. Here's another variation: "I don't see any use playing the game if you don't win—do you?" "Personality: Babe Didrikson Zaharias," *Time* (February 2, 1953), p. 41.
18. Bill Cunningham, "Texas Flash," *Colliers* 90 (August 6, 1932), p. 104.

19. Pieroth, *Their Day in the Sun*, pp. 101–2.
20. Johnson and Williamson, *"Whatta-Gal,"* p. 105.
21. *Ibid.*, p. 107.
22. Cayleff, *Babe*, p. 95; Cahn, *Coming On Strong*, p. 112. Cahn thinks that Didrikson may have been part of the problem: "In the long run, however, 'the Babe's' success did as much to harm as to help the reputation of the sport. Didrikson's disdain for dresses, men, and middle-class etiquette as well as her later involvement with commercial promotions made her the perfect target for horrified foes of track and field" (p. 116).
23. The impact of the Depression haunts the stories of many athletes who competed. Jean Shiley for one remembered the plentiful food at their training table: "I was just glad there was something on the table. I didn't care *what* it was." [Pieroth, *Their Day in the Sun*, p. 86.] Evelyn Hall missed out on the post-Olympic party at Pickfair, the home of Hollywood's most famous couple, Mary Pickford and Douglas Fairbanks, because she had cashed in the train ticket provided by the Olympic committee to drive home with her family, none of whom could afford to spend an extra night in Los Angeles. [*Ibid.*, p. 135.]
24. Johnson and Williamson, *"Whatta-Gal,"* p. 121.
25. BDZ, *This Life I've Led*, pp. 85, 5.
26. Cayleff, *Babe*, 109; BDZ, *This Life I've Led*, p. 73. The quote continued: "I want to live my life outdoors. I want to play golf." Cayleff (pp. 103–4) and BDZ's autobiography (pp. 70–73) have good descriptions of the vaudeville act; Cayleff's photo section has a picture of the marquee.
27. Cayleff, *Babe*, p. 108. This fairly risqué remark for the times was widely circulated in sports columns, hardly the thing to build up her reputation as a respectable athlete.
28. *Ibid.*, p. 113; "Whatever became of . . . ", *Saturday Evening Post* 216 (November 20, 1943), p. 91.
29. Cayleff, *Babe*, p. 89.
30. *Ibid.*, pp. 124, 100.
31. Mildred (Babe) Didrikson, "I Blow My Own Horn," *American Magazine* 121 (June 1936), p. 104.
32. *Ibid.*
33. Cayleff, *Babe*, p. 138.
34. Johnson and Williamson, *"Whatta-Gal,"* p. 163; Cayleff, *Babe*, p. 143.
35. BDZ, *This Life I've Led*, pp. 124–25.
36. Cayleff, *Babe*, p. 2; BDZ, *This Life I've Led*, pp. 103–4.
37. Cayleff, *Babe*, p. 114.
38. Cahn, *Coming On Strong*, p. 209.
39. *New York Times*, July 24, 1931, p. 16.
40. Paul Gallico, *Farewell to Sport* (New York: Knopf, 1938), p. 233. Gallico disguised his most negative portrait of Didrikson as fiction in an absolutely appalling story called "Honey" published in *Vanity Fair* (April 1933), pp. 46–48. The short story was accompanied by pictures of Didrikson herself. For a more positive view of the athlete by a sportswriter, see "The World-Beating Girl Viking of Texas," *Literary Digest* 114 (August 27, 1932), pp. 26–28.

Notes

3 2 5

41. Paul Gallico, "The Little Babe," Esquire (March 1955), p. 48. The "transcriptions" by sportswriters of Didrikson's Texas drawl into a kind of pidgin English provided another way of belittling the athlete. Here is how Paul Gallico butchered her description of her crossover to femininity: "Ah got so tired of being a tomboy, so Ah quit, Ah'm a business woman golfer now, so Ah guess Ah hyev to look th' part." [Johnson and Williamson, "Whatta-Gal," p. 153.] This is reminiscent of racist white renditions of the patterns of African-American speech.
42. Paul Gallico, "The Texas Babe," Vanity Fair (October 1932), p. 36.
43. Betty Hicks, "The Legendary Babe Didrikson Zaharias," in Greta Cohen, ed., Women in Sport: Issues and Controversies (New York: Sage, 1993), p. 42.
44. Cunningham, "Texas Flash," p. 49.
45. Johnson and Williamson, "Whatta-Gal," p. 21.
46. Gallico, "The Little Babe," p. 48.
47. Cayleff, Babe, p. 127; Johnson and Williamson, "Whatta-Gal," p. 153.
48. Cayleff, Babe, p. 137; BDZ, This Life I've Led, p. 131.
49. George Farmer, "Babe Is a Lady Now," Life 22 (June 23, 1947), p. 90.
50. For example, her obituary in Time 68 (October 8, 1956), p. 92, highlighted how she "matured from a pugnacious girl into a talented housewife who could design her own clothes."
51. Cayleff, Babe, p. 159; Pete Martin, "Babe Didrikson Takes Off Her Mask," Saturday Evening Post 220 (September 20, 1947), p. 27; BDZ, This Life I've Led, p. 129. For background on women in golf, see Elinor Nickerson, Golf: A Woman's History (Jefferson, N.C.: McFarland, 1987), and Glenna Collett, Ladies in the Rough (New York: Knopf, 1928).
52. Ibid., p. 180.
53. Cayleff, Babe, p. 187.
54. "Babe Didrikson Zaharias," Current Biography (1947), p. 703; Johnson and Williamson, "Whatta-Gal," p. 183; BDZ, This Life I've Led, pp. 84, 223.
55. "Big Business Babe," Time 57 (June 11, 1951), p. 66. Her detractors on the tour noted this was true: "With a crowd, Babe, she'd really put out, but if there was no crowd, she wasn't worth a damn." Johnson and Williamson, "Whatta-Gal," p. 129.
56. Cayleff, Babe, p. 164; Hicks, "The Legendary Babe Didrikson Zaharias," p. 42; Cayleff, Babe, p. 123. Here's another variation on the girdle line from her autobiography: "You've got to loosen your girdle and really let the ball have it." [BDZ, This Life I've Led, p. 46.]
57. Johnson and Williamson, "Whatta-Gal," pp. 149, 91–92, 175.
58. Martin, "Babe Didrikson Takes Off Her Mask," p. 27+.
59. BDZ, This Life I've Led, pp. 83–84; Cayleff, Babe, pp. 109–11. The Associated Press also had a panel of Babe doing ten different sports, dating from around 1932, which was reproduced in some of her obituaries.
60. Johnson and Williamson, "Whatta-Gal," p. 15; Hicks, "The Legendary Babe Didrikson Zaharias," p. 46; Cayleff, Babe, pp. 211–12.
61. Hicks, "The Legendary Babe Didrikson Zaharias," p. 46; Cayleff, Babe, p. 194; Johnson and Williamson, "Whatta-Gal," p. 190; Cayleff, Babe, p. 190.
62. Ibid., p. 182; Johnson and Williamson, "Whatta-Gal," pp. 190–91. Like Babe

Didrikson, Betty Hicks couldn't imagine a life without golf: "If I am ever tempted to complain about the strain of tournaments and the woes of traveling, I remember the poor girls back home, slaving over hot stoves and cold typewriters. And then I know how lucky I am to own a golf swing that will keep me going on the LPGA circuit." [Hicks, "Next to Marriage We'll Take Golf," p. 95.]

63. Johnson and Williamson, *"Whatta-Gal,"* p. 165; BDZ, *This Life I've Led*, p. 225.

64. *Ibid.*, p. 142.

65. Hicks, "The Legendary Babe Didrikson Zaharias," p. 44; Johnson and Williamson, *"Whatta-Gal,"* p. 157; Cayleff, *Babe*, p. 199.

66. *Ibid.*, pp. 97, 215; Johnson and Williamson, *"Whatta-Gal,"* p. 167; Hicks, "Next to Marriage We'll Take Golf," p. 37.

67. BDZ, *This Life I've Led*, p. 204; Babe Didrikson Zaharias as told to Booton Herndon, "I'm Not Out of the Rough—Yet!," *Cosmopolitan* 135 (October 1953), p. 80. Sometimes Dodd was referred to as Didrikson's "protege," but she said this was not really an accurate description: "She never taught me anything. She wasn't interested in teaching me how to play golf, she was interested in winning her own deal." Dodd captured the underlying inequality of this relationship: "Babe didn't just take up with me because I was a cute kid. She thought I had a lot of talent. And in one way she wanted to help me and in another way she did not want me to beat her." (Cayleff, *Babe*, p. 209)

68. Susan Cayleff interviewed Dodd for her biography, although Dodd died before the book was published. Quotations from those interviews, in addition to the interviews with Dodd done by William Oscar Johnson and Nancy P. Williamson for their 1975 book, are very important for gauging the Dodd-Didrikson relationship.

69. BDZ, *This Life I've Led*, p. 227; Martin, "Babe Didrikson Takes Off Her Mask," p. 27.

70. BDZ, *This Life I've Led*, p. 191.

71. Cayleff, *Babe*, p. 203.

72. Johnson and Williamson, *"Whatta-Gal,"* p. 196; Cayleff, *Babe*, pp. 215, 203.

73. BDZ, *This Life I've Led*, pp. 228, 221–22.

74. Arthur Daley, "A One-Woman Team," *New York Times Book Review* (December 11, 1955), p. 22.

75. BDZ, *This Life I've Led*, p. 232.

76. Transcript of Eisenhower press conference, *New York Times*, September 28, 1956, p. 14; Editorial, *ibid.*, p. 26.

77. BDZ, *This Life I've Led*, p. 228.

78. Another example is Arthur Daley's "Sports of the Times" column several days after her death, which refers to "a tender awkwardness to her romance with George Zaharias, the massive wrestler. They were mutually attracted the moment they met and their love story was a rich and rewarding one through courtship, matrimony and beyond." *New York Times*, September 30, 1956, Section V, p. 2.

79. Fred Wittner, "Shall the Ladies Join Us?" *Literary Digest* (May 19, 1934), p. 42.

80. This quotation came from the wonderful piece that editor Charles McGrath wrote about what Babe Didrikson Zaharias had meant to his mother for the special *New York Times Magazine* issue on Heroine Worship (November 24, 1996, p. 62). Here is the full quote: "Part of Babe's appeal for my mother and other women of her wifely, house-bound generation was that she was so modest and unpretentious—a regular gal. But these women must have responded to something else in Babe too: something that my mother, at least, would have been unwilling, or unable, to articulate—a dream of prowess and success, of being able to beat the men at their own games."

CHAPTER 6: FRONT AND CENTER: MARTHA GRAHAM

1. Martha Graham, *Blood Memory: An Autobiography* (New York: Doubleday, 1991), pp. 3, 5; Joseph H. Mazo, *Prime Movers: The Makers of Modern Dance in America* (New York: William Morrow, 1977), p. 154; Marian Horosko, "Frontier of the Mind: Martha Graham at 95," *Dance Magazine* 63 (May 1989), p. 57.

2. Robert Tracy and Elizabeth Kaye, "I See You as a Goddess," *Mirabella* (July 1991), p. 42; Merle Armitage, ed., *Martha Graham: The Early Years* (New York: Da Capa Press, 1978), p. 8; Mazo, *Prime Movers*, p. 161; Tobi Tobias, "A Conversation with Martha Graham," *Dance Magazine* 58 (March 1984), p. 64; Graham, *Blood Memory*, pp. 255–56.

3. Emily Coleman, "Martha Graham Still Leaps Forward," *New York Times Magazine* (April 9, 1961), p. 49. Mazo, *Prime Movers*, p. 186, has another version of the quote, slightly fuller.

4. Joseph H. Mazo, "Martha Remembered," *Dance Magazine* 65 (July 1991), p. 44; Jennifer Copaken, "From the Domestic Sphere to the Artistic Cube: The Feminist Impulse in the Modern Dance Movement," Senior Honors Thesis, Harvard University, 1990, p. 3; Deborah Jowitt, *Time and the Dancing Image* (New York: William Morrow, 1988), p. 152.

5. Don McDonagh, *Martha Graham* (New York: Popular Library, 1973), p. 284; Walter Terry, "At Seventy-five, a New 'Frontier,' " *Saturday Review* 52 (May 3, 1969), p. 42.

6. Graham, *Blood Memory*, p. 18; McDonagh, *Martha Graham*, p. 13. Agnes de Mille, *Martha: The Life and Work of Martha Graham* (New York: Random House, 1991), p. 17, has a slightly different version of the first part of the quote, which I used.

7. Graham, *Blood Memory*, pp. 9–10.

8. *Ibid.*, p. 32.

9. Howard Gardner, *Creating Minds: An Anatomy of Creativity Seen Through the Lives of Freud, Einstein, Picasso, Stravinsky, Eliot, Graham, and Gandhi* (New York: Basic Books, 1993), p. 268.

10. Walter Terry, *The Dance in America* (New York: Harper and Row, 1971), p. 87.

11. Walter Terry, *Frontiers of Dance: The Life of Martha Graham* (New York: Thomas Y. Crowell, 1975), p. 42.

12. Clive Barnes, "The Untamed Surge of Modern Dance," *Life* 59 (November 12, 1965), p. 107.

13. Elizabeth Kendall, *Where She Danced: The Birth of American Art-Dance* (New York: Knopf, 1979), p. 174.

14. Graham, *Blood Memory*, p. 113.

15. De Mille, *Martha*, p. 377.

16. McDonagh, *Martha Graham*, p. 50.

17. Terry, *The Dance in America*, p. 90; Copaken, "From the Domestic Sphere to the Artistic Cube," p. 38; Jowitt, *Time and the Dancing Image*, p. 227. This quote is from 1944, but it is true of her entire repertoire.

18. Susan Leigh Foster, *Reading Dancing: Bodies and Subjects in Contemporary American Dance* (Berkeley: University of California Press, 1986), p. 44; Barbara Morgan, *Martha Graham: Sixteen Dances in Photographs* (New York: Duell, Sloan and Pearce, 1941), no page.

19. Ernestine Stodelle, *Deep Song: The Dance Story of Martha Graham* (New York: Schirmer Books, 1984), p. 81; Jowitt, *Time and the Dancing Image*, p. 157; Ethel Butler oral history, found in Copaken, "From the Domestic Sphere to the Artistic Cube."

20. De Mille, *Martha*, p. 135; Molly McQuade, "Agnes de Mille," *Publishers Weekly* (August 23, 1991), p. 40.

21. Barnes, "The Untamed Surge of Modern Dance," p. 103; Mazo, "Martha Remembered," p. 44; Martha Duffy, "The Deity of Modern Dance," *Time* 137 (April 15, 1991), p. 69; Mazo, "Martha Remembered," pp. 39, 41.

22. Martha Graham, "A Modern Dancer's Primer for Action" (1941) in Cobbett Steinberg, *The Dance Anthology* (New York: New American Library, 1980), pp. 47, 52; McDonagh, p. 53.

23. Jowitt, *Time and the Dancing Image*, p. 154. The quotation is from dance critic Elizabeth Selden.

24. Walter Terry, *I Was There: Selected Dance Reviews and Articles, 1936–1976* (New York: Audience Arts, 1978), p. 6; Terry, *The Dance in America*, p. 84.

25. Armitage, *Martha Graham: The Early Years*, p. 61; Mazo, "Martha Remembered," p. 43. Another example of her phenomenal concentration and identification with her character came during a performance of *Judith* in Washington, D.C., where she had to be careful about rings imbedded in the stage floor. "I looked at those rings and said to myself, 'One more hazard for Judith to face.' " Terry, *The Frontiers of Dance*, p. 122.

26. Coleman, "Martha Graham Still Leaps Forward," p. 49; Terry, *The Frontiers of Dance*, p. 62.

27. Helen Thomas, *Dance, Modernity and Culture: Explorations in the Sociology of Dance* (New York: Routledge, 1995), p. 130.

28. Angelica Gibbs, "The Absolute Frontier," *New Yorker* 23 (December 27, 1947), p. 34; Terry, *I Was There*, p. 160. Another, unintentionally humorous reaction was recounted in Jowitt, *Time and the Dancing Image*, p. 214: "The thing to keep in mind is that everything is a point of departure." Or these two dowagers overheard in 1942: "Either she is deteriorating or we're getting better, because we liked her." [McDonagh, *Martha Graham*, p. 159.]

29. Mazo, "Martha Remembered," p. 39.

30. Graham, *Blood Memory*, p. 163.

31. McDonagh, *Martha Graham*, and de Mille, *Martha*, contain biographical material on Erick Hawkins.

32. From the beginning, rumors and speculation circulated widely among the company. Perhaps the most extreme was the rumor that Hawkins had once tried to push Graham over the edge of the Grand Canyon. McDonagh, *Martha Graham*, p. 154.

33. Mazo, "Martha Remembered," p. 42.

34. Gardner, *Creating Minds*, p. 286; Terry, *I Was There*, p. 54.

35. Tim Wengerd, "Martha's Men," *Dance Magazine* 65 (July 1991), p. 52.

36. Martha Graham, *The Notebooks of Martha Graham* (New York: Harcourt Brace Jovanovich, 1973), p. xi. Here is the same idea in variation: "I am a thief, but I give it all back . . . as I see it." Stodelle, *Deep Song*, p. 85.

37. There are many parallels, which were obvious to observers at the time, between the Graham-Hawkins marriage and that of Ruth St. Denis and Ted Shawn, including the intense personality and artistic clashes as well as the age difference between an older (and dominant) woman and her younger husband. Moaned Louis Horst about Hawkin's ascendancy, "This is Shawn all over again, and she swore it would never happen in her life." De Mille, *Martha*, p. 231.

38. Agnes de Mille, *Dance to the Piper* (Boston: Little, Brown, 1952), p. 148.

39. Graham, *Blood Memory*, p. 171. Agnes de Mille (*Martha*, p. 293) suggests that Hawkins may have deliberately contributed to the injury in a domestic dispute, a highly controversial statement. The more accepted chronology is that Martha Graham injured herself in the Paris debut, and then reinjured her knee several weeks later when she tried to salvage the London part of the tour. Eleanor Roosevelt had been in the audience the night of the Paris performance.

40. Gibbs, "The Absolute Frontier," p. 34. Of course, being the subject of a *New Yorker* profile also showed the company she kept. Of the subjects in this book, Thompson, Mead, and Hepburn were also profiled. Babe Didrikson appeared in *New Yorker* articles, especially by writers such as Herbert Wind Warren, before and after her death, but did not ever have an entire article devoted to her; Graham's brother-in-law Winthrop Sargeant covered Marian Anderson's later singing career, but never profiled her. Eleanor Roosevelt was probably too famous to be the subject of a profile.

41. "Impossible Interviews: Sally Rand vs. Martha Graham," *Vanity Fair* (December 1934), p. 40.

42. Jowitt, *Time and the Dancing Image*, p. 151. Martha Graham would continue to be spoofed in popular culture throughout her career. For example, Danny Kaye did a real number on her in *The Kid from Brooklyn*, which has a skit called "Diesel Engine 45" in which a character called Graham is the engine and her "six little Graham crackers" are the spark plugs. [McDonagh, *Martha Graham*, p. 212.] And English actor Cyril Ritchard once presented a drag performance of *Frontier*. Graham admitted in her autobiography that she had never really liked the idea of female impersonators, but had to admit that there was something to be said for Mae West's attitude: "What's wrong with it? Women have been doing it for years." Graham, *Blood Memory*, p. 127.

43. Graham, *Blood Memory*, p. 153; de Mille, *Martha*, pp. 221–22. See also McDonagh, *Martha Graham*, p. 120. In her autobiography, Graham notes that she and Eleanor became good friends in the 1940s, and tells the story of

appearing with her at a United Jewish Appeal meeting that was being pick-
eted by Orthodox Jews. Finally, Eleanor had had enough, and she announced
they were going through the picket line. Graham, who had never crossed a
picket line in her life, remembers Eleanor telling her to come with her. "And
Martha came." Graham, *Blood Memory*, p. 153.

44. McDonagh, *Martha Graham*, pp. 201–2, has the best description of the Miss
Hush episode, and decodes all the clues: listeners guessed dancer as her profession by the reindeer reference; her initials M.G. were revealed as the thir-
teenth and seventh letters of the alphabet; there was a Graham auto; and
finally they caught the reference to dance technique at the end. The winner
got $21,500 worth of prizes.
45. Graham, *Blood Memory*, p. 77.
46. Stodelle, *Deep Song*, p. 67; de Mille, *Dance to the Piper*, p. 152.
47. Stodelle, *Deep Song*, p. 13; Mazo, "Martha Remembered," p. 42.
48. De Mille, *Martha*, p. 189.
49. Leo Leatherman, *Martha Graham: Portrait of the Lady as an Artist*, pp. 134–35.
50. For more on Humphrey, see Selma Jeanne Cohen, ed., *Doris Humphrey: An
Artist First* (Pennington, N.J.: Princeton Book Company, 1972); Terry, *The
Dance in America*; Jill Johnston, "Of Course, Martha Graham, But Especially
Doris Humphrey," *Ms.* (December 1978), pp. 57–60, 101; and Beatrice Gottlieb, "Choreographic Contrast," *Theatre Arts* 34 (June 1950), pp. 24–28.
51. Cohen, *Doris Humphrey*, p. 128.
52. McDonagh, *Martha Graham*, p. 55; de Mille, *Martha*, p. 130; Marie Marchowsky oral history, found in Copaken, "From the Domestic Sphere to the
Artistic Cube."
53. Tracy and Kaye, "I See You as a Goddess," p. 46. The dancer quoted is Robert
Cohan, but many others have said the same thing.
54. Mazo, *Prime Movers*, p. 188.
55. Graham, *Blood Memory*, pp. 211, 212.
56. Lynn Garafola, "Books," *The Drama Review* 37 (Spring 1993), p. 171; Tobi
Tobias, "Cherchez la Femme," *New York* (October 10, 1994), p. 81; Coleman,
"Martha Graham Still Leaps Forward," p. 57.
57. Mazo, *Prime Movers*, p. 16; Jennifer Dunning, "Martha in Present Tense," *New
York Times*, September 25, 1994, p. 27.
58. McDonagh, *Martha Graham*, p. 225; Mazo, "Martha Remembered," p. 43.
59. Coleman, "Martha Graham Still Leaps Forward," p. 57; Arlene Croce, "Agnes
and Martha," *New Yorker* (October 14, 1991), p. 124; Croce, *After Images* (New
York: Knopf, 1978), p. 53.
60. Graham, *Blood Memory*, p. 25.
61. Tobias, "A Conversation with Martha Graham," p. 65.
62. *Ibid.*, p. 64; Graham, *Blood Memory*, p. 26.
63. Graham, *Blood Memory*, p. 174.
64. *Ibid.*, p. 160.
65. Coleman, "Martha Graham Still Leaps Forward," p. 57.
66. Elinor Rogosin, *The Dance Makers: Conversations with American Choreographers*
(New York: Walker and Company, 1980), p. 28; Duffy, "The Deity of Modern
Dance," p. 69. On alcohol, see McDonagh, *Martha Graham*, p. 260. Dancer
Gus Solomon remembered those later years in this way: "I saw her as a funny

little old lady who drank too much most of the time and didn't have too much concentration. She would come to rehearse a dance and get everyone hysterically angry at each other, at the dance, at Martha herself." Tracy and Kaye, "I See You as a Goddess," p. 44.

67. Croce, *After Images*, p. 297.
68. Stodelle, *Deep Song*, p. 260.
69. Graham, *Blood Memory*, p. 237.
70. Carolyn G. Heilbrun, "Exceptions and Rules," *Women's Review of Books* 9 (November 1991), pp. 15–16. She was referring to Juan Hamilton's role in the later years of Georgia O'Keeffe.
71. De Mille, *Martha*, pp. 400, 366.
72. Rogosin, *The Dance Makers*, p. 30.
73. Laura Shapiro, "Martha Graham at 90," *Newsweek* 103 (March 12, 1984), p. 55.
74. Terry, *Frontiers of Dance*, p. 155.
75. Mazo, *Prime Movers*, p. 182.
76. Clive Barnes, "Graham Tomorrow," *Dance Magazine* 63 (December 1989), p. 130.
77. Croce, "Agnes and Martha," p. 120. Croce was far more sympathetic to the Agnes de Mille biography, which she reviewed in the same piece. The book had been finished several years earlier, but its publication had been held up out of deference to Graham until her death.
78. Armitage, *Martha Graham: The Early Years*, p. 103; Laura Shapiro, "After the Ball Is Over," *Newsweek* 116 (October 15, 1990), p. 70.

CHAPTER 7: ACROSS THE COLOR LINE: MARIAN ANDERSON

1. Marian Anderson, *My Lord, What a Morning* (New York: Viking, 1956), p. 158. Anderson was always quite embarrassed that this private comment was repeated by an acquaintance to the press, and circulated without the Maestro's permission. Nonetheless, the quote was repeatedly used in publicity surrounding the singer and, in the way that is true of all the subjects in this book, entered the popular discourse as a must-use quotation.
2. *Ibid.*, p. 149; Sol Hurok, *Impresario* (New York: Random House, 1946), pp. 237–38; Jessye Norman, "Grace Under Fire," *New York Times Magazine* (November 24, 1996), p. 59.
3. "Marian Anderson," *Current Biography* (1940), p. 18.
4. Harold Schonberg, "Music: Marian Anderson," *New York Times*, April 19, 1965, p. 38.
5. Anderson, *My Lord, What a Morning*, pp. 187–89; Nellie McKay, "Introduction," to the 1992 University of Wisconsin Press edition of *My Lord, What a Morning*, p. xvi.
6. T. H. Watkins, *The Great Depression* (Boston: Little, Brown, 1993), pp. 325, 328.
7. McKay, "Introduction," p. xxxiii.
8. W. E. Burghardt Du Bois, *The Philadelphia Negro: A Social Study* (New York: Benjamin Blom, 1899), p. 315.

9. For example, she allowed her seventy-fifth birthday to be celebrated in 1977, and her eightieth birthday gala was in 1982. In fact, she would have been five years older each time.

10. Damon Kerby, "Noted Singer's Spiritual Depth," *St. Louis Post-Dispatch*, March 22, 1938, found in Marian Anderson papers, University of Pennsylvania [hereafter MA, Penn].

11. Hurok souvenir program, 1939–1940, MA, Penn; Anderson, *My Lord, What a Morning*, p. 3; Felicia Warburg Roosevelt, *Doers and Dowagers* (Garden City, N.Y.: Doubleday, 1975), p. 142. Frank J. Sulloway, *Born to Rebel: Birth Order, Family Dynamics, and Creative Lives* (New York: Pantheon, 1996), offers a theory about the importance of birth order on adult development.

12. Roosevelt, *Doers and Dowagers*, p. 142.

13. Du Bois, *The Philadelphia Negro*, p. 204.

14. Anderson, *My Lord, What a Morning*, p. 11.

15. Marian Anderson, "My Mother's Gift," in Norman Vincent Peale, *Guideposts* (1954), reprinted in Hurok souvenir program, c. 1954–1955, MA, Penn; Edwin R. Embree, *13 Against the Odds* (New York: Viking Press, 1944), p. 143. Dr. Wilson was also instrumental in arranging for Anderson to study with the noted voice teacher, Guiseppe Borghetti. Wilson was the first woman to win the prestigious Bok award for service to Philadelphia in 1934. Marian Anderson would become the first black to win the award in 1940.

16. Du Bois, *The Philadelphia Negro*, p. 350; Marian Anderson with Emily Kimbrough, "My Life in a White World," *Ladies' Home Journal* 77 (September 1960), p. 173. The music school in question was not the famed Curtis Institute of Music, which was not founded until 1923.

17. Barbara Klaw, "A Voice One Hears Once in a Hundred Years," *American Heritage* 28 (February 1977), p. 54; Roosevelt, *Doers and Dowagers*, p. 144.

18. Margaret Truman, *Women of Courage* (New York: William Morrow, 1976), p. 167.

19. "Marian Anderson," *Current Biography* (1950), p. 10.

20. Anderson, *My Lord, What a Morning*, pp. 144, 141. References to her race were rife in the early years of her career, although by the 1940s and 1950s they had subsided. For example, the *Times-Herald* article about the Easter concert, April 10, 1939, used this language, "This Negro girl, born in poverty, lifted to fame by her gifts of voice . . . . " The *New York Times*, February 17, 1935, referred to her as a "colored contralto", as did Eleanor Roosevelt in a blurb for Hurok promotional material in 1936–1937. All found in MA, Penn.

21. Anderson, *My Lord, What a Morning*, p. 159.

22. Langston Hughes, *Famous American Negroes* (New York: Dodd, Mead, 1954), p. 129; Kosti Vehanen, *Marian Anderson: A Portrait* (New York: McGraw Hill, 1941), p. 265.

23. Hurok, *Impresario*, pp. 237–38; "Marian Anderson," WETA documentary (1991).

24. Anderson, *My Lord, What a Morning*, p. 160. In one unnamed Southern city, the local manager told the Hurok representative in a huff that the audience would never stand for Anderson's holding her accompanist's hand at the end of the performance, and she should be instructed not to do so. This ultimatum

was not passed on to the singer, who went ahead with her usual custom. No riot ensued; instead they were met by deafening applause. *Ibid.*, pp. 245–46.
25. *Ibid.*, p. 165.
26. Vehanen, *Marian Anderson*, pp. 267–70.
27. Anderson, *My Lord, What a Morning*, p. 169.
28. Arthur Bronson, "Marian Anderson," *American Mercury* 61 (September 1945), p. 286.
29. Mrs. Anderson was not a demonstrative person. At the end of one concert, the dowager seated next to her said, "Good heavens, woman, how can you sit there like a bump on a log? Don't you know a great artist when you hear one?" Hurok, *Impresario*, p. 248.
30. Vehanen, *Marian Anderson*, p. 223; Anderson, *My Lord, What a Morning*, p. 194. Anderson's autobiography places this episode in 1939, but it seems far more likely to have occurred in 1936 at the earlier recital where she certainly would have met the president along with her mother.
31. Anderson, *My Lord, What a Morning*, p. 196. For Eleanor Roosevelt's role, see Allida M. Black, "Championing a Champion: Eleanor Roosevelt and the Marian Anderson 'Freedom Concert,' " *Presidential Studies Quarterly* 20 (Fall 1990), pp. 719–36, and Black, "A Reluctant but Persistent Warrior: Eleanor Roosevelt and the Early Civil Rights Movement," in Vicki Crawford, Jacqueline Ann Rouse, and Barbara Woods, eds., *Women in the Civil Rights Movement: Trailblazers and Torchbearers* (Bloomington: Indiana University Press, 1990).
32. *New York Times*, March 19, 1939, cited in Janet L. Sims, *Marian Anderson: An Annotated Bibliography and Discography* (Westport, Conn.: Greenwood Press, 1981), p.60; Martha Graham, *Blood Memory: An Autobiography* (New York: Doubleday, 1991), pp. 153–55. Graham supported the artist in other ways, protesting an occasion when Anderson had not been welcome at New York's Algonquin Hotel.
33. Black, "A Reluctant but Persistent Warrior," p. 241. See also Scott A. Sandage, "A Marble House Divided: The Lincoln Memorial, the Civil Rights Movement, and the Politics of Memory, 1939–1963," *Journal of American History* (June 1993), pp. 135–67.
34. Anderson, *My Lord, What a Morning*, pp. 187–89; Hurok souvenir program, 1965 Farewell Tour, MA, Penn.
35. Vehanen, *Marian Anderson*, p. 244.
36. *New York Times*, July 3, 1939, in Sims, *Marian Anderson*, p. 207.
37. Hurok, *Impresario*, p. 258; Vincent Sheean, "The Voice of the American Soul," in Hurok souvenir program, 1965 Farewell Tour, MA, Penn.
38. Carl Van Vechten quoted in Hurok souvenir program, no date (1940s), MA, Penn.
39. Anderson, *My Lord, What a Morning*, p. 173.
40. Hurok, *Impresario*, p. 250; Anderson, *My Lord, What a Morning*, p. 214.
41. *Ibid.*, p. 157; "Marian Anderson," *Current Biography* (1940), p. 18.
42. Marcia Davenport, "Music Will Out," *Colliers* 102 (December 3, 1938), p. 40.
43. Anderson, *My Lord, What a Morning*, p. 250.
44. Robert T. Jones, "Anderson and Maynor: Two Who Paved The Way," *New York Times*, June 29, 1969, p. 27.

45. Anderson, *My Lord, What a Morning*, pp. 167, 279.
46. Fan mail and copies of her often belated replies are found in MA, Penn.
47. Anderson, "My Life in a White World," p. 54; Anderson, *My Lord, What a Morning*, pp. 240, 239.
48. Sims, *Marian Anderson*, p. 227.
49. Anderson, *My Lord, What a Morning*, p. 244.
50. Anderson, "My Life in a White World," p. 174.
51. Anderson, *My Lord, What a Morning*, pp. 217, 219.
52. When she disembarked from the ship in December 1935 just prior to her Town Hall concert with her injured ankle, she still insisted on wearing a favorite pair of brown shoes: "I was as fond of them as of any shoes I had ever had, including the Buster Brown pair of my childhood." Plus they went with the nice outfit she had chosen for her homecoming. "I had not been home for a long time; I knew that there would be many special people to meet me at the pier and I did not wish to alarm anyone. Oh, yes, there was vanity in it, too." *Ibid.*, pp. 11, 163.
53. In one of her daybooks from the 1950s (MA, Penn), there is a formula for removing hair dye stains from clothing, another piece of evidence. Her hair stayed black through her eightieth birthday gala, and then suddenly went white in the photographs in the last years of her life.
54. Anderson, *My Lord, What a Morning*, p. 11.
55. Anderson, "My Mother's Gift"; Aylesa Forsee, *American Women Who Scored Firsts* (Philadelphia: Macrae Smith Company, 1958), p. 35.
56. Anthony Heilbut, "Postscript: Marian Anderson," *New Yorker* 69 (April 26, 1993), p. 82; McKay, "Introduction," p. xxix. Wayne Koestenbaum defines a diva as "a woman opera singer of great fame and brilliance" but the term also has connotations of flamboyant and often temperamental behavior on stage and off, as well as a highly theatrical approach to life in general. One unintended, indeed ironic, legacy of Marian Anderson was to create the equal opportunity for a black artist to be just as much a diva as any white. Koestenbaum, *The Queen's Throat: Opera, Homosexuality, and the Mystery of Desire* (New York: Random House, 1993), p. 111.
57. Vehanen, *Marian Anderson*, p. 219; McKay, "Introduction," p. xxix.
58. Gwendolyn Cherry, *Portraits of Color* (New York: Pageant Press, 1962), p. 66.
59. K. Sue Jewell, *From Mammy to Miss America and Beyond: Cultural Images and the Shaping of U.S. Social Policy* (New York: Routledge, 1993), Chapter 3.
60. For general background, see Paula Giddings, *When and Where I Enter: The Impact of Black Women on Race and Sex in America* (New York: William Morrow, 1984); Glenda Gilmore, *Gender and Jim Crow* (Chapel Hill: University of North Carolina Press, 1995); Stephanie J. Shaw, *What a Black Woman Ought to Be and to Do: Black Professional Women Workers during the Jim Crow Era* (Chicago: University of Chicago Press, 1996); Hazel Carby, *Reconstructing Womanhood: The Emergence of the African-American Woman Novelist* (New York: Oxford University Press, 1987).
61. Evelyn Brooks Higginbotham, *Righteous Discontent: The Women's Movement in the Black Baptist Church, 1880–1920* (Cambridge: Harvard University Press, 1993), p. 187.

62. "A Day at Marian Anderson's Country Hideaway," *Ebony* 12 (April 1947), p. 10; Associated Press Biographical Service, Sketch #3005 (December 1, 1942), MA, Penn.
63. Roosevelt, *Doers and Dowagers*, p. 147; Anderson, *My Lord, What a Morning*, p. 83.
64. Anderson, "My Life in a White World," p. 176.
65. "A Day at Marian Anderson's Country Hideaway," p. 10; Bill Ryan, "Serene Marian Anderson Lives on Danbury Farm," *Hartford Times*, May 5, 1964, p. 16.
66. "Of Men and Music," *Ebony* 6 (May 1951), p. 52; Anderson, *My Lord, What a Morning*, p. 291. I do not know if these servants were black or white, but my guess is that they were local Connecticut people, most likely white.
67. "At Home with Marian Anderson," *Ebony* 9 (February 1954), p. 55. The *Hartford Times* interview, May 5, 1964, cited above refers to Orpheus Fisher as white, presumably based on the reporter's meeting him rather than his presenting himself as white.
68. Anderson, "My Life in a White World," p. 174. At various points in his career, Fisher had worked on such large projects as the Empire State Building, Rockefeller Center, and the 1939 World's Fair, although it is not clear in what specific capacity. See Richard C. Wald, "How to Live with a Famous Wife," *Ebony* 13 (August 1958), pp. 52–54, 56.
69. Anderson, *My Lord, What a Morning*, p. 285.
70. Wald, "How to Live with a Famous Wife," p. 56; Rita Reif, "Marian Anderson at 70, Reflecting: On a Life's Work," *New York Times*, February 28, 1972, p. 36.
71. Roosevelt, *Doers and Dowagers*, p. 147; Anderson, *My Lord, What a Morning*, p. 292.
72. Reif, "Marian Anderson at 70, Reflecting," p. 36; Roosevelt, *Doers and Dowagers*, p. 147.
73. Klaw, "A Voice One Hears Once in a Hundred Years," p. 57. Anderson was not, however, the first black to appear with the company. Dancer Janet Collins had performed in a Met production in 1952. Nor was she the first black to sing opera, of course. In the 1940s Mary Caldwell Dawson organized a National Negro Opera Company, which presented *Aida* in Chicago in 1942 and *La Traviata* in New York in 1944. In 1946 the New York City Opera Company was the first major opera company to employ black singers Todd Duncan, Camilla Williams, and Laurence Winters as principals. Southern, *The Music of Black Americans*, pp. 500–1.
74. Anderson, *My Lord, What a Morning*, p. 304; "Now One Is Speechless," *Time* 64 (October 18, 1954), p. 87.
75. Anderson, *My Lord, What a Morning*, p. 177; Michael Sweeley, "The First Lady," *National Review* 41 (September 29, 1989), p. 66.
76. Anderson, *My Lord, What a Morning*, p. 304.
77. *Ibid.*, p. 305.
78. "Now One Is Speechless," p. 87.
79. Althea Gibson, "I Always Wanted to Be Somebody," *Saturday Evening Post* (September 6, 1958), p. 78.

80. McKay, "Introduction," p. xxvi.
81. Dorothy Thompson, "On the Record," February 3, 1958, and Thompson to Cosmopolitan Club, January 30, 1958, both found in Dorothy Thompson papers, Syracuse University. Anderson had been proposed by Emily Kimbrough, who later collaborated with Anderson on her powerful *Ladies' Home Journal* article, "My Life in a White World."
82. Harold Schonberg, "The Other Voice of Marian Anderson," *New York Times Magazine*, August 10, 1958, p. 17; Roosevelt, *Doers and Dowagers*, pp. 146–47.
83. Clipping from *Boston Globe*, October 30, 1976, found in Biography File, Schlesinger Library, Radcliffe College; Harold Taubman, *New York Times*, December 31, 1935, clipping found in MA, Penn.
84. "An 80th Birthday Tribute to Marian Anderson," *Ebony* 37 (May, 1982), p. 49.
85. Anderson, *My Lord, What a Morning*, p. 45.

INDEX

Page numbers in *italics* refer to illustrations.